THE PRIVATE LIFE OF OLD HONG KONG

Western Women in the British Colony 1841–1941

The Private Life of Old Hong Kong

Western Women in the British Colony
1841–1941

SUSANNA HOE

HONG KONG
OXFORD UNIVERSITY PRESS
OXFORD NEW YORK
1991

Oxford University Press

Oxford   New York   Toronto
Petaling Jaya   Singapore   Hong Kong   Tokyo
Delhi   Bombay   Calcutta   Madras   Karachi
Nairobi   Dar es Salaam   Cape Town
Melbourne   Auckland

and associated companies in
Berlin   Ibadan

First published 1991
Published in the United States
by Oxford University Press, Inc., New York

British Library Cataloguing in Publication Data

Hoe, Susanna 1945–
The private life of Old Hong Kong: western women in the
British colony 1841–1941.
1. Hong Kong. Social life, 1843–1945 — Biographies — Collections
I. Title
951.25040922
ISBN 0–19–582797–X

Library of Congress Cataloging-in-Publication Data available

Printed in Hong Kong by Calay Printing Co., Ltd.
Published by Oxford University Press, Warwick House, Hong Kong

Although this book is about women and,
mostly, for their descendants,
I dedicate it to four men,
fine historians, dear friends.

Sione Latukefu

Derek Roebuck

Carl T. Smith

and in memory of Arthur Bryant

PREFACE

*T*his book had an inspiration, a constant reminder, and a prod with the force of electricity. In early 1987, my husband and I were passing through Hong Kong so that he could be interviewed for a job. I was reading Joanna Trollope's *Britannia's Daughters* at the time and came across the information that Flora Shaw Lugard had been governor's wife here at the beginning of the twentieth century.

The story was more subtle an inspiration than that. Before her marriage, Flora Shaw had been a famous expert on Africa and an influential journalist on *The Times*. Some time after she married, she was seated between two diplomats at a dinner party. Afterwards, they asked who their impressive companion had been. 'Lady Lugard,' replied their hostess, and added, 'She was Miss Flora Shaw.' The diplomats threw up their hands. 'What, *the* Miss Shaw.'

Flora Lugard's name is unknown in Hong Kong too, in spite of her past and what she quietly achieved here. When my husband got the job, I knew that I had to write a history about expatriate women in the colony, that I had to give Flora back her due. To have written of Chinese women, except where their lives are inextricably bound with those of Western women, would have been presumptuous on my part; there are many rather better qualified to explore what was, until after World War II, a separate world.

Once we settled here and I started my research, I used to sit in the evening on our balcony overlooking the harbour. In the fading opalescent light, the cargo vessels riding at anchor grew misty and the derricks transformed them into sailing ships. I was constantly reminded of August 1839 when British men, women, and children had to leave the Portuguese trading enclave of Macau in a hurry and live for some weeks on the sixty or so merchant ships sheltering in what was to become Hong Kong harbour.

Then there is the prod. If ever I needed an incentive, it came from two remarks made when my project became known. 'Why is she writing about expatriate women?' a British male academic asked a mutual acquaintance. 'They didn't amount to much.' The second question was asked to my face: 'But is there any expatriate woman who achieved anything?' I smiled. But I did not forget and I have tried to keep faith with my sisters.

Several strands have emerged. One of them determined my final title. Women lived a private, not a public life. They created, therefore, their own thought world; they had different needs and different values from men and their own ways of fulfilling them. The most outstanding value was that of mutual support, not necessarily limited to the circle determined by their husband's status. As for the more obvious connotation of 'private life', there is one chapter on love affairs and one on Western prostitutes!

The second strand is how women progressed as people in an integrating world over more than a century. I have cheated a bit by starting with life in Macau. It seems unnatural not to do so for that life, transferred as it was by force of arms to Hong Kong, influenced the future, and continues to influence the present. Julia Baynes, in the first chapter, is a brave and beautiful woman with seven children. But she is a pawn. Nobly she goes to out-of-bounds Canton in 1830 because her husband wants to make a political gesture against the Chinese. In the last chapter, Hilda Selwyn-Clarke is a brave and beautiful woman with one child. Her husband supports her in the stands she takes over major social and political issues affecting the Chinese. Although she has sacrificed a political career in Britain to accompany him to Hong Kong, she retrieves it on her return home.

Julia Baynes, an East India Company wife, follows the Company's policy of ostracizing non-Company merchants and their wives, such as Elizabeth Fearon, until the Company changes its policy. Then Elizabeth can enter the magic circle. After the book ends, Hilda Selwyn-Clarke and her close friend from Hong Kong, Margaret Watson Sloss, help the American radical writer Agnes Smedley, whom they knew in Hong Kong, to a less lonely and bitter death in

England in 1950, although Agnes is being reviled as a Communist spy.

By the twentieth century a few women spoke out, they appeared to lead a public life (as well as a more determined private one); but they did so against the grain, not as of right. It can still be judged private. In retrospect, though, it was progress — it was pulling the levers of public affairs on tiptoe. The number of doctors and teachers increased, too. There was barely representation, though, in the executive branch of the Civil Service — Phyllis Harrop just counts — and the first lawyer and the first political representative did not appear until after World War II.

It is not often that one has the opportunity of looking at such a neat and self-contained women's world over time closely enough and in enough detail to discern such changes; I think, therefore, that the private life of women in Hong Kong has something to reveal about the history of women more generally. Not surprisingly, it also gives a new and essential perspective to Hong Kong's own history. That history came to an abrupt end in December 1941. The book has a similar ending for after the War Hong Kong was a quite different place, one that had, in every sense, to be built anew.

The book could not have been written without the help of many people and I have made many new friends, women and men, in Hong Kong and elsewhere. Those in Hong Kong have added immeasurably to my happiness here. They are all thanked in the acknowledgements. I should have liked the dedication to be to two women, Dr Maria Jaschok and Dr Elizabeth Sinn. I did not know them before, now I thank them for their friendship, their support, and their practical help. Elizabeth, apart from directing me towards sources, read the manuscript, Maria, part of it. But I have earlier and even heavier debts.

The late Arthur Bryant was my role model when I started writing. I worked for him then and he helped my first book towards publication. Sione Latukefu was my mentor at the University of Papua New Guinea where, in my maturity, I got a BA in history. Carl Smith is the doyen of Hong Kong's historians and what is not in his head is on his card index research system that is one of our national treasures. His scholarly generosity towards me defies adequate description or thanks. He, too, has read the manuscript. I thank my husband, Derek Roebuck — legal historian, teacher, feminist, and everything to me. When we both had books to get to the same publisher by the same heated deadline, he put his aside to read mine, and improve it, and was gentle when I fought back.

SUSANNA HOE
HONG KONG
FEBRUARY 1990

ACKNOWLEDGEMENTS

I should like to thank, firstly, descendants and relatives for their help and permission to quote. They are listed in alphabetical order of the historical character that appears in the book: Colonel Sir John Baynes Bt and Simon Baynes; Sir Peter Osborne Bt (Edith Blake); Major General John Bowring, and Peter Bowring; Dr James Cantlie, Eva Cantlie, Colin Cantlie and Jean Cantlie Stewart; Alwin (Clementi) Ovenell; Brigadier Cree; John F. Fletcher and Elizabeth Kiddle (Emily Davis); Lord Pender (Marion Des Voeux); Lady Badenoch (née Forster), Helen (Forster) Clemetson, and Lindsay Badenoch; John Meade (Georgiana Kennedy); Arthur Hummel junior (Harriet Low); Brian McElney; Lord Napier and Priscilla Napier; Peggy Gotto, Ann Satchell, and Sir Cecil Burney Bt (Sybil Neville-Rolfe); Diana Piggott; David Egerton (Susanna Pottinger); Susan Milln, and Viscount Valentia (Nea Robinson); Dr Mary (Selwyn-Clarke) Seed; Claudia Severn; Richard Webster (Matilda Sharp); Cecilia Colledge (Caroline Shillaber); Clare Sack (Bella Woolf Southorn).

I thank those who have talked to me or answered letters who also appear in their own right: Dr Irene Cheng, Maria Fincher, Emily Hahn, Eric Himsworth, Dr Ellen Li, Margaret (Watson) Sloss, Joyce Symons.

I thank the following archivists, librarians, libraries publishers, societies, and government departments, mostly for their help but also for permission to quote: Terry Barringer (Royal Commonwealth Society); E.G.W. Bill (Lambeth Palace); as always, the staff of the British Library; D.J. Burkett (Kensal Green Cemetery); Dr Raymond C.I. Chen (Nethersole Hospital); Sarah Choy and other staff (Public Record Office, Hong Kong); Church Missionary Society; David Doughan (Fawcett Library); Ian F. Green (Protocol and Conference Department, Foreign and Commonwealth Office); Waltraud Haas (Basle Mission); Penelope Harland (Martyn Gregory); C.G. Harris (Bodleian

Library); Joy Herring (Library and Records Department, Foreign and Commonwealth Office); Historical Society of Pennsylvania; Eileen Ho (Jardine Matheson Archives, Hong Kong); the staff of the India Office Library; Rosemary Keen (Church Missionary Society); Patricia Moore (Glamorgan Archive Service); Virginia Murray (John Murray); National Library of Scotland, Trustees and Olive Geddes; Michael Page (King's College, London); Christine Penney (University of Birmingham); Kate Perry (Girton College); Gerald Pollinger (Laurence Pollinger Ltd); Stephen Rabson (P & O Library); Alan Reid (Jardine Matheson Archives); Rhodes House Library, Oxford; Barrie D. Scopes (The Council for World Mission — LMS); Rosemary Seton and staff (SOAS Library); Squadron Leader W.B. Sowerby and Major General D.H.G. Rice (Central Chancery of the Orders of Knighthood); Lily Sung (Hongkong and Shanghai Bank Archives); The Syndics of Cambridge University Library, and A.E.B. Owen, Margaret Pamplin, and Godfrey Waller (Manuscript Room); Leonore Thompson (Royal Botanical Gardens, Kew); Peter Travers-Laney (Cable & Wireless); Katherine Vaughan (Times Newspapers); Barbara McLean Ward (Essex Institute); Air Commodore Vivian Warrington (Protocol, Hong Kong Government); Dr Linda Washington (National Army Museum); Michael Webb and Dr Roger Morriss (National Maritime Museum, Greenwich) Margaret Welsh (Salvation Army Archives); Mrs Wong (Tsan Yuk Hospital); Peter Yeung and staff (Special Collection, Library, University of Hong Kong).

I thank the following scholars and informants for often putting aside their own work to help me with mine: Shiona Airlie, Martin Barrow, Jim Biddulph, Dr Alan Birch, R.J.F. Brothers, Belinda Brown, Philip Bruce, Nigel Cameron, Austin Coates, Leon Comber, Father Diederich, Sylvia Doulton, Professor Dafydd Evans, Diane Fearon, Francesca Fearon, and Jo Fearon (none of them any relation to Elizabeth Fearon, but hooked, nevertheless), Sir Charles Frederick, Valery Garrett, Alexis Gavriloff, Dr Joy Grant, Alan Harper, Dr James Hayes, Robin Hutcheon, Dr Ronald Hyam, The Earl of Iddesleigh, Dr Barbara Kaulbach, Maggie

Keswick, Elim Lau, Professor H.J. Lethbridge, Dr Norman Miners, Jan Morris, Myrtle Munroe, Professor Dorothy O. Helly, Dr E.H. Paterson, Lauren Pfister, Lady Ride, Sister Lina Riva, Stephen Selby, Sister Joyce Smith, Dr Tony Sweeting (who read the three chapters on education), Father Manuel Teixeira, Ken Vernon, Father Dr Vogt, Mrs Kenneth Watson, Professor Peter Wesley-Smith, Sir David Wilson, Lady Wilson.

The editorial staff at Oxford University Press prefer to remain anonymous, but will know who they are when I offer them warm thanks.

AUTHOR'S NOTE

*T*he words expatriate, white, Caucasian, Western and European are interchangeable; European includes American, as it used to. Until after World War II, women referred to each other as Mrs, Miss, or Lady, rather than by their first name, even when they were quite intimate. But since today we use first names very easily, I have often done so in the book, in an attempt to bring our sisters closer. Where a single woman has married during the course of the narrative I have sometimes when mentioning her later used both single and married names; it was not common then as it is today. I have used the more familiar Wade-Giles system of transcription, rather than the Pinyin Romanization. Most of the reference numbers in the text give only sources. They are for the sake of those who wish to follow up quotations of often unpublished papers or contentious claims or refutations on my part. General readers may want to ignore them, but they should perhaps have a quick look at the sprinkling of elaborations before putting the book down. My interest in women who lived in Hong Kong is continuing, so I should be glad to hear of anything I have missed.

CONTENTS

PLATES

MAPS

I
BEFORE HONG KONG
1830–1841

CHAPTER ONE

LADY NAPIER
LEAVES MACAU

'We managed to get on well enough until about the 19th of July,' wrote Clara Elliot, wife of Britain's Plenipotentiary on the China Coast to her sister-in-law in November 1839. Then, as she explained, the Chinese claimed that a drunken English sailor had killed a Chinese, and 'Because Charlie could neither prove the murder or give any of us up to the Commissioner, we were on the 15th August turned out of our Home in five hours notice and driven on board ship for safety.'[1]

That incident, and the First Opium War that followed, was the culmination of decades of interchange, misunderstanding and intransigence between British merchants and Chinese officials in the Pearl River delta, with the large Chinese city of Canton at one end and the Portuguese enclave of Macau 100 miles away on the coast. Forming a triangle with them was the shadowy island that was to become, as a result of the war, the British colony of Hong Kong.

Clara had lived in Macau since 1834 when Captain Charles Elliot RN accompanied Lord Napier and his commission on its mission to formalize and stabilize relations between the European maritime power and China. But she and other women like her lived there not from choice. The wives of foreigners were not allowed to visit Canton, let alone live there — a prohibition that had been explicitly spelt out since 1751 when a woman accompanying a Dutch merchant was sent back to Macau in custody.

China and Hong Kong

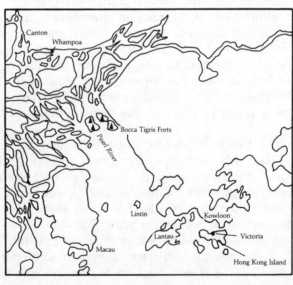

The absence of their wives from Canton was only one of the restraints on foreign merchants on the China Coast. More important to them was that they were allowed to trade only through Canton, and then only from September to March. As a concession, any business left unfinished then could be concluded from Macau.

The Portuguese had been trading with the Chinese through Macau for hundreds of years but since the eighteenth century they had been edged out by the British who, through a Parliamentary Act of 1786, had imposed their own restrictions on China trade. Only merchants of the East India Company — the 'Company' or 'Factory', as it was known for short — could take part in the trade. All other British subjects — specifically those independent merchants known as 'Country Traders' — were kept out. What is more, until the early years of the nineteenth century, Company ships had not carried women out to Macau, as they carried wives to Calcutta and other parts of the British Empire in India. In spite of that, there were British wives in Macau before 1800, and thereafter they drifted in in considerable numbers, creating there a varied European society.

The main reason for the growing number of women was that in the years following the Napoleonic Wars the Company monopoly had come under increasing pressure. By 1830 there were numerous Country Traders and non-British, particularly American, traders based in Macau. But the Chinese, for their part, remained obdurate on all points.

There had been attempts in 1829–30 to force the hands of the Chinese on a variety of issues by a number of ploys. The most obvious, in February 1830, was when Julia Baynes, wife of the President of the Select Committee of the Company, travelled to Canton together with her children, and stayed there for a while. She was followed a few days later by Elizabeth Fearon, wife of a Country Trader, and Mrs George Robinson, wife of a Company supercargo. The reaction then was stronger from the foreign confirmed bachelors trading in Canton than from the Chinese authorities, but in October Julia went to Canton again and stayed even longer. Exchanges between the British merchants and the Chinese grew increasingly hostile but did not lead to open conflict. Both sides managed to save face, at least in their own eyes. Indeed, Julia's father, General John Smith, wrote to her: 'Your adventure to Canton has proved you to be a heroine.'[2]

Keeping women out of Canton was no mere whim. An American trader who explains how much most foreign men in Canton missed feminine company, also suggests the rationale behind the ban on women when he wrote that it was 'on the principle that if foreigners were allowed their families here, they would sooner or later endanger the rights of sovereignty'.[3] But more unsettling to the Chinese after 1834 and the ending of the Company's monopoly was that there was now seemingly no control over foreign traders. Lord Napier was only of interest to them if he could solve that problem — the Chinese authorities were unconcerned about relations between the two powers, for they did not regard Britain as a power with which to negotiate.

Lord Napier's mission and its failure has been much discussed as a prelude to Hong Kong's history. What is rather less familiar is what went on behind the scenes; both Napier and his master attendant, Charles Elliot, whose name is most commonly associated with the taking of Hong Kong, travelled out to China with their wives.

The day after their arrival in Macau, on 15 July 1834, A. Robertson wrote to William Jardine, the most forceful of the Country Traders, that Napier's wife 'looks more delicate and his daughters rather good looking than otherwise'.[4] A few days later, 48-year-old Napier set off for Canton, against Chinese regulations, leaving 40-year-old Eliza (Elizabeth) and two teenage daughters comfortably enough installed in Macau. The Napiers had left six children behind in Scotland — one only a year old. Eliza returned home barely six months later a widow.

The private face of Napier's failure to prevent a move inexorably to force of arms between Britain and China is only fleetingly glimpsed as only one letter describing Lady Napier's life in Macau survives, but there are quite a number of letters from Charles and Clara Elliot, their travelling companions on the *Andromache*.

The Elliot letters home to his sister, Lady Hislop, do not appear to have been used before for historical reconstruction.[5] They provide a wealth of detail concerning the private life of a man who has, hitherto, only been seen as a public figure. Clara has previously been granted only one line in Hong Kong's early history. The letters also reveal a range of emotions and reactions to Elliot's treatment by Napier and the British government, as well as the Chinese and China Coast merchants, and Clara's version gives them a distinctive zest.

The position of 33-year-old Charles Elliot was relatively lowly in the hierarchy of Napier's Commission; three others were ahead of him in seniority. Whether or not Napier's preoccupation on board ship was intended to exclude his master attendant, Elliot felt ignored. As far as birth and connections were concerned, he did not consider himself inferior to Napier. Elliot's cousin, the Earl of Minto, was Ambassador to Berlin and was about to be appointed First Lord of the Admiralty, a post held by another cousin, Lord Auckland who would be appointed Governor General of India (with considerable responsibility for operations in China) soon after the *Andromache* arrived in Macau.

Elliot had been recalled from British Guiana, where his title was 'protector of slaves', to discuss the question of slavery at a time when it was an important one in Whitehall. He had been recommended to the China post by his friend John Davis, Napier's number two, a man already acknowledged as a China hand. Davis had been with the Company since 1813 and was to become Hong Kong's second Governor in 1844.

But there was more to Charles and Clara Elliot's sensitivity about a lack of friendliness between the two families than, presumably, the Napiers could know. The Elliot letters make it clear that Charles was deeply in debt and saw the China job as a means to earn money, live cheaply, and pay off his debts. Added to that, he had not been happy in his job in Guiana; he had felt put upon and he did not intend to be taken advantage of in China. He did not even feel that his appointment was adequate for his experience, talents and aspirations. Then there was Clara, his wife of six years. Her reaction on being told of the China posting was bitter. But she had, after, as Charles put it, talking 'her full share of nonsense', come round.[6] Difficult decisions had still to be made, however. In the end they had left behind with Emma and Sir Thomas Hislop, baby Gibby, only a year old, and taken with them young Harriet and little Hughie.

There was also Clara's appearance which, given the lack of sociability displayed in her letters, may have been important. One Opium War historian writes of her 'red nose'.[7] That she had some recurring trouble with her nose is obvious from her letters.[8] It appears that the infection dated from their stay in British Guiana and was by 1835 being treated as ringworm.

Clara's health problems were more severe than her inflamed nose. On her way to Calcutta in August 1840 to stay with Charles's cousins Lord Auckland and Emily Eden at Government House, Clara wrote to her sister-in-law, 'One thing only I hope that idiotical feeling which you must have observed tho' you were too kind to notice it will not seize upon me as on former occasions when I wished most to appear to advantage. At that time dearest Emma my health had failed me and I was otherwise crushed by various causes.'[9]

On board the *Andromache*, therefore, Charles Elliot was crushed by debt and an appointment he felt was beneath him; he was also as upset as Clara about leaving his baby son behind; and Clara's health and nerves were undermined. Not a promising start. On top of that they felt slighted by the Napiers. In writing to his sister on that subject, Charles pretended he only did so to amuse her and that it was nothing to him; but the joke wore thin.

Eliza Napier was also in poor health. Charles Elliot described her as being confined to her cabin until Madeira and the ship being held up at the Cape on account of Lady Napier's ill health. Delay mattered to the Elliots in the cramped conditions in which they were housed. In one letter Charles Elliot called the Napiers the 'Emperor' and 'Empress'; later he remarks, 'I do not like the ladies. She is sly and her young ladies unmitigatedly disagreeable. If we were intimate we should very soon quarrel, that is to say, I should, for the manner disputatious always provokes me excessively, as it is we are not likely to fall into collision.'[10]

Clara, born the daughter of untitled Robert Harley Windsor, got on well enough with Lord Napier — Charles suggested it was because she knew her place. She remarked, 'I am such a favourite with Lord Napier and he has been so kind to *me* that I do not like to say a word of ill nature about him.'[11]

The two women arrived to a society in Macau which was in a state of flux, a society which has some bearing on the early days of Hong Kong and the tensions that were to occur between different interest groups — within government circles, between them and merchants, and between merchants and traders, or shopkeepers. Tensions which were, therefore, not caused by women but reflected by wives.

Before 1834 the Company had done all it could to discourage the Country Traders. What that confrontation had meant in social or personal terms has not been explored, either in the histories of the East India Company in China or in those of the First Opium War which followed on from the end of the Company's monopoly. An entry in the diary of a young American woman who lived in Macau between 1829 and 1834, Harriet Low, gives a clear idea of the implications. 20-year-old Harriet was the niece of the senior partner in the American trading firm Russell and Company and she wrote on 8 February 1830, a few days before Julia Baynes set out for Canton for the first time, 'Heard today that the ladies of the factory have called on Mrs Fearon. Was very happy to hear it, as she has heretofore been excluded.'[12]

It might be that Harriet is talking simply of the unprecedented plans to visit Canton but I think it is more likely to mean that since 1826, when Elizabeth Fearon came to live in Macau, she had been ostracized by the East India Company wives and that she had not been part of that surprisingly gracious and elegant, though small society that revolved round the Company.

It could hardly be argued that 36-year-old Elizabeth was excluded on her own account. Apart from the fact that she was, as her husband carefully explained to Harriet, to her disgust, the daughter of a baronet, 'well-born and well bred',[13] she was, as Harriet recorded, 'a very lively pleasant woman'[14] with 'the sweetest disposition possible'.[15] And then there was her house. Inside, Harriet saw Elizabeth 'surrounded by everything comfortable and elegant'.[16] As for the garden, where Harriet went to walk as often as possible, it was a paradise. Those who today visit the public gardens alongside the Camoens Museum can imagine what it must have been like over 150 years ago when it was all one and belonged to a private house. From there could be seen the sweep of Macau Bay, with fine Company houses following its curve, and Portuguese churches with their bell towers on the hills that overlooked it, as well as the narrow and teeming Chinese streets.

Elizabeth's exclusion is more likely to have been on account of her husband. Christopher Fearon had once been a Company man; but since 1825 he had been a Country Trader, enabled by the device of calling himself the Hanoverian Consul, to evade the Parliamentary sanction against British subjects trading independently.

The relationship between Emily Davis, wife of Company officer John Davis, and American Harriet Low is less clear. Davis, as Governor of Hong Kong, was to be a man so caught between his Company and administrative background and the demands and attitudes of Hong Kong's merchants that he left Hong Kong reviled. His wife Emily did not accompany him to Hong Kong, perhaps to the detriment of his governorship. The reasons for her absence are discernible in what it is possible to piece together from her days in Macau. The coolness that developed between Emily and Harriet Low may well reflect the tensions between Company and outsiders, in this case the Americans, though obviously other more personal factors may have been involved.

Emily had been in Macau since her husband arrived back in Chinese waters in November 1830, and probably on and off since her marriage in 1822. At one time she and Harriet were the best of friends. On 15 April 1831 Harriet wrote:

Our dear friend Mrs Davis spent 2 hours with us this morning. We read French together, says I shall read very well in a little while — encouraging but she does read it so smoothly and elegantly that I feel almost ashamed to read it to her. Before Mrs D went we had some carmine come from Canton, to *colour stockings* (mind ye). We thought we would see *how* it would look, on our cheeks, so I painted Mrs D and Aunt ... We washed ours directly off but Mrs D said she would go home and see what Davis would do.[17]

At the beginning of 1832, John Davis was President of the Company's Select Committee for six months. Harriet mocked him and Emily as 'The King and Queen' when they were delayed by a visit from a mandarin and made a picnic late; but they were still friends.[18] On 3 July 1833, however, Harriet wrote, 'Called on Mrs Davis. Found her very agreeable apparently although I believe she cares very little about seeing us, that is she would much rather not. Oh the hypocrisy of this world.'[19]

Emily Davis had problems of her own, as Harriet had recorded in May 1831: 'Went to Church. Mrs Davis came in after. Poor soul, she has troubles too as well as the rest of the world, and lovely as she is, I would not change places with her.'[20] The Davis family went home at the beginning of 1835 and Emily spent the rest of her life in England. Doubtless she had had enough: married at 21 in India where her father was in the army; twin daughters born at sea in 1824, and seven children born by the time she was 38, in 1839.[21]

Harriet Low had left by the time Eliza Napier arrived, and the Company's monopoly was newly ended. Eliza's impressions of the opening of a new era are, therefore, of some interest. She described Mrs Davis and the newly elevated Lady Robinson, wives of the senior members of her husband's commission, and Mrs Daniell, wife of the principal agent of the Company, as 'all pleasant people in their various ways, and gentlewomen'. She observed more generally a month after her arrival:

Hitherto the Gentlemen of the Factory have always had their wives here, and till the last few years there were scarce any merchants. Now the Company is dissolved the Society must deteriorate still more, because the private merchants, though respectable men, are not educated ones, and if they bring their wives they have probably risen with themselves ... Besides the persons I have mentioned, there are the captains of what are called the *Country Ships*, that is, traders between this and India, they are here during 4 months of every year and bring their wives, these are not fine ladies, and being respectable though not refined I said I should be happy to receive them and return their visits. It is absurd in a place like this to be *exclusive*, and civility is easy and intimacy need not follow.[22]

Clara Elliot is most unrevealing about other women and their lives, her letters being almost wholly concerned with family affairs, including her husband's work. The inflammation of her nose, having cleared up soon after her arrival in Macau, flared up again later which may have exacerbated a natural reserve. She wrote in March 1836 of the imminent arrival in England of J.F.N. Daniell and Mrs Daniell, 'Should you ever meet them pray be good-natured to them as nothing could have exceeded their kindness and hospitality to us and the children.' But she continues, 'Nice people here Emma are very scarce.'[23] It was not just her and Macau, it was the eternal cry of the expatriate throughout the ages, and a continuing problem for women with too much time on their hands.

It would be a pity, and a mistake, to think that Company ethos or even ordinary British snobbery dominated the relations between women in Macau in the 1830s. Half the time Harriet Low bemoaned the lack of congenial company but the other half she extolled the virtues of her 'sisters' and her diary shows many examples not only of women from different milieux who found themselves in alien surroundings caring for each other's well-being, but also of their simple, unaffected pleasures together. Her description in November 1831 of a 'lady party', which aptly equates with a '*tai tai* lunch' in Hong Kong today, is one of the most appealing:

Went to Mrs Thornhill's in the evening. As a specimen of the company we take at these lady parties I'll just tell you how we were situated tonight. We took our tea at the center table, then had a couch on each side of the table, Mrs Fearon on one, Mrs Davis on another, Mrs Low on the third, Miss Low on the fourth, our feet up, which is generally the custom when no gents are present.[24]

Lady Napier was in Macau only a short time but it was a crucial moment in the unfolding of the events that were to follow. Her husband's mission failed. At various stages the Chinese authorities stopped trading and resorted, as they were increasingly to do in the 1830s, to removing the servants from expatriate households in Macau, where their writ, not that of the Portuguese Governor, applied at the most basic level. Rumours abounded; as Clara Elliot reported home, 'All Europeans were to be murdered except Lady Napier and her two daughters who were to be taken as hostages. We laugh *now* at these idle tales but I assure you at the time we were all much alarmed, the husbands being absent in Canton and the poor women alone.'[25]

Napier returned to Macau in October 1834, rejected as Plenipotentiary from the King of England, and dying of a fever he had contracted up river. Clara Elliot wrote of Eliza Napier that she 'has had much suffering of late and I sincerely sympathise with her and feel for her how differently she will return home, how dreary and miserable — poor thing.'[26] It was Mrs Thornhill, Harriet Low's friend — 'Irish and has all the open frankness of manner belonging to the Irish, enthusiastic, affectionate and hospitable'[27] — who took the Napier women into her house during those dreadful days following his death.

CHAPTER TWO

MRS KING
AND THE OPIUM

*I*n March 1839 Clara Elliot wrote a distraught letter to her sister-in-law Emma Hislop. It was carried on the *Melbourne* to England and with it went young Harriet and Hughie Elliot. Their continued presence in Macau had become too much of a risk.

Following Lord Napier's death five years earlier, many changes had taken place. Charles Elliot had worked his way through the ranks of the commission, moving higher as John Davis, Sir George Robinson and J.H. Astell left. He became Britain's senior representative in China in December 1836. His opinion of his friend John Davis had remained warm; indeed, he regretted Davis leaving for, although it made him more senior, which in turn meant more money to pay off his debts, it also elevated Sir George Robinson. In his letters, Elliot was unabashedly scathing about everyone else connected with the Commission and claimed to carry the whole burden of the work and responsibility long before he did so in name.

It is obvious that as early as 1828 the Select Committee of the East India Company were dissatisfied with George Robinson, and yet he had risen, then been appointed to Lord Napier's commission, and continued to rise after the latter's death. Clara Elliot's letter of March 1836 gives a flavour of the disagreements in policy:

Charlie leads a sad life with Sir George Robinson, who has not a spark of manly feeling, or of truth or of integrity in him; he is detested by the Chinese and a disgrace to the English. I would not write this strongly, were it not the truth and did I not know, he had done his best to injure Charlie. I wish I could tell you distinctly all that has taken place but it would be far too long a task for me and besides I feel convinced that the government will ultimately do Charlie justice. It is utterly impossible that they can sanction Sir G's conduct in going [moving his headquarters] to Lintin in spite of his instructions and Charlie's entreaties — a place where the opium or smuggling trade is carried on and then forwarding home his own reasons for doing so and suppressing the minutes in which Charlie advises him not to go to Lintin.[1]

Under Robinson the opium trade had flourished, and not only for the British merchants and British India. However, although many officers in the Chinese administration and, even it is said, the Emperor, made money from it, the Emperor chose now to intensify the fight against what was seen as a menace to China. The drug undermined the health of his people, and the silver which bought it was a drain on the economy. In addition, the trade, illegal as it was as far as China was concerned, created unsettling incidents as from time to time corrupt officials made a show of suppressing it.

At the end of 1838 the Emperor appointed Commissioner Lin Tse-hsü to deal once and for all with the 'foreign mud' and re-establish trade on a proper footing. Unlike corruptible officials, Lin acted swiftly and uncompromisingly. Having arrived in Canton on 10 March 1839, eight days later he issued an order that all the opium stored in the foreign factories in Canton and at Whampoa just downstream was to be handed over to him.

In view of what was to follow, the Elliots' decision to send the children away was a wise one. But only two children had gone, for by now there was a new baby in the family, and he was to remain through the drama of 1839. From the private correspondence of Charles and Clara Elliot and the interspersing in the letters of family matters and the news of the difficulties and responsibilities of Charles's work, comes an unparalleled view, not just of the contrast

between the public and private domain but of the inter-
dependence of the two.

It is not often in the private correspondence of the nineteenth century that one gets an insight into the bodily and
reproductive functions of its women and yet, looking at the
large families of the women who pass through these pages,
and the emotional and physical strains which they must
have produced, the subject is a serious one. Clara and
Charles are more forthcoming than is usual.

The constant appearance of new babies played some part
in the problems that had led to them going to China. Gibby,
the baby they left behind, had been born the year before.
Part of Clara's misery at the time of the decision must have
been the fear that she was once again pregnant, for soon
after their arrival in Macau, she talks of Harriet and Hughie
having been well buffeted about, metaphorically as well as
physically, and adds, 'and what do you say to *me* dear
Emma — am I not behaving well — not the slightest appearance of another, it is indeed a happy escape'.[2]

The Elliot's celebrated their escape too soon for in
February 1837 Charles wrote to tell Emma that 'Clara grows
round, I regret to say.'[3] The baby was born on 9 October
1837 when Charles wrote, trying to make light of the matter,

To get away, however, from death to life, be it known to you that
my fourth child has been introduced into this Christian family, by
the name of "Frederick Eden". Fred for dear old Fred's sake [his
brother]; and by the high and mighty name [that of his cousin
Lord Auckland] that he may some day beg a [favour] from the
byegone governor general.

Clara wrote with more resignation, 'Of course you have
heard of my ill luck in adding another Boy to our Hearth.
Foolish is it not but unavoidable, in spite of grand resolutions.'[4] Fred was not the last but that is another story!

The agony of parting from their two middle children at
the time of Commissioner Lin's edict was to last with them
both. An idea of how they felt is given at the end of the
letter from Clara that accompanied the children:

I am sure you love Charlie too dearly to regret my final determination to remain with him instead of accompanying my
darlings home, the pain of this separation is indeed intense and
we pray God that they may be rewarded by the advantage and
good they will experience by it. My poor heart is so full that I
cannot write more just now.

Charles's letter is no less anguished as he describes, 'my
own darling Hughie, the plague and pleasure of my life
... with a bottle of quicksilver dancing through his veins
instead of blood'.[5]

Clara writes of 22 March, the day the children left, 'on
our return on shore late in the evening we found the dis-
quieting news of the stoppage of trade and all communication between Macau and Canton with threats of punishment ... towards the British merchants until they had given
up every chest of opium in their possession'.[6] Charles left
for Canton in his cutter immediately, rather like the traditional knight on a white charger, and it was probably the
last time the merchants approved of his actions. Clara was
not to see him again until the end of May for he, with the
other British in Canton, remained under house arrest there
for nine weeks. Then, persuaded by Elliot, the merchants
handed over the opium.

Nearly all the merchants on the China coast were involved in the opium trade. One particular exception was the
American Charles W. King who actively campaigned against
what he saw as an evil trade. He and his wife were to be
uniquely involved in the destruction of 20,000 cases of
opium that followed. In August 1830 Harriet Low had referred to King as

certainly one of the best young [men] I should think that ever
lived so long in this country. I mean he is really good, religious.
He is very strict, and it quite astonishes me that a young man
should leave home so young as he did, and come to Canton and
Manila and reside for so many years as he has, and still be so
correct as he is. His health is very poor is one reason I presume.
His habits are sedentary — has always been a great student —
but if he would be a little more cheerful (which I think one so

thoroughly good as he is should be) he would do more for the cause of religion. But he certainly is very much to be respected. He is now about 22 . . .[7]

Some time before 1837 Charles King married Charlotte Mathews, daughter of an American minister, and brought her out to China. By then he was working for the American trading company of Olyphants and in July that year he, Charlotte, and the missionaries Dr Peter Parker, Samuel Wells Williams and Charles Gutzlaff went on a mission to Japan in the company's ship the *Morrison*. The object of the mission, instigated by Charles King, was, as Williams put it, 'the extension of civilisation and Christianity'.[8] The second aim, which it was hoped would facilitate the first, was to return home some Japanese sailors who had been ship-wrecked.

The mission, to a country which had been completely closed to the outside world for a long period, was a failure on both counts. What Charlotte King made of it does not seem to have been recorded but Williams reports that she was 'somewhat indisposed during this voyage, from the heat and the reflection from the water'.[9] No doubt she took comfort from being the first American woman to have had contact, however tenuous, with Japan. All that we can guess about her from the fact that, unusually, she spoke Cantonese and accompanied her husband as she did, is that she was a woman of some determination and application. Her next mission on the *Morrison* was even more startling.

Commissioner Lin knew exactly who the opium traders were; King was not one of them. When, therefore, King asked if he could watch some of the opium being destroyed, his request was granted and on 14 June 1839 he took a party, including Charlotte, up the Pearl River. They trans-ferred to a war junk and landed near what is now called Humen. There they watched as the sickly sweet smelling opium balls and cakes were broken up, pushed into water scattered with lime and salt, and stirred vigorously. The mixture was then allowed to run into the creek and so into the sea.

Today there is a disappointing museum celebrating the Chinese side of the First Opium War. In its grounds are still three of the ponds where the opium was made to decompose. When I visited the place in 1989, exactly a hundred and fifty years later, and stood by the pools, I was absurdly conscious of Charlotte King sitting there watching. Afterwards the men were taken for an interview with Commissioner Lin, while Charlotte was kept comfortable. Her presence was all the more extraordinary because she was the first Western woman granted permission to visit China — a fact of which nothing has ever been made.

Charles Elliot was much plagued by King's anti-opium activities, not because Elliot supported the opium trade — he did not — but because he had his own views on how the matter should be handled, and he was in charge. King, and his so-called anonymous pamphlet addressed as an open letter to Elliot, caused him embarrassment. Even his sister Emma wrote to him about it and he took time patiently to explain to her about Charles King and his own position and activities.

Clara was less patient. She wrote to Emma on 4 May 1840,

If our kind friend and well-wisher [King] should pay you a visit, pray do not allow him to prejudice or deceive you by his plausibility, humility and sincerity. A greater hypocrite never existed and it is odd enough I *knew* him almost the first time we met and made Charlie angry by my description and my warning not to be too confiding.

Charles Elliot was being attacked, and would continue to be so even after his return to Britain, on so many sides that Charles King's endeavours have left little trace on his reputation, though King's own moral stand allows him to be better appreciated today than he was then. Charlotte King, an unusual woman for her day, about whom too little is known, appears as hardly more than a name in the continuing story. The Kings left for home in January 1840. Clara Elliot, with a young child and a husband weighed

down by intractable problems to worry about, saw more of
the drama out; for the destruction of the opium was by no
means the end of the matter.

CHAPTER THREE

MRS ELLIOT GOES TO SEA

So volatile did the situation become after the destruction of the opium in June 1839, so full of negotiations which failed, and agreements that were betrayed, that in many ways the hostilities which followed were inevitable. And yet that July not everyone can have been feeling the strain and tension. On 4 August the American missionary Henrietta Shuck sent home from Macau an account of a trip to Hong Kong harbour on board the *Scaleby Castle* that was both cheerful and prescient:

We remained at Hong Kong, about one week, were greatly bene-fited by a change of air, and returned to our happy home and pleasant labors. Hong Kong is indeed, a most romantic spot, and said to be the finest harbor in the world. There were forty-five square rigged vessels anchored in different directions, during the time we were there, which presented a lovely aspect. The lofty and green covered hills surrounded us on all sides.[1]

One of the most awful moments for a writer recon-structing the past with the help of personal documents such as the letters of Clara and Charles Elliot is to come across a letter that reads, as does Clara Elliot's to Emma of November 1839, 'I have written to my aunt fully on this subject and probably she will have shown you my letters, so I need not repeat the story.'[2] The letters to her aunt do not survive. All that is left from Clara about the events of August 1839 is the account with which this story began of the alleged murder of a Chinese by a drunken English sailor and the information that the Elliots had to leave Macau.

The reason for the evacuation of 15 August seems to have been that it was known Commissioner Lin was to leave on a journey to the enclave that day, and Charles had just sent off a reply to the Chinese saying he would not give up the English murderer. It was assumed that the two were connected.

Lin's visit was, according to Chinese sources, pre-planned, but in his reply to Elliot he did threaten that the British in Macau were to be cut off from all supplies.[3] Only some British families left with Clara and Charles; at least another 57 families left ten days later when there was a threat that Chinese troops were to surround British dwellings. Some stories have it that the Portuguese Governor of Macau refused to protect the British; others that they left so as not to embarrass the Portuguese administration.[4]

In a later letter, looking back, Clara writes, 'Freddy is too young to be inconvenienced. He was as happy as possible on board the *Fort William* and is as merry and as impudent here as he can well be.'[5] How women with slightly older children, and more of them, managed can be imagined, as the sailing ships — about sixty in the end — rode at anchor for weeks in what is today Hong Kong harbour. It was August, the height of heat, humidity, rain and the menace of typhoons. Even the Star Ferry — an eight minute crossing today — makes one distinctly queasy when a stiff breeze gets under the waves.

We know that there were pregnant women among the evacuees because the *Canton Register* reports that 'ladies in the last stages of pregnancy, were hurried off on the decks of schooners'.[6] Only one new mother termed 'temporarily at Hong Kong' is noted in the baptismal records of St John's Cathedral Hong Kong, but it only needs one confirmed birth under those circumstances to stir the imagination.

Only the British had to leave Macau. Caroline Squire's husband, an English missionary with the Church Missionary Society (CMS), left, but the Squires shared their house with American missionaries so Caroline, who was ill, could stay behind. She talks of 'hardly experiencing any hindrance save confinement in the house'.[7] She says, too, that she was lonely and rather overcome by the responsibility. Her husband returned quite soon and they remained quietly in the house; in October other evacuees started to drift back. But Elliot wanted an agreement that they could do so officially and that trade could resume on British terms, and was negotiating for it.

At the end of October, negotiations foundered again. An English ship, the *Thomas Coutts*, disobeyed Elliot's instructions about presenting a united front against Chinese demands, thus opening the way for new pressure from them. Elliot, with his negotiating power reduced, nevertheless took up a further letter himself on board the man-of-war the *Volage*, seeking to safeguard British interests. It was returned unanswered, and a fleet of junks was sent out to turn Elliot back. There was a 24-hour stand off and then a confrontation at Chu'an-pi on 2 November, the first blow in the war. Clara Elliot, describing this incident in a letter to Emma from Macau two days later, continued:

The *Volage* sailed here as fast as possible to advise the English once more to embark. My maid who had lived with me for upwards of two years would not again undertake the inconvenience of living on board ship and refused to accompany me. By dint of entreaty therefore Charlie was persuaded to leave me here. He is gone on board the *Volage*. The Chinese [servants are all] gone so I am obliged to confine myself to the House all shut up and keep very quiet with everything packed up for an instantaneous move if necessary. I am strongly urged to go for a few months to Manila or Singapore. But as long as I am of the least service to Charlie and he does not express a wish for me to be out of the way I do not mind discomforts and will not forsake him. I have however written and told him to do with me as he thinks best. My heart aches dear Emma not at the loss of fortune or comfort but at the knowledge of His broken spirit. Hitherto he has gone through his troubles with surprising courage and strength of mind but this last treachery of the Commissioner's together with the discontent and ill feeling of his own countrymen . . . Never was I so brought in contact with the mercantile world as of late and truly they have lowered the English character in *my* eyes — they sacrifice every thing, every feeling, for *dollar making*.[8]

For those not immediately involved, the experience was, once again, fairly painless, as Caroline Squire records:

The ships came at once to Macao, and during the night of Sunday, took off the English ladies and children, and nearly all the British subjects, fearing in revenge for their defeat, the Chinese would secure them. This sudden flight astonished the Chinese greatly. We knew nothing of the flight till it was over, and ourselves, with the few others who remained, confined themselves to their houses; within the last two days, we hear that Englishmen are seen in the streets once more. We consider it prudent to keep very quiet, it would be not a little distressing to be ordered away at present, when I am in bad health, and our children might suffer, and we should not be inclined again to separate.[9]

In the midst of unsettled conditions that Christmas, Clara and Charles Elliot managed to find one moment of happiness. They received a letter from Emma telling them that Harriet and Hughie had arrived safely in England. Clara wrote to her sister-in-law how,

Charlie in spite of the Chinese and other difficulties brought it to me *himself* on Christmas day and my heart rejoiced to hear his voice again in its natural tone call out 'I have *such* a Christmas box for you,' and to see his face beaming once more with joy. We read the happy letter over and over again, wept and then frolicked about like two mad creatures.[10]

The joy was fleeting for, at the beginning of 1840, presumably about the 4 February when HMS *Hyacinth* sailed into Macau harbour to evacuate the British once more following the exhibition of murder notices, Charles and Clara made a heartbreaking decision: she left for Singapore with little Fred. Charles wrote to his sister:

My single hearted, wise wife (for she is wise in the best sense of the word) has resolved to spare me the pain of constant anxiety whilst she is here, and to take the whole bitter burden to her own heart. She [leaves] for Singapore where she will remain till the troubles have either blown over or till I can join her ... I owe it to my countrymen to leave no hostages here ...[11]

And in a longer letter of 25 February, giving Emma more details of the political situation, he became sentimental about his wife, pouring out his heart to his sister who he knew would understand, and ending:

I have never known her virtues and never felt how helpless I am without her till now that she has left me. She is an excellent woman in every sense of the word, and has displayed so much real tenderness, and so much wisdom during the *desperate* year I have passed, that at least it has had the one salutary effect of making me understand and love her better than I ever did.

By now, Lord Palmerston, the British Foreign Secretary, and Lord Auckland, Governor General of India, from where help would come, had put in train an expedition to sort out the China problem or, as Clara put it, 'It is whispered that Lord Auckland is to take up the cudgels and teach them better manners.'[12] Clara waited in Singapore for events to resolve themselves, uncertain about whether or not to return to England. She stayed with a merchant called Johnston and on 5 May 1840 wrote, 'He is good and hospitable but his house is mercantile and dirty. I remain with him for prudential reasons (of the purse).' She was saved from having to make a final decision by an invitation from Lord Auckland and Emily Eden to visit them in Calcutta — a great kindness on Emily's part for they hardly knew each other. Clara had explained to Emma over a year earlier that 'I have managed to win a corner in Miss Eden and Lord Auckland's heart by doing 2 or 3 little commissions for them, as a proof of this her first letter ended sincerely, her next affectionately, and her last, your very affectionate *cousin*.'[13]

Clara left for Calcutta in August 1840. Meanwhile, the expedition, under the overall command of Charles's cousin Admiral George Elliot, with Charles as number two Plenipotentiary, had arrived in Hong Kong waters. Commissioner Lin's immediate response was to issue a proclamation offering rewards for the destruction or capture of various parts of the force, including any British person, combatant or non-combatant, alive or dead.

Among the forces was a brig called the *Kite* which had brought stores out for the expedition and was now borrowed and armed by the Royal Navy to take dispatches to ships surveying the Yangtze river. The *Kite*'s civilian captain was John Noble, who had with him on board his 26-year-old wife Anne and their five-month-old son. On 15 September the *Kite* foundered. Anne heard her husband call out, 'Hold on, Anne', but never saw him nor their baby again.

Anne and several members of the crew managed to save themselves and drifted helplessly again and again past the *Kite*, Anne always hoping desperately that her family had somehow survived. At first the Chinese they met treated them kindly enough, but then information was obviously received about the proclamation and they were attacked. Chains were placed round their necks and they were dragged on foot for twenty miles or so over a period of days; later they were put into bamboo cages. Meanwhile Anne, dressed as she says 'in a thin morning gown, no bonnet, no shawl and no shoes', had her wedding ring snatched from her finger, was spat upon, and denied food. What she did not write in a 'letter' apparently written in Ningpo prison but probably written later for publication, was that she was also pregnant.

At one stage of the journey Anne recorded:

In the evening I was taken to see the Mandarin's wife and daughters, but although my appearance must have been wretched in the extreme, they did not evince the least feeling towards me, but rather treated me as an object of scorn. This I felt the more, as I was enabled to make them understand, that I had lost both my dear husband and child in the wreck.[14]

On 23 September the party reached Ningpo and, there-after, Anne, at least, was reasonably treated. The only hint she gives of her state of health is, 'On the 8th October I was far from well; two days afterward I suffered much from violent pain, and was not able to lie down during the whole night, on account of the pain.'[15] She was allowed to receive letters and clothes and at one stage 'I went to see the Mandarin's lady, who gave me some fruit and artificial flowers, the first mark of kindness I had received from a lady'.[16] From the questioning Anne received, she drew the impression that they thought she was Queen Victoria's sister.[17]

In the outside world, the capture of the *Kite* party, particularly Anne, and two other individuals at about the same time, generated high feeling. Edward Cree, a ship's surgeon whose journal, part of it published, will provide useful information from now on, had met Anne, and wrote, by the side of a drawing of her in a bamboo cage slung on two poles, 'Mrs Noble is a raw-boned, red-headed Scotch-woman poor thing. This has caused great indignation in the force against the Chinese who won't get much mercy when a chance comes of retaliation.'[18]

Meanwhile, Charles Elliot was doing all he could for the hostages; in October he had a meeting with a mandarin on a beach at Tinghai. He made it clear that they must be released if recent negotiations were to have a peaceful conclusion.

Tinghai, on the island of Chusan, had been taken in July 1840, following the blockade of Canton when the expeditionary force first arrived, and after that a fair-sized European community sprang up there. Under the protection of the Force it was safer than Macau. Conditions were obviously pleasant because later, when Hong Kong Island had been taken, there were complaints that Chusan would have been a better prize.

Among the new residents were Mary Gutzlaff, and Mary's two grown-up nieces, Catherine and Isabella Parkes. Mary was the second wife of Charles Gutzlaff, the eccentric, Pomeranian-born missionary closely associated with the proliferation of missionary endeavours in the Far East. She is important to the story not only because she is one of the few women about whom there are details for this transitionary period but also because she was a particularly interesting example of the sort of missionary wife who contributed to Hong Kong's early education, as well as being a precursor — rather a maverick one, as Chapter 11 shows — of the unmarried missionary teacher.

Mary Wanstall had arrived in Malacca as a missionary teacher in 1832, and married the widower Gutzlaff in 1834. When in that year the Napier commission needed a new interpreter, Gutzlaff was appointed and moved with Mary to Macau. There she set up a school which very soon concentrated its efforts on blind Chinese girls.

During the evacuation of Macau, many people had gone quite away from the area, Mary Gutzlaff and her nieces for example, after six weeks afloat in Hong Kong harbour, going to Manila. But in 1840 Charles Gutzlaff had gone to Tinghai as part of the Expedition; Mary Gutzlaff and her nieces, sailed from Macau to Chusan in October and Mary started planning a school there. Edward Cree talks of going for a walk on Chusan on 7 December 1840, 'Met Mr Gutzlaff with his pretty step daughter and their band of Chinese children.'[19] In October he had drawn a picture entitled, 'The Chinese ladies overhauling Mrs Bull' beside a story in which he recounted how Mrs Bull, the wife of the Botswain of his ship the *Rattlesnake*, 'went on shore with her husband and excited intense excitement amongst the Chinese here — who believed her to be the Queen of England. The Chinese ladies came out of their houses and overhauled her well, her shoes and dress especially.'[20]

Throughout the last weeks of 1840 and the first week of the new year, after his cousin George had returned home ill and he was the sole Plenipotentiary, Charles Elliot negotiated with Kishen, the Chinese representative. On 7 January 1841, in an effort to break the impasse, Elliot issued an ultimatum that unless by 8 o'clock the following morning the Chinese had become less intransigent, he would seize the Bocca Tigris forts that dominated the Pearl River leading to Canton. The second battle of Ch'uan-pi took place when there was no response. On 20 January preliminary negotiations for a peace treaty were announced, ceding Hong Kong Island to the British. On 26 January the navy took possession of the island.

Under the terms of the Convention of Ch'uan-pi, Chusan

was to be evacuated. Mary Gutzlaff and the Misses Parkes, therefore, embarked for Macau, on 23 February, on the transport ship *Blundell*. Chusan's small missionary community also included Dr William Lockhart. In his diary he wrote on 24 February, 'Early this morning a Chinese boat came into the harbour, bringing Mrs Noble and one of the officers of the *Kite*. Mrs Noble joined Mr Gutzlaff's family on board the *Blundell*.'[21] That entry must be taken as the clue needed to solve the mystery of which 'dear friend' Anne Noble's published letter was addressed to, for she ends her account, 'Being most anxious to see you, my dear friend, and, Dr Lockhart being in waiting to accompany me, I lost no time in hastening to the ship *Blundell*, where you had so carefully provided for my comfort.'[22] Anne and her new baby sailed for England in June 1841. $10,000 had been raised for her by public subscription and her reminiscences had gone into their second edition.

That spring in Macau was a time of rejoicing, for at last feeling secure. Catherine Parkes became engaged to William Lockhart and they were married in May. Lockhart wrote to the London Missionary Society (LMS), 'She already possesses a good knowledge of the language and a ready aptitude in speaking to people and joined to this . . . piety and a strong and constant desire to spend her strength in our Saviour's service.'[23] About that time Mary Gutzlaff must have conceived her first child, but it was born dead in January 1842, leaving Mary ill and depressed. She would sail for New York with three little blind Chinese girls.

Kishen was dismissed and as his last action, in an effort to redeem himself, he repudiated his agreement with Elliot and ordered an attack on British shipping — the third Battle of Ch'uan-pi (26 February 1841). But before that Charles Elliot had celebrated the taking of Hong Kong by sending for Clara and Fred to come back from Calcutta.

The surviving Elliot letters do not cover this later period, but Clara was seen in Hong Kong waters. Captain Hall RN of the *Nemesis* remembers how on 10 May 1841 Elliot 'resolved to go in person to Canton in the *Nemesis*, and in order the better to impress the Chinese with the opinion which he still wished them to believe he retained of their good faith, he even took up Mrs Elliot with him; probably the first time an English female had ever set foot in Canton'.[24] Julia Baynes was already forgotten!

On 20 July Charles was travelling from Macau to Hong Kong in the cutter *Louisa* when it was shipwrecked in a typhoon. The Chinese who rescued him and his companions had, happily, not heard of the $5,000 ransom on his head and he arrived back in Macau safely in a Manila hat, a jacket, no shirt, and a pair of striped trousers. As Captain Belcher of the *Sulphur*, who saw him arrive, put it, 'What must have been the state of poor Mrs E, who must have given her husband up for lost.'[25]

In August, Henry Pottinger, sent from London as the new Plenipotentiary, arrived in Macau to relieve Charles Elliot of his command. He was to receive double Elliot's salary. Palmerston had not been pleased with the taking of Hong Kong. Charles Elliot justifies his conduct in the letters he wrote to his sister Emma on board ship. He, Clara, and Fred, left for England on the *Atlanta* on 26 August 1841.

If one needed final proof that Clara had returned to the turmoil of China waters, it is provided in Charles's letter of 26 October 1841, written off Malta: 'Clara has borne the fatigue admirably, but you will consider how desperate an effort it has been when I tell you, for our sins, she is five months gone in the family way.'

Charles's next posting was as Chargé d'Affaires to the newly independent state of Texas; he was to be paid half his previous salary. He was not popular in London. 'All we wanted, we might have got,' wrote Queen Victoria, 'if it had not been for the unaccountably strange behaviour of Charles Elliot ... who completely disobeyed his instructions and *tried* to get the lowest terms he could'.[26] And so, as a 'lowest term', the British colony of Hong Kong came into being.

II
EARLY DAYS
1842 – 1860

CHAPTER FOUR

MARY ANN HICKSON
HAS FUN

*T*he typhoon that shipwrecked Charles Elliot on 20 July 1841, was the same one that wreaked such havoc in the very early days of Hong Kong. What is more, a second typhoon struck four days later. There was much distress among the Chinese population, both indigenous islanders and those who had begun to arrive following the taking of the island by the British. And there was a lot of damage, most of it superficial, to the ships, both merchant and naval, lying in the harbour. The regiments on shore were left without supplies, their tents and flimsy wooden barracks destroyed. But were any Western women hurt? Indeed, were there any in Hong Kong at that time?

Although the British had taken Hong Kong in January that year, the Chinese had almost immediately repudiated the terms of the convention that followed; it was not until the Treaty of Nanking, signed over a year later, in August 1842, that Hong Kong became truly British. Nevertheless, Western women did arrive to live in Hong Kong before then, probably following Henry Pottinger's removal in February 1842 of his office as Superintendent of Trade from Macau to Hong Kong. Henrietta Shuck, a missionary who had been in Macau with her husband and family since 1836, claims to have been the first and she arrived in March.

According to Henrietta, she was closely followed, by Mrs Ramsey, the wife of James, a captain in the 35th Bengal Army. It should be added, however, that, according to the

HONG KONG ISLAND *c.* 1860

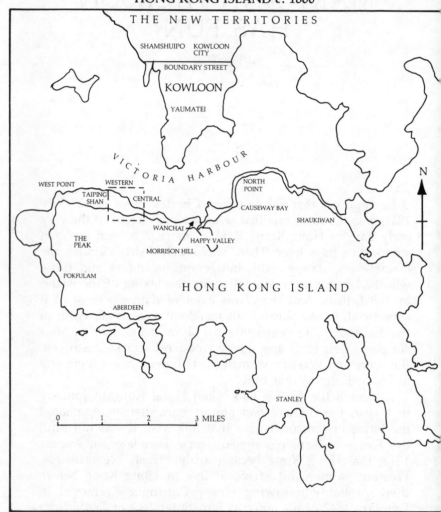

VICTORIA c. 1930

CANOSSIAN MISSION

UNIVERSITY
BONHAM ROAD
TANK LANE
HOLLYWOOD ROAD
CLEVERLEY STREET
BONHAM STRAND
TRAM LINE
GOUGH STREET
STAUNTON STREET
ROAD
ELGIN STREET
ROAD
STREET
GRAHAM STREET
ROAD
CAINE
OLD BAILEY STREET
COCHRANE STREET
CENTRAL MARKET
CHANCERY LANE
HOLLYWOOD
LYNDHURST TERRACE
STREET
POTTINGER STREET
DES VOEUX ROAD
CONNAUGHT ROAD
WELLINGTON
STANLEY
QUEEN'S ROAD
D'AGUILAR STREET
WYNDHAM STREET
HONG KONG HOTEL
FLAGSTAFF HOUSE
DUDDELL STREET
GOVERNMENT HOUSE
ICE HOUSE STREET
STAR FERRY PIER
PEAK TRAM
ST JOHN'S CATHEDRAL
ROAD
QUEEN'S
ROAD
CHATER
HONG KONG CLUB

1/4 MILE
1/8
0

baptismal register, Captain Mitchel Sparks of the 49th Regiment, and his wife Sarah, had their daughter baptized in Hong Kong on 13 February that year. We know, then, that there were at least two army wives in Hong Kong by March 1842, and many more were to follow, but it is fair to assume that there were none on shore at the time of those July 1841 typhoons.

There were, however, captains' wives on board the merchant ships in the harbour. Many accompanied their husbands on voyages to and from China, India, Britain and Australia. Sometimes the wives lived in Macau for a time, while their husbands carried on their business in the Pearl River area; just as often they remained on board ship. Harriet Low wrote in 1831 how one such wife, Mrs Crockett, 'was giving us an account of the dreadful shipwreck she once experienced. It is astonishing to hear the variety of dreadful scenes these ladies go through who go to sea with their husbands'.[1] But were any 'floating wives' hurt, or worse, in the July typhoons?

Edward Cree, the ship's surgeon notes how 'the *Bulah* was totally demasted and got foul of the *Wellesley*, the master and crew left her thinking she was going down, the master's wife was amongst them and was accommodated by a suit of clothes of the chaplain'.[2] A contemporary journalist, William Tarrant, tells how the *James Laing* 'parted from its anchor in Hong Kong harbour and drifted right down to Cow-ee-chow [an island between Green Island and Lantau], where it was stranded and the captain's wife drowned while attempting to land.'[3] So, at least one Western woman lost her life in the typhoons.

The floating wives were not necessarily as brave as their experiences would suggest. Mrs Bull, wife of the botswain of the *Rattlesnake*, part of the force that took Chusan, had, during that incident, felt very insecure. Cree tells how she 'was told off to assist in attending to the wounded under my care, but when the firing had ceased, she was nowhere to be found, till at last she was discovered in the chain locker at the lowest part of the ship, where she had jumped in her fright and could not get up without help'.[4]

Hong Kong and its environs were to be a frightening place for some years to come — frightening, exciting, unhealthy, scandalous, a place for adventurers, rascals, the strong and the brave. It was the men who made the running but strong traces remain of women, their virtue, or lack of it, bravery or lack of it, their death or survival or their return home in sickness or disgust.

Lord Palmerston had disparagingly called Hong Kong a barren island with hardly a house on it; in reality between four and seven thousand Chinese already lived on the island a mere eight miles long and never more than five miles wide. The houses, in about eleven scattered villages, were built very close together, rather as squatter settlements still are today, and there were no public buildings, though there was at least one schoolmaster. More of the villages were on the south side of the island than the north where the British settlement, christened Victoria, began to be built facing Kowloon, still part of China, across the harbour. Above the new town, falling almost to the water's edge, was what is today simply called the Peak, and a string of other hills.

Henrietta Shuck had first seen the unspoilt scene in August, the height of the wet season; she described it as green and pleasant, while later descriptions are of bareness and starkness. It seems, firstly, that there were villages in what early on became known as Happy Valley, and that there was greenery — rice paddies and the verdure with which Chinese traditionally like to surround themselves — watered by the streams that still gush down the gullies. The crags and slopes seem to have been covered by a sort of fern which from a distance, even from a ship in the harbour, would give the appearance of a green hill. Even today, with the hills thickly wooded, bold rock formations stand out, giving a craggy feeling to the scene.

The expeditionary forces immediately put up sheds and tents; the merchants who had had fine homes in Macau for half a century were slower to follow. Osmond Tiffany junior was in Hong Kong between September and November 1844; then there was one street fit for horses and carriages which ran parallel with the water. He describes the shops as being 'of the most wretched order, there being no rich natives on the island and the Europeans being supplied from several shops kept by English in which the wares of London are retailed at enormous profit'.[5] But he also talks of the buildings going up: 'Go where you would, your ears were met with the clink of hammers and chisels and your eyes were in danger of sparks of stone at every corner.'[6] In October that year Edward Cree wrote, 'Hong Kong is still flourishing and some handsome houses have been finished since we were last here.'[7]

An example of such a house was that of Crawford Kerr of Lindsay and Company and his wife Emily. He had been in the area since at least 1837 and on 29 June 1840 married Emily Eva Gribble. She was in Macau in the company of Captain Henry Gribble, probably her brother, who had been a ship's captain with the East India Company, and later a merchant among the first to buy land in Hong Kong. By then the expeditionary force was in Chinese waters and providing security that encouraged family life, but six months earlier Emily and Gribble's wife Harriet, newly arrived from Calcutta, had a frightening introduction to China. On 26 December 1839 Gribble was seized by the Chinese, taken before Commissioner Lin for questioning and held for a time for contravening a rule which prohibited the British from being carried as passengers in small Chinese (smuggling) boats.

Emily Eva Gribble Kerr was a pretty woman, according to Lord Saltoun who saw her in Macau in June 1843. The American Quaker, Rebecca Kinsman, described her in December 1843, in spite of the fact that she had by then had three children in quick succession under what must have been difficult conditions, as 'An English lady of very pleasing appearance and manners.'[8] Emily made friends among the more religious elements of the community, in both Macau and Hong Kong, and it is from an unpublished letter she wrote to another sober American woman, Mary Sword, that we get details of the Kerr's home. She wrote in November 1844:

My new home is everything I could wish. It is quite as large as our last and at the same time more compact. The drawing room is a very pretty room, very nearly as long as the one at Macau, and much wider, and is therefore square. My bedroom leads out of it, which is large, and my dear husband has had it fresh carpeted and a new sprung couch covered with morocco leather placed for me. Attached to it is a water closet for my own use, and Bath, and the same in the opposite end of the house for Eliza and the children, and on top of the house are two cisterns for each of the bath rooms from which are got all the water used for the baths, and there is also an outlet to each with sewers, so that not a drop of water has to be carried up or down anywhere. The verandah is open towards the sea, and venetianed on the road side and laid with marble, besides this, the roof is flat, which gives us a long walk when we wish. We also have a little pony carriage to go out in.

I think Hong Kong is not at all a despicable place, on the contrary, is making as rapid strides toward a flourishing town, as any *reasonable* [person] can expect: as Rome was not built in a day, we cannot expect Hong Kong with its twice 'seven hills' will be. At present houses are springing up everywhere, and roads cut up and down, and across. In a few years I predict that it will be a better place than Macao.[9]

The rest of Emily's letter provides some help in investigating one of the less attractive aspects of Hong Kong's past: a pronounced divisiveness in society that has been blamed on the colony's women. Typical of the material that has gone to feed such an impression is a comment of Henry T. Ellis drawn from his visit to Hong Kong in 1855:

The English residents of Hong Kong, like many other small communities, were divided by exclusive feelings which rendered society far less agreeable than it might have been had a better understanding existed among them. As each little coterie was headed by its own particular lady patroness, it was a difficult matter to find any half-dozen who would meet any other half-dozen, without their evincing mutual marks of contempt or dislike.[10]

Such divisions were not unique to Hong Kong, nor even to the China Coast, and it may be worth contrasting the reality of Emily's life with that of another woman to put the criticism into perspective. The most striking fact is how few women there were in the early days. As late as 1848, Edward Cree says of a ball given by the officers of the 95th Regiment, 'all the principle people of the island were there, but they could only muster 30 ladies'.[11] That is ignoring ordinary soldiers' wives and those belonging to the religious community, but it still gives a fair idea of size.

Emily Kerr describes relationships with women friends who would not have been at the ball, regimental or any other — Mrs Brown and Mrs Hepburn are missionary wives, and Mrs Stanton's husband is the colony's chaplain — in the rest of her letter to Mary Sword:

I have seen 4 or 5 ladies and returned their calls and now hope to be very quiet, as there are no *notes* to answer and we are quite as dependent upon our domestic occupations as Macao. I have seen Mr and Mrs Stanton several times and attended the first of what will, I am sure, prove a very interesting meeting at his house, last Wednesday, for studying the Bible, and he expounded the 1st Chapter of 1st Thess[alonians], & he wishes us all to make observations on the subject, and we are to study the chapter beforehand. They seem a sweet Christian couple. I have only seen Mrs Hepburn twice — once at Mrs Brown's and yesterday I spent a portion of the morning at Mrs Stanton's where she was spending the day.

I am sorry you think it necessary [to go to the ball] — if Mr Sword did not particularly request it. I certainly should not care about giving offence in a matter between my conscience and myself — look at Ch 15 St John 18–19 verse. If I had been at Macau, I should not have gone, nor do I think because you are an American, that you are to put yourself out of your Christian profession, in order to please worldly people.[12]

In April 1845 Emily wrote to Mary, 'I derive no pleasure from society of any English ladies here, except Mrs Stanton whom I greatly regard.' And in May, 'We see scarcely any company & are I daresay considered very unsociable, but in Hong Kong if we did not appear disinclined, it would lay us open, to having our house full of loungers of military and naval officers — as it is, we see only those who are most agreeable.'[13] Emily Kerr had better things to do with her time:

I am trying to get passage to England for a poor woman left with 2 children, one a helpless cripple, whose husband sailed off for Calcutta. You cannot think how many objects of distress come before us here. People come up from New South Wales in search of employment, and finding none, and an expensive place, are frequently found almost starving. Mr and Mrs Stanton are most persevering in finding every one out, and it is then I hear of objects of pity, of course it is our duty to relieve them and I am only too thankful when I can assist.[14]

Emily Kerr was a worthy woman, not to be sneered at. The sort of young woman whom she obviously avoided formed part of a circle which the naval surgeon Edward Cree enjoyed whenever his ship put into port over the years 1840–1850. Whatever Emily Kerr may have thought of Mary Ann Hickson, we can only rejoice in the charming portrait that Cree presents of her and her friends.

Mary Ann was the eldest stepdaughter of Thomas McKnight, a purser in the Royal Navy who arrived in Hong Kong as naval storekeeper in June 1843, and took a house near the dockyard at West Point. He was, according to Cree, 'a fat old fellow,' but he had 'three pretty step daughters . . . a pleasant addition to Hong Kong society. This is a good place for marriageable girls.'[15]

Whenever he was in Hong Kong, Cree visited the Hickson girls and they and their girl friends were in constant demand at social functions. On 14 February 1845 there was a Royal Navy regatta followed by a dinner on board the Agincourt. Only a hundred and forty could sit down for dinner at 6 o'clock so there were two sittings. Of the forty women present, 'the Belles of the party were Miss Hickson and Miss Bowra'.[16]

The following day, Cree called on the McKnight family: 'Had a long chat with Miss Hickson, who is a pretty, fresh complexioned, Devonshire girl, jolly and good.' And the day after that, the McKnight family came on board Cree's ship. At the same time, another officer invited Mr Pett, ordnance storekeeper, his wife, and 'two of their three little girls, the second about fifteen and very pretty'.

In March Cree wrote, 'Often of an evening, when not otherwise engaged, Willcox and I go down to West Cottage to enjoy some music and a chat with the girls.'[17] And a few days later there was a sail across the bay in a cutter. 'We landed on the opposite side, scrambling through brambles and over rocks, to the detriment of the ladies' dresses.' Dunlop tore his trousers and was most mortified because, as Cree suggests, 'He is dreadfully spoony with Miss Hickson, who was so cruel as to laugh immoderately.'[18]

The next day there was another ball, where there were ten men to every woman, not all of them as pretty as Mary Ann; her mother was nicknamed Mrs Nickleby, so much did she resemble the Dickens character. Cree tells how,

Mrs Nickleby was elated at the attention paid to all three pretty daughters, and as I took her down to supper, had the benefit of her talk under the tongue-loosening effects of champagne, when she expiated on the virtues of her three girls. One young lady there we nicknamed Miss Jack Horner, a hoydenish lady who loved champagne, not wisely, but too well.[19]

And a few days later, yet another picnic. And so it went on, until poor Dunlop could take it no more and called on the McKnights. Cree recorded, 'Found poor Dunlop had been there and popped the question to which the lady had answered No!' The refusal meant that Miss Hickson had no one to escort her to a musical party that evening,

So I persuaded her that it would be quite proper if she put herself under her medical adviser's care. So I walked into the room with the Belle of Hong Kong on the day she rejected a gallant officer of the 4th. Her pretty sister Alice gave me a sly look and a flower for my button hole. There was a large party and some good music, champagne iced, and a capital supper, dancing and green-tea punch to finish. I escorted my fair friend home about 2 o'clock.[20]

And so Cree sailed away, no harm done, until the next time. In October that year he was back. The Chinese Commissioner Keying was in town and Cree wrote,

A grand review of all the troops, in Victoria Road, before Government House, where the mandarins were, and all the Hong Kong ladies, now amounting to about fifty, in their gayest attire ... the mandarins dine with the Governor, who gives a ball in the evening at which I had great fun. Keying evidently admired the English ladies, especially Miss Hickson, and praised her beautiful black ringlets, and called her the Queen of Beauty.[21]

The next night the Admiral gave a party: 'The polka was danced by Miss Hickson with a French gentleman, and attracted a great deal of attention from the mandarins. Keying wanted to know what Miss Hickson's bustle was made of.' And the following day, 'The mandarins dine with the General, and some of the ladies go in the evening. Keying presented Miss Hickson with a beautifully embroidered cap, and exchanged handkerchiefs with another lady.'

On 29 October it was Mary Ann's 21st birthday party. Among the guests was 'a new devoted admirer of Miss Hickson, Mr Cleverly of the Land Office'.[22] And off Cree goes again. In March 1848 he writes,

At a gay wedding breakfast: the pretty little Alice Hickson married to E Sargent of the 18th Reg, ADC to the Governor, Sir J. Davis who was present, & a large party: the two sisters and four other girls made a pretty set of bridesmaids. 50 people present. A splendid breakfast. As Sargent's ADCship is over, they go to India immediately to join his regiment'.[23]

Then it was Mary Ann Hickson's turn to marry and that is where Cree's account leads the unwary reader astray and one has to stop being charmed by him and become a serious historian!

In the version of his diaries published in 1981, he tells of a party in October 1849 at which he met a member of

Keying's suite who asked about 'the pretty black-haired girl, Miss Hickson, and was not surprised when I told him she was married'.[24] In Cree's unpublished diaries we are hardly surprised on 11 March 1849 to find him describing a picnic on top of Victoria Peak attended by 'Most of Hong Kong society', including 'Mrs Cleverly, late Miss Hickson the Belle of Hong Kong . . .'[25] But Miss Hickson did not marry Mr Cleverly. The marriage register is quite clear: on 8 June 1847 Charles St George Cleverly, bachelor of Hong Kong, married Mary Pope, spinster of Hong Kong; and on 1 April 1848 William Wilkinson Dale married Mary Ann Hickson.

Mary Ann Hickson Dale, unhappily, slips from the history of Hong Kong. The list of residents in China in the *Chinese Repository* shows W.W. Dale and family in Canton in 1849 and 1850, and in Shanghai in 1851 (when the *Repository* ceased publication). Mary Pope Cleverly is mentioned briefly from time to time in historical sources, for her husband remained some years in Hong Kong, and was responsible for many of its early buildings, such as Government House. As for Emily Kerr, she was to have one more child before she and her husband departed for England in 1847; she was left a widow with four young children when he died four years later.

Emily and Mary Ann were very different women, and they could be said to move in different circles, circles that did not touch. But within those circles was understanding and friendship — a point that seems to have been ignored in socio-historical studies of Hong Kong. And in those early days they were not necessarily circles practising sharp class distinction. Neither of the first two Governors, Henry Pottinger and John Davis, brought their wives with them; nor was there a fixed Government House. There was not a formal first lady until Mrs Bonham arrived in 1848; and she left because of ill health in February 1851. That might have led to other women attempting to fill the first lady vacuum but neither Emily nor Mary Ann could be described as a 'patroness' of a 'coterie'. The Bowrings were the first to move into the newly completed Government House in 1854. Even after their arrival, divisions were caused more by personality clashes and incompatible activities between men, as will be explored in a later chapter, than by hierarchical class distinctions practised by women. Perhaps Henry T. Ellis, the transient visitor, would have been snubbed by Emily if he came to scrounge, by Mary Ann if he were dull! Thus are historical impressions created.

The lives of those two women were comparatively easy and comfortable. It was not the same, as Emily has suggested, for all women in the early days of Hong Kong. And the Chinese, after all, as the next chapter shows, had never wanted them there.

CHAPTER FIVE

POOR MARY ANN
AND THE ROBBERS

*T*he indigenous inhabitants of Hong Kong Island before and after 1841 were, on the whole, peaceful, and not hostile towards the Westerners who came to settle. Those Chinese who started immediately to arrive from the mainland were of a different mind; like many of the Westerners, they were there for the pickings. Robbery and piracy were rife.

Brigandage was not the only problem. The August 1842 Treaty of Nanking was meant to end the First Opium War; Hong Kong was in British hands and five mainland ports, including Canton, were opened up to foreign trade. In Canton, trading was no longer to be only through designated Chinese merchants, and families were allowed to live in the foreign factories. In practice it was not quite so easy.

In the 1840s the watery triangle of Canton, Hong Kong and Macau was to become a well-travelled trail. If there was too much heat, too much illness, or too much trouble in one place, residents, particularly women and children, would move for a few weeks. Friendship between women then was important, as mothers with a brood of children in tow would descend on each other to escape their usual environment.

One of the factors forcing women temporarily out of Canton was that the ordinary Chinese there took time to accept them. What happened in December 1842 was the most violent manifestation of a series of upsets. The riots were a natural result of a treaty under which the Chinese had finally to accept defeat; it created fertile soil for rumour and increased fear and hatred of the barbarian.

It is said that the riots were caused by the thoughtless appearance in Canton of 'three or four English ladies (wives of captains of the ships at Whampoa) in the streets of Canton'.[1] It was not just that they were foreign women, according to W.D. Bernard of the *Nemesis*, but that the sight of women was so against custom: Chinese 'ladies' were never seen in public except in secluded sedan chairs. A few days after that first expedition, the same women came to live in one of the factories, which was then the first to be attacked during the riots.

Who were those women? It is no doubt out of delicacy that Bernard fails to name them but the lack of a name under such circumstances always arouses suspicion. After the riots, a group of foreign merchants in Canton wrote to Sir Henry Pottinger, the British Plenipotentiary, about them. They talked of the wives being those of 'accidental visitors', not resident merchants. Again, no names.

One named woman was in Canton during that period and was involved in those riots, but she was not British, and she was not a merchant's wife or a captain's wife. She was Harriet Parker, wife of the American medical missionary Dr Peter Parker. He had been practising in Canton for some years and had only recently brought back from America with him the former Miss Webster — young, 'very pretty and amiable', and pious.[2]

Peter Parker at first left Harriet in Macau but having re-established himself in his hospital in Canton, he took her there on 5 November 1842. She is known as the first Western woman to live, rather than stay temporarily, in China, and she took great pains to be discreet. Parker wrote about that first day: 'It was not perceived that a foreign lady was in the boat as we came up the river, and, wishing to avoid a tumult immediately on landing, we walked to the American factory. As we passed through the company's factory the crowd began to collect to see the foreign lady.'[3]

A linguist was sent by the Chinese authorities to ascertain the Parkers' intentions and was reassured; although Mrs

Parker was there permanently, she did not want to cause trouble and would not venture into the streets. But from the terrace where she walked in the evening she could be seen from the tops of the houses.

On 23 December, Parker wrote to his sister about what had happened:

Alas! in an evil hour our peace and quietness were disturbed from our proximity to the English, who, in the course of the late war, had rendered themselves particularly obnoxious to the Chinese. On the eighth instant, a quarrel with a lascar [Indian sailor] became the occasion for the pent-up feeling to manifest itself in the burning of the English factory and the plunder of nearly half a million dollars in specie [coins].

The scene was one that defies description. Hatty, with her friend, Mrs Isaacson, an English lady who was making her a visit, were early moved to Mingkwa's factory, the Chinese factory next to the American ... and the next morning without any difficulty was removed to Whampoa, where she has since been kindly and hospitably entertained on board the *Splendid* and the *Oneida*. In one or two days more I think of her returning with me to Canton, as all is quiet now, and I have so many friends among the Chinese, as well as foreigners, that, on the approach of a similar riot, it would be easy for her to escape; besides there is no present prospect of such an occurrence again.[4]

In Bernard's version, he reports that the anonymous English merchants' wives 'escaped, with the utmost difficulty and danger, by a back way, and were received in one of the Hong merchants warehouses until they could be conveyed down the river. But the mob destroyed and tore into shreds every article of their wardrobe which they could find.'[5]

Harriet Parker returned to Canton on the evening of Christmas day, and stayed, though there are constant sightings of her visiting Macau and Hong Kong in the years that followed. Eighteen months later, a *Friend of China* editorial declared:

There is a continued manifestation of the ill feeling entertained towards foreigners by the Chinese, which have resulted in one or two riots which although not of a very serious nature, tend, with other circumstances, to make Canton a disagreeable and dangerous place of residence. Numbers of idle vagabonds keep prowling round the factories, bent upon mischief; and the sight of a lady walking in the Company's garden is quite enough to cause an excitement, the mob getting upon the walls and staring in the most annoying manner.[6]

The next time the newspaper discussed the issue, it was used as an occasion to belabour Admiral Cochrane, the naval commander; he seemed to care little that 'many of his fair countrywomen are exposed to the brutality of degraded beings, whom we are ashamed to be compelled to look upon as fellow men'.[7]

It was six months after Harriet Parker's escape, that Elizabeth Brown experienced similar unpleasantness, in Hong Kong, and barely a year after that it was Mary Ann Le Foy's turn. In both those last two cases, however, the motive appeared to be robbery, rather than a manifestation of hatred; destruction, though, was once again a feature.

The *Friend of China* wrote of the first incident on 9 May 1843:

An attack was made by Robbers upon the house of the Morrisonian Education Society; Mr Brown was stabbed in two places. The robbers drove all the inmates from the house, of which they had full possession for two hours and only decamped at daylight. Dr Hobson, Mr Brown, and Mr Morrison lost some property, and HE the Plenipotentiary's great seal was stolen.[8]

What that report omits to say is that the Reverend Samuel Brown had a wife, and that she was with him. In his detailed account of the incident, Brown's biographer mentions only Samuel and Elizabeth Brown, their two children, Julia aged four, Robert a babe in arms, Dr McCartee, a visiting missionary, and some Chinese boys — pupils who lived in.

Elizabeth Brown was not a nonentity whose presence might have been missed by any but a careless reporter. The American educationalist and missionary, Samuel Robbins Brown, married Elizabeth Bartlet, daughter of a Connecticut clergyman, on 10 October 1838 and sailed with her for China a week later. They arrived in Macau in February 1839. The most appealing account of Elizabeth is by William Low, Harriet Low's brother, who arrived in China as a clerk after she had left. He went to tea with Elizabeth in August 1839 and wrote:

It did me good to see some white ladies I assure you. Mrs Brown is a very good looking woman indeed, and quite young. I hauled alongside of her as quick as possible, and had quite a confab. She looked good enough to eat, I did not talk as long with her, as I should like to have done, as I wanted to give others a chance, and then I did not want her hubby to get jealous — hem . . .[9]

Brown had been recruited to run the Morrison Education Society's school in Macau and he opened it soon after his arrival in the house that Mary Gutzlaff had used for her school before the August 1839 evacuation. The school was removed from Macau to Hong Kong in November 1842, to what is today called Morrison Hill — but in those days it was a hill; developers razed it in 1924. By 1844 the house had 44 inhabitants. As Samuel Brown so rightly wrote, in a letter to his sister in March 1844, 'Elizabeth's hands are very full of work . . . what with teaching a class or two, and superintending her household affairs.'[10] But that was after the attack.

On that May night in 1843, the Browns were wakened at midnight by loud talking in Chinese outside their window. They assumed it was quarrelling workmen and Samuel Brown shouted out for them to keep quiet. The reverse happened, so he went to the front door. He could see nothing but he soon felt the sharp pain of a spear entering his leg and he shouted out to Elizabeth to get to the henhouse with the children.

Brown himself, losing blood rapidly, grabbed a box of valuables and threw it over the side of the hill before joining his wife in the henhouse where they managed to staunch his wound. The pirates, as they were called for they had come from the sea, vented their frustration at finding nothing of value by breaking down the doors and windows, cutting up the beds and setting fire to piled up clothes.

Elizabeth may have recovered from that ordeal, but her health had been shaky since her arrival in China — the LMS records are dotted with remarks such as the one on 20 January 1841, 'We gratefully record the mercy of God in restoring Mrs Brown to health.'[11] The family left Hong Kong on account of Elizabeth's health in 1847.

The next violent robbery to shock Hong Kong was at James White's house in February 1844 and involved his niece Mary Ann Le Foy. The merchant James White, formerly a City of London Alderman, and his family arrived in Hong Kong in October 1843. Edward Cree describes Mary Ann Le Foy as 'a nice buxom London girl of 16, a desirable addition to Hong Kong Society'.[12] A few days later he dined with them and suggested to his diary, 'I make out that Alderman White has lived too fast in London and has come out on spec & the neice has come out on spec also.'[13] Two days later he 'Called on Mrs Alderman White & the blooming neice. Found them very pleasant so put them up to the "ropes" at Hong Kong.'[14] His interest by no means diminished, Cree added on 22 October, 'After dinner we called on Mrs White & her neice, the lovely Mary Ann & brought them off to the *Vixen* & afterwards escorted them home.'[15]

Whatever drove the 34-year-old former alderman away from London, he settled quickly in Hong Kong, which was made for men of his kind; he was an expert in silk and had a smooth pen — which he used briefly as editor of *Friend of China*; and he became a Justice of the Peace (JP). The night of the robbery he was away in Shanghai where he was soon to set up in business and make enough money to go back to England and become a Member of Parliament. His wife Mary and Mary Ann were alone in the house.

It is difficult to tell which of Cree's descriptions is the more evocative, the pictorial one that so appealed to me that I chose it for the front cover, or the verbal one:

Called on Mrs Alderman White whose house has been broken into by a party of Chinese robbers. She gave a graphic description of the affair and Miss Le Foy added she had 50 Chinamen in her bedroom. That she jumped out of bed & without dressing ran down to the 41st quarters to fetch up the guard. But before she got back the robbers had decamped. Mrs White did not lose much by the Chinese plunderers, some clothes & nothing of value. Poor Mary Ann lost the clothes she was going to put on — but they had a great fright. These affairs are constantly occuring at Hong Kong where the Chinese are most expert & daring robbers.[16]

In March 1848, four years later, Cree wrote, 'Call on the Misses Hickson & with them to see Mrs Makrel Smith, formerly Miss Le Foy, or Poor Mary Ann, who had the 50 Chinese robbers in her room. We had a good laugh over the incident. She is still a very lively young lady.'[17] Mary Ann Le Foy disappeared to Shanghai where her husband sold superior pale Sherry, Port and Madeira, and was a broker. No doubt she and Mary Ann Hickson Dale remained friends there.

Some of the incidents could be viewed less philosophically. Cree writes on 8 October 1845, 'Some Chinese pirates have been at their old diabolical work. An English blacksmith in the civil engineering department, went home from his work and found his wife murdered and house plundered, and the pirates escaped, but hopes are entertained of their capture.'[18]

It may be that the situation would have improved with the passage of time and all that meant in terms of the development of law, administration, policing and different cultures getting used to each other, but the so-called 'Lorcha Incident' of October 1856 — when a vessel flying the British flag was boarded by Chinese officials — led to a period of incidents between China and Britain, and subsequently to war.

When the British flag was insulted, John Bowring, Governor of Hong Kong, an experienced China hand, oriental scholar and man of peace felt obliged to act militantly. It emerged that Commissioner Yeh, Governor of Kwangtung province, was testing Britain's strength with a view to ridding Canton of the British factories. John Cowper senior was one of the early victims.

The John Cowpers, father and son, had been responsible between 1851 and 1854 for constructing the dry docks at Whampoa, down river from Canton. Thereafter, the father settled with his wife on their chop — the floating, two-storey houseboat ubiquitous in the Pearl River delta. At 5 p.m. on Saturday, 20 December 1856, a sampan came alongside the chop with a letter for Cowper. Husband and wife were walking on the upper deck when their daughter called up to him and he reached out for the letter. As he did so, several men who had been hidden in the sampan lunged at him. Mother and daughter fought frantically to prevent him being pulled overboard, but they failed. Cowper's daughter then jumped into a punt and with the help of two servants tried to follow, but the attack had been well-organized and night was falling; she was forced to give up. On her return to the chop she found her mother lying face downwards and unconscious. It was learnt later that two days after the British opened fire on Canton, Commissioner Yeh issued a proclamation offering 30 silver dollars for every foreign head.

One source says of the Cowpers that 'the couple were found murdered in their boat'.[19] Austin Coates, in his book *Whampoa* says that old John Cowper 'was never seen or heard of again'.[20] As for Mrs Cowper, the impressario Albert Smith met her after the incident, in September 1858, during his three week visit to Hong Kong and Canton. He recorded how he breakfasted on Mr Cowpers chop, 'His mother and sister joined us. The old lady was very weary of China and longed to be home again.'[21]

In order to put pressure on the British, it was also common practice for the Chinese authorities on the mainland to manipulate those of its citizens who had flocked to Hong Kong and who served in the early days mainly as servants and coolies. They had done it in Macau, too, and were to continue to do so well into the twentieth century. Usually the result was the withdrawing of labour. In January 1857, however, a more dramatic event aimed at the expatriate population took place. The motive behind the plot to poison all bread eaters (which excluded the Chinese) was never established in a court of law, but its timing coincided with the upset between the two powers.

Fortunately for all concerned, the baker put so much arsenic in the colony's morning bread supply that it acted as an emetic, but many people were very ill that day. No one died then, but it was always maintained that Lady Bowring died the following year as a result of the strain put on her system by the poison. Evidence suggests that both her physical and emotional well-being were already undermined enough to make her, at her age, vulnerable.

Like most of the early governors' wives, Maria Bowring is a shadowy figure, but there are some descriptions of her by George Preble (an American naval officer attached to Commander Perry's expedition to open up Japan, but seconded to the Hong Kong authorities to help in their fight against piracy) which supply some flesh and blood. Research done by her youngest daughter's biographer shows the strain that she may have been under.

Preble met Lady Bowring quite frequently; on 25 February, 1855, he remarked, 'I had a pleasant talk with Lady Bowring who is lame, and uses crutches.'[22] And in November that year he breakfasted with the Bowrings and noted, 'Lady Bowring is very lame, and has been so for seven years. She told me it was with great difficulty she got up and down stairs.'[23] The change in weather, then, made no difference to her lameness; in February it is usually cold, grey and very damp; in November it can be crisp, warm, and dry. At Christmas that year — the first Christmas in the new Government House — Preble was among the guests and was again struck by Maria Bowring's disablement but he added, 'She told me the other day she was sixty two years old, just the age of the [American] Commodore [Abbott] at his death. The instant she heard of his death the other day she went in her carriage a mile to tender her sympathy and assistance.'[24]

But Maria Bowring, wife of a convinced Unitarian whom she married in 1816 when she was 22, had more to contend with than physical disability. Three of her nine children, including her daughter Emily who was with her in Hong

Kong, had become Roman Catholic by 1855. A letter from John Bowring to his son Frederick in 1855 suggests that Emily's parents knew of her conversion in 1853. He refers to a tendency in her towards a 'conventual life which to all of us would be eminently repulsive'.[25] What is more, Emily's eldest sister, Mary, had already become an Anglican nun; whether or not she then left holy orders, Mary seems to have been with the family in Hong Kong.[26] There must have been considerable tension within the family which would further undermine Lady Bowring's health. And, as a later chapter shows, war with China and intransigent children were by no means the only worries the Governor, and therefore his wife, had to contend with.

Then on 15 January 1857 Maria Bowring was poisoned. It appears that she was delirious for a time and her husband wrote, 'Lady Bowring has been a bad case, as it is thought some arsenic got into her lungs, but the danger is now over.'[27] In 1858 she travelled home to England, accompanied by Emily, and she died in Somerset in September. The death certificate gives as the cause, 'Ulceration of the stomach — long standing atrophy — 4 months certified.'[28]

As a result of all the violent incidents of that period, armed Malayan guards were commonplace in the halls of merchant houses, and a host seeing his guests out would buckle on a revolver.[29] A man walking alone outside the city limits by day was quite likely to be mugged.[30] A woman would venture out only in a large party.

Every effort was made to protect Westerners who travelled by boat; in spite of that, a Frenchwoman, Fanny Loviot, was kidnapped when pirates boarded the ship, the *Caldera*, in which she was travelling from Hong Kong in 1854. Ida Pfeiffer, an Austrian woman travelling round the world, passed through Hong Kong and Canton in 1847. She could not afford to travel by steamer, so went by Chinese junk to Canton, taking care to put her pistols in order before she did so. Arriving at Canton, she walked boldly through the streets. She noted later, 'I was told I might regard it as a quite peculiar piece of good fortune that I had not been grossly insulted and even stoned by the populace.'[31]

Women residents, as opposed to those fearlessly passing through, left their houses in Canton only in a closed litter. And even in Hong Kong they must have felt their lives circumscribed. One must be careful, though, not to over-emphasize the constraints in Hong Kong: when living in insecure places in insecure times, the only way to survive is to have a fairly relaxed attitude. The light-hearted way that the two Mary Anns looked back on the robbery was more natural than it was insensible. Soon after 1857, too, the news of the horrors of the Indian Mutiny will have reached Hong Kong and people must have felt their little local difficulties rather insignificant. Nevertheless, the strain must sometimes have affected the behaviour of women, and men, and their relations with each other.

CHAPTER SIX

MARY ANNE MITCHELL IS DIVORCED

Colonial life is always seen as a hotbed of scandal and gossip, and Hong Kong, from its earliest days, was affected by financial corruption, administrative infighting, and permissive attitudes. But where did women fit into the shenanigans of ambitious men, first of all where sexual morality was concerned?

Mary Ann Hickson and her sisters, the Misses Bowra, the Misses Pett, and Mary Ann Le Foy were all pretty, jolly young girls, flighty perhaps, but innocent. They settled down, as far as it is possible to tell, to be respectable wives and mothers. But side by side with them were women who felt unfettered or frustrated by their marriage bonds. In this chapter, Mary Anne Mitchell with her divorce, unusual, even scandalous, in her day, is symbolic of them.

As for the effect on women of the corruptions of money and power-seeking, that is a feature of the next chapter, 'Mary Ann Caine Leaves Hong Kong'. Again, she is just one example, highlighted partly because her name is Mary Ann. The prevalence of that name during these years is too striking totally to ignore. Mary Ann Kingsmill, the policeman's wife in the title of Chapter 8, epitomises the victim; her social position made it less easy for her to extricate herself than it was for middle-class women. A later chapter, 'Queen's Women', is about European prostitutes. They at least had a solution.

Edward Cree, the naval surgeon, had just the sort of irreverent touch to give an honest impression of morals in the 1840s, when Queen Victoria had not yet put her stamp upon her subjects. He wrote on 14 May 1843, when there were still few women in Hong Kong — the merchants had not yet moved their families over from Macau: 'In the evening, took a walk with Harshaw along the new road and heard lots of scandal about the English ladies, married and single. Met Mrs Morgan, a pretty little woman, wife of an invalid merchant on a visit to the Plenipo.'[1]

The Plenipotentiary, was Sir Henry Pottinger, who had been administrator since 1841, but was not yet formally Governor. He had left his Irish wife Susanna in Britain and thus obviously felt unconstrained about seeking solace elsewhere. It would not, perhaps, be so interesting to recount his relationship with Mrs Morgan were it not for the fact that he left his subsequent posting, the Cape in South Africa, under a cloud after six months for 'No other governor of the Colony ever lived in such open licentiousness as he. His amours would have been inexcusable in a young man; in one approaching his sixtieth year, they were scandalous.'[2]

Amours are particularly interesting — apart from the delights of prurience — when they affect the governing of a country or colony. Where Pottinger and Hong Kong are concerned, although he was sent as a famous soldier to put right what Captain Charles Elliot had got so wrong, not everyone viewed him as an unqualified success. The journalist William Tarrant — whose pen was notoriously dipped in vitriol — wrote that

During the last few months of his stay in China, (he) exercised a wayward discretion, was petulant to a degree, and, excepting those whose obsequiousness formed a special qualification for his company, his deportment was hardly bearable by those about him ... to some Sir Henry seemed to have become prematurely senile, his eye, so sharp and piercing when he arrived in China, assuming that sluggish, leaden look invariably marking the tired politician.[3]

That Harriet Morgan was Pottinger's mistress, known about quite openly, is confirmed by Cree's diary entry on 16 July 1843: 'Captain Morgan, husband of the lady of the

Plenipo scandal has died suddenly of fever and the pretty Mrs M, fair, fat and forty, is left a disconsolate widdy. As he was captain of one of [Jardine] Matheson's opium clippers, all their flags are at half mast.'[4] The discreetly tenuous connection drawn between the Plenipo and the continuing sale of opium adds a nice touch. Another more subtle Cree allusion — if that is what it is — is to a remark made by William Jardine, when he left the China Coast in January 1839. He had answered the toast at his farewell dinner wishing him health and 'a charming wife', with the riposte that the best he 'could hope for was fair, fat and forty'.[5] He died a bachelor.

Lord Saltoun, the Commander in Chief, was only slightly less open in his letters home, though his hints about Mrs Morgan might not have been so obvious today without Cree's contribution. Saltoun rented a house from Captain Morgan when he first arrived in Hong Kong, in November 1842. Eventually he met his landlord's wife and at first he described her innocently enough as 'a fat little woman with pretty eyes in a way likely to increase the race of Morgans'.[6] He wrote more fully on 13 December 1842:

We had a very nice party yesterday at Sir Henry Pottinger's and he gave us an excellent dinner, and the soup and fish, the only dressed things I eat, were very nice and clean, and spoke well for his China cook; we had besides a roast turkey. They have no turkeys in this country, but they have them at Manila, and very fine ones after they have been fattened here; and Mrs Morgan, a Bombay lady, ... has these turkeys brought over regularly, and fattens them, and sent this one as a present to Sir Henry, who is an old acquaintance of hers, he having been employed in the Bombay presidency during his service in India, before he was sent on this service.[7]

Saltoun followed that up on 29 December:

Yesterday [Sir Hope] Grant and [Captain Arthur] Cunynghame, and I dined with Mr and Mrs Morgan. The only other person was a Doctor Young from Macao, who is the first doctor there, and I presume is over here living in the house till Mrs Morgan is

confined, which, to all appearances must soon take place. He is
quite in favour of the merchants' side of the question, which did
not please the lady, with whom Sir Henry is an old acquaintance
and a great favourite.[8]

The baptismal records show that Harriet called her son,
baptized on 2 March 1843, before her husband's death,
Henry William Herbert. He was named firstly, presumably,
after her lover, and only secondly after her husband. The
Morgans had been married since at least 20 December 1836,
when shipping records show Mrs Morgan arriving in Macau
on the *Pascoa*. Her husband was the captain of that ship, so
it is likely that she travelled as a 'floating wife', particularly
as the records show her continuing to arrive and depart.
Morgan was also the captain, in 1839, of the *Scaleby Castle*,
on which the missionary Henrietta Shuck and her family
had a jaunt to Hong Kong, so Harriet was undoubtedly
among the women caught up in the evacuation of August
1839, and she was probably in Hong Kong harbour on board
the *General Wood* during the typhoons of July 1841.

It looks as though when he died William Morgan left
Harriet well provided for. Saltoun's first mention of Morgan
was, 'He lives at the upper end of the anchorage in a sort
of palace he has there.'[9] Records suggest that Morgan's
executor dealt with $8,000, a 'bungalow' (his 'palace' was
known as 'Morgan's Bungalow') and a row of houses.[10]

When Pottinger was invested as Governor of Hong Kong
in May 1843, Harriet Morgan, wife of a merchant captain,
was 'handed out' by the Commander in Chief, Lord Saltoun;
but after Cree's mention of her husband's death in July there
seems to be no further record of her. Pottinger, so often
away fighting, left Hong Kong in May 1844, and after his
six months in South Africa, he was appointed Governor of
Madras — a post in which he did not distinguish himself.
Perhaps Harriet went back to India.

It has been said that it was difficult for a single unaccom-
panied woman to live in Hong Kong; even a widow's
activities could be open to misconstruction. Cree seems to
confirm that when he related on 17 October 1845:

There has been an amusing bit of scandal amongst the English ladies here. It seems, a gay young widow, rather pretty, has arrived from Sydney, where it said she kept a boarding house: some of the ladies, jealous, I suppose of her good looks, have been saying spiteful things about her, which has given work to the Hong Kong lawyers.[11]

In spite of that, the marriage register regularly records the remarriage of widows. It is possible that usually they came out specifically to remarry from India, Britain, or Australia. There is certainly considerable evidence that men sent off for women, sight unseen, to come to the colonies to marry, or that, having met elsewhere, they sent for them at a later date.

Endings could be happy or, as Major Poyntse relates, they might be otherwise. In 1858 a nameless 'officer of high naval rank' wrote home for 'a young lady to whom he was engaged to come out and marry him.' The steamer was expected, the Bishop ready but 'poor fellow, an awful disappointment awaited him, when he learned his inamorata had married a military officer ... on arrival at Singapore, who had come out on the same steamer with her'.[12]

Poyntse describes that as an 'amusing episode' and Saltoun and Cree write with an equally light heart. So, men were no less averse to a little gossip than women! Saltoun was not yet finished with the women of Hong Kong. At that same investiture of Sir Henry Pottinger where he escorted Harriet Morgan, he espied Joanna Matthysson and wrote:

We had besides a very pretty woman, a Mrs Mathieson, a native, I heard, of New South Wales. She is wife of a clerk, or, as they call them here, writer in Dent's house and was over with her husband from Macao to see the place, and probably to look after a residence here ...[13]

It is natural to assume that the British expatriates who quickly flocked to Hong Kong were from Britain; but just as often they were from India, as Captain and Mrs Morgan were, or from Australia, as Mr and Mrs Matthysson were. By the 1830s and 1840s, Australia was by no means a land only of convicts, but one of opportunity, a place for a new start. Charles Elliot himself dreamed of going to Van Diemen's Land (Tasmania). Many Hong Kong residents were, therefore, doubly colonial, with all that might imply, and to gain the broadest perspective on them, curiosity about the British in India and the development of Australia is useful.

Very pretty Joanna Matthysson caused something of a sensation in Hong Kong when in 1846 her husband Edward divorced her. It had to be done by means of a special Bill brought before Parliament in London as it was not until 1857 that the Matrimonial Causes Act became law and divorce became, if still uncommon, at least possible under English Common Law.

Joanna's lover was George Thomas Braine, a senior partner in Dent's, the firm second only to Jardine Matheson, and the Matthyssons lived in a house owned by Braine in Hong Kong. While Edward Matthysson was on a business trip to Australia, the Bill claimed, Joanna, left under the protection of her brother Adam Elmslie, secretary to Sir Henry Pottinger, 'carried on adulterous intercourse' with Braine.[14] The adultery must have taken place before Pottinger left Hong Kong for good in May 1844; indeed, he was called as a witness.

A London news item of 20 October 1847 reports the death of Joanna Braine, confirming that they married after the divorce — it was not just a fling — but she must have died almost immediately afterwards.[15] Soon after her death, Braine, known as the man responsible for the foundation of the Hong Kong Club and a founder of Rio Tinto Zinc, was in financial difficulties.

Mary Anne Mitchell's life and divorce were even more complicated and bizarre. *The Times* (of London) of 8 July 1853 describes the case in the Court of Queen's Bench: *Mitchell v. The Prince of Armenia*. The charge: the seduction of Mitchell's wife.[16]

William Henry Mitchell, arriving in China in 1843, had been a merchant in Amoy and then held the post of clerk in the consulate there under the Consul, George Tradescant

Lay. His business not doing so well, he turned to journalism, harassing the Hong Kong government as an independent contributor, turning pro-government when he became editor of *The Hong Kong Register*. That turnabout was rewarded by the post of assistant police magistrate and sheriff in 1850. Two years earlier, he had married Mary Anne, the widow of the merchant Thomas Kirby.

Mary Anne, described as 'very beautiful' and about 30 years old in *The Times* report, had had two children by Kirby — Catherine, born in 1844 and William Henry born in 1847. The boy died five months later and his short life becomes memorable because his names, William Henry, were the same as Mitchell's. Five days after the death of the boy in Hong Kong, Thomas Kirby died in England, suggesting that he may have left Mary Anne even before the birth of her son. *The Times* reported that Mrs Kirby was left a widow in not very prosperous circumstances. Whether or not she was already Mitchell's mistress, they were married eight months after Kirby's death, in 1848. But they only lived together until the end of 1851.

The Times says that Mary Anne Mitchell left for England 'partly for the benefit of health, and partly for education of her child.' The latter seems unlikely, as in June 1856 there is a note of the death at the orphanage of La Sainte Enfance in Hong Kong of 'Kate, daughter of late Thomas Kirby.'[17] It looks as though Mary Anne left her daughter in Hong Kong when she went to England.

In London, Mary Anne took advantage of China Coast female friendships and went to live with Mary Lay, widow of Amoy's former Consul (and niece of Horatio Nelson). Then she moved to Mrs Mullings, whose husband had been killed in a mutiny of coolies on board his ship the *Victory*. It was presumably there that Mary Anne was seduced by the 'Prince of Armenia'. The jury found the co-respondent guilty and he was fined £700. What happened to the Prince or Mary Anne Mitchell is as mysterious as their relationship. As for William Mitchell, he was to become involved in another sort of Hong Kong scandal.

CHAPTER SEVEN

MARY ANN CAINE
LEAVES HONG KONG

While affairs of the heart were often not taken too seriously in the early days of Hong Kong, the scandals of corruption were intense. The best known is that which ravaged a group of administrators in the 1850s — on one side the allegedly corrupt, and on the other the incorruptible. How, one wonders, would the wives of the the men on the different sides have acted towards each other in such a small community?

Over all Hong Kong loomed the figure of Major William Caine. Today's Caine Road is not so much named after him, in his honour, as because he owned tracts of it. The apocryphal story goes that when a newcomer asked the name of the governor, the Chinese bystanders looked blank, but when asked who was the most important man, 'Major Caine' was the answer.

William Tarrant, who worked in the office of the Surveyor General, Charles Cleverly, accused Caine's comprador (Chinese intermediary) of corruption in 1847 in connection with the stall holders in Central Market. Tarrant lost his job as a result, became a journalist and editor of the *Friend of China*, and remained locked in mortal combat with Caine until 1859 when Caine reached retirement age, sued Tarrant for libel, hired every lawyer in town, thus depriving Tarrant of a defence, and won. Tarrant was sent to prison for a year.

A year earlier, in 1858, the government had sued Tarrant for publishing material leaked to him from a Commission of Enquiry. Then he was defended by Thomas Chisholm Anstey who, when he was still Attorney General, had been responsible for the Enquiry being instituted. Tarrant was acquitted. The two men had something in common — a determination to fight corruption and a tendency to do so with a passion that suggested a lack of stability, or at least of wisdom. It was their passion that rocked Hong Kong in the late 1850s.

Anstey, son of one of the earliest settlers in Van Diemen's Land, but educated and called to the Bar in England, had come out as Attorney General in 1856, after a career as an academic and politician, during which he harassed the British government on its Irish policy. Within a year, starting immediately on his arrival in Hong Kong, he had attacked William Thomas Bridges, a leading barrister and later Acting Colonial Secretary, criticized Charles Batten Hillier, the Chief Magistrate, accused Chief Justice Hulme of 'exceeding the bounds of temperance', attacked William Henry Mitchell, erstwhile husband of Mary Anne and Assistant Magistrate, for extorting money from prisoners, openly quarrelled with the Governor, Sir John Bowring, and accused Daniel Richard Caldwell, Registrar General and Protector of the Chinese, of owning brothels and protecting pirates. Sides were taken and much fur flew. No wonder Hong Kong was at that time ungovernable by Bowring, regarded by the Home government as a liability, and by visitors as incomprehensible.

But the above tangle, which forms a feature of histories of Hong Kong, can usefully be looked at in a new light through the women connected with the men. In the exploration, major themes, such as the relationship between foreign men and Chinese women, emerge. Of all the men involved, the only one for whom there is no woman is the sea-green incorruptible, Anstey.

It was written of Anstey, 'He has clean hands and a keen sense of public duty, and had we had a Governor who could have restrained his impetuosity, instead of arousing his indignation, he would have been a blessing to this colony.'[1] Why did John Bowring fail so miserably in harnessing Anstey's anti-corruption drive for Hong Kong's good and, instead, allow him to rampage destructively through the colony? It is particularly strange when Bowring himself was a man of radical politics and acknowledged intellectual powers, a Governor who intended to administer Hong Kong very well but who left — indeed, he was virtually recalled — despised by all but the Chinese. To find a simple answer which has not yet been tried, we should look at Bowring's daughter Emily.

In the chapter 'Poor Mary Ann and the Robbers', Emily's conversion to Roman Catholicism was put forward as a contributory factor in the undermining of her mother's health, because of the tension it must have produced in a Unitarian household where the father was strong-willed and highly committed to his Nonconformist beliefs. Emily and her two brothers had come to Roman Catholicism through Cardinal Newman's New Oxford Movement. That was also how Thomas Anstey had become a Roman Catholic and, thereafter during his political career, he fought unremittingly for the rights of Catholics.

I think that given the relationship between a beloved youngest daughter and a father, and the disappointment Emily's conversion must have caused, John Bowring's ability to cope with Anstey may well have been seriously impaired. He baulked Anstey's moves against men, some of whom were undoubtedly corrupt or, at the very least, lacked integrity — men whom, under other circumstances, Bowring's past suggests he would not have tolerated, let alone supported.

Added to his feelings about Anstey's religion and his own advancing age — he was 65 in 1857 — it is worth remembering the health of his wife during the period of uncontrolled scandal: she had been poisoned in January 1857 and went back to England at the beginning of 1858, to die that September. Not only that but Emily, who might have provided invaluable moral support to her beleaguered father in spite of their differences — her integrity was unimpeachable — accompanied her mother to England, and did not return until late 1858.

William Caine's motives are less opaque: he supported the

officials Anstey attacked because they were his friends and because Anstey was supported by Tarrant who was his enemy. The ramifications of Caine's effect on Hong Kong are too deep to elaborate on here, and they have undoubtedly been distorted by the fact that Tarrant left a written record and Caine did not. But Caine's relations with his wife, as far as they can be reconstructed, add some shadows to the picture.

There seems to be only one Hong Kong public record that shows there was a Mrs Caine. There is no marriage or death or birth of children recorded but when William Caine died in England in 1872, twelve years after retirement, Mrs Caine wrote to claim his pension. The Hong Kong administration refused her request. From the very brief resumé of the interchange that exists in the Colonial Office records, it is obvious that the Caines were no longer living together at his death.[2]

Family information shows that Caine married Mary Ann Vallancey, widow, in India in 1830, when he was serving there in the army. By the time Caine came to Chinese waters as part of the expeditionary force in 1840, leaving his wife in India, they had three sons.[3] He left the army with the rank of Major and became Chief Magistrate of the new colony. He immediately began to make his mark, for there was really no one but him to organize the maintenance of law and order.

How do we know that Mary Ann Caine ever came to join her husband? Once again Edward Cree obliges, intriguingly. On 21 March 1845, he describes how he and a friend made a round of calls, how they called on 'Mrs Caine, wife of the Chief Magistrate — a lively little woman full of fun'. On 10 April and 5 May there were musical parties at Mrs Caine's; on that second day there were some 'famous German performers there'.[4] On 6 May, Cree's ship was about to leave Hong Kong and he made calls on friends to say goodbye, including Mrs Caine.

By 8 September that year Cree is back in Hong Kong. He calls on Major Caine, and thereafter over the years he often does so, but he never again mentions his friend Mrs Caine.

What happened? And why is there no sign in the baptismal records of the boy whom descendants believe was born in Hong Kong in 1846?

There is an inscription in the Roman Catholic cemetery in Happy Valley that reads, 'Elizabeth Caine, died 5 December 1890, aged 47 years.' And in the baptismal records of the Roman Catholic Cathedral, Hong Kong, is one that reads, 'Baptised 1890, 17 October, aged 47 years, Chinese illegitimate parent ex Protestante Colonello Caine — Elizabeth Maria Magdelena Caine, sponsor Lucia Lau-ngan.'[5] The shipping records show the arrival on 25 January 1845 on the *Humayson* of Mrs Caine; and on 26 July that year her departure for England on the *Emerald Isle*.[6]

Based on the above, it is possible to suggest the following: that William Caine took a Chinese mistress in the early days of Hong Kong and that some time in 1843 she had a daughter, Elizabeth. His wife Mary Ann, arriving to join him in Hong Kong in January 1845, either attempted to live with his union and its result, and found after six months that she could not do so, or discovered the facts just before July and decided to leave on the first available ship. There is one other question to be explored. She did have a son, probably in 1846, month unknown. He was christened Charles Henry Fearon Caine.

We have come across the Fearons, Elizabeth and Christopher, in Macau in the 1820s and 1830s. One of their sons was Charles, another Samuel, born in 1819. Samuel was a clerk of the Magistrates Court and its interpreter in the early days of Hong Kong, then coroner. He travelled to England on 26 July 1845 on the *Emerald Isle*, a fellow passenger of Mary Ann Caine.

Although Harriet Morgan and Mary Anne Kirby (Mitchell) seem to have named their children after their lovers, it was quite common for the names — Christian or family — of friends to be used when christening a new baby. Samuel worked in William Caine's court; he was probably a friend of the family. He was due for leave that July. If Mary Ann Caine was fleeing an intolerable situation, he may well have taken her side and been kind to her on the ship. She may have named her son Fearon to honour his kindness, and the use of the name of his brother Charles may have been a coincidence.

On 30 January 1846, six months after the ship left Hong Kong, Fearon was gazetted Registrar General and Collector of Chinese Revenue in Hong Kong, a position he had already been acting in. In December 1845 he decided, instead, to take up the appointment of Professor of Chinese Language and Literature at King's College, London. He did not return to Hong Kong. Did he feel unable to do so, either because of disgust at Caine's behaviour, or because of a relationship with Mary Ann Caine? Or was his new appointment simply a fascinating change of job? It is impossible to know. King's College records only show that he did not marry Mary Ann of whom nothing more is known.

Caine's relationship with his wife does not necessarily reflect badly on him, but his relations with the Chinese mother of his child introduce a Hong Kong phenomenon that bears exploration. It also creates a link with another Anstey protagonist, Daniel Richard Caldwell, whose behaviour under similar circumstances was unusual.

The scarcity of Western women on the China Coast contributed to the quite common establishment of relations between foreign men and Chinese women. Sometimes they were long-lasting and resulted in children. That created a Eurasian population which is now an integral part of Hong Kong society, often at the highest echelons, but which was earlier an excluded and anomalous segment.

Osmund Cleverly, the merchant shipping captain, (brother of Mary Ann Hickson's admirer — Charles Cleverly) provides a good example of the phenomenon. The baptismal records show two children christened on 9 September 1845: Charles Osmund, born February 1842, and Emily Osmund, born April 1845. There is no mother's name, and the children's surname is their father's first name. On 31 October that year Osmund Cleverly married Ellen Fagin, and they had at least one child, Ellen, born in 1853. Thus Osmund Cleverly had two families. He may well have cut off relations with the first upon his Christian marriage but it was not unprecedented for the new Western wife of a man with a family by a previous, Chinese, union, to act with grace and generosity towards the earlier family. Often the man at least made provision for that family when he married.[7] Cleverly's will shows that he did not do so there, though he may have done so earlier.

Caldwell's own will reads quite otherwise and reading it and finding out a bit more about his relations with Mary Ayow, gives a different perspective to the accusations Anstey levelled against him of owning brothels and protecting pirates. Unlike nearly every other European man who had relations with a Chinese woman in the early days, Daniel Caldwell married Mary Ayow on 12 March 1851 at St John's Cathedral. Thereafter, they had nine children, all baptized at St John's. Before their Christian marriage, but following their traditional Chinese marriage, they had three children.

It is clear that they married officially either because or after Mary Ayow became a Christian in 1850. She was a woman of character, who not only reared her own family but brought into the Caldwell household a collection of displaced or homeless Chinese. She was a member and benefactor of the Chinese congregation of the London Missionary Society.

In his will Caldwell named his wife and ten children then surviving and added, 'some of these children were born in the interval between my being married to my wife Mary Ayow according to Chinese usages and the subsequent ceremony according to the established church, and some after such ceremony but by the ten children where used in this my will I intend to include all my children'.[8]

Many Eurasian children were brought up by their mothers in the Chinese tradition and never knew their fathers; Daniel and Mary Caldwell brought theirs up knowing both parents and both cultures, at a time when that must be considered rather advanced. There is an attractive description of Caldwell family life, written by the impresario Albert Smith in September 1858: 'At 6.30 to dine with Mr Caldwell, passing one of the most agreeable evenings with his family that I spent in Hong Kong. Mrs Caldwell is

Chinese, and the little children speak in the language.'[9] Several of the older Caldwell children, at least, studied in England.

How Hong Kong Western society received Mrs Caldwell is not altogether clear. Mary Ayow entertained in a cosmopolitan way, obviously, and at least three of the children married Westerners. Young Daniel, the eldest son, became a solicitor and just before he qualified he married Mary, daughter of Francis William Mitchell, the Postmaster General.

The missionary James Legge attended the wedding breakfast, along with 50 others, and noted the absence of the bride's father, who had planned a trip outside Hong Kong to coincide with the wedding. But gossip had it that Mitchell, however competent he was at his job, treated his wife and daughters badly and that Mary Mitchell was lucky to marry Daniel Caldwell. As Legge put it, 'The girl has no chances of being sought by any other young Englishmen about the place, and I do not wonder at her accepting young Caldwell whom she has known for many years.'[10] One can therefore deduce that Mitchell's wife had not been averse to being friends with Mary Ayow Caldwell, for at least one parent of friendly children would probably have been friendly. More generally, however, a canard was spread, later proved unfounded, that Mary Ayow had been a prostitute.[11]

Anstey began his attacks on Caldwell in 1857, and they culminated in an enquiry in 1858; Caldwell was found not guilty of 15 of the 19 charges, and was deemed, therefore, not guilty. Anstey was suspended by the Governor and left Hong Kong in 1859 but pursued his accusations, so that under the new Governor, Sir Hercules Robinson, a new enquiry was set up in 1861 which found Caldwell guilty. He was dismissed. During that period 1857 to 1861, Mary Ayow Caldwell had three children. She provided a stable home life for a husband in trouble, but it must have been rather a strain on a constantly pregnant woman.

The same, no doubt, applied to Frances Bridges who had a son in 1859. She was the wife of lawyer William Bridges,

Caldwell's friend. The two had become friends because Caldwell provided Bridges with Chinese clients and Bridges became involved in the Caldwell case because Anstey accused the laywer of burning papers which would have incriminated Caldwell. Charles May, Superintendent of Police, did not tell Anstey direct that he had found papers in Caldwell's writing on an arrested pirate, but leaked it to William Tarrant for publication in his newspaper. Bridges and Tarrant were already locked in conflict over an earlier case.

Harriet May, wife of the Superintendent, cut off by the affair from a whole segment of administrative society, may have been able to seek solace with a little group of isolated Tarrant women. Eliza Whitlock had married Tarrant in 1845, witnessed by Charles Cleverly. But Cleverly's wife, Mary, will have had to be most circumspect because her husband was chairman of the Caldwell Commission of Enquiry. Eliza Tarrant had two sisters-in-law, Martha Urmson and Eleanor Tarrant, who had a son in May 1859. No doubt the new baby in the family was a consolation during the time Tarrant was in prison.

Meanwhile, George Caine, the eldest son of Tarrant's mortal enemy, and his wife Emily, had two children during the period of conflict. One cannot help but picture Mary Ayow Caldwell, Frances Bridges, and Emily Caine passing Eleanor Tarrant — all of them pregnant — in Hong Kong's two main streets, and being compelled to look the other way, when usually Western women made 'a point of looking at each other well in passing, as if the sight were of no everyday occurrence'.[12]

Anstey and Tarrant were of a type that the world will continue to need; men like Caine and Bridges were of their time. One of Hong Kong's historians G.B. Endacott, writes of Bridges, 'He was a thoroughly able lawyer and a strong, determined, but rather unscrupulous character. He was typical of the adventuring class of Englishmen of that period.'[13] As for the women that accompanied them, whatever their own preferences might have been, who suffered alongside them when things went wrong, and enjoyed the good times, their type is not so easy to discern. Indeed nearly everything about them is speculative, based on hardly more than a skeleton of birth, death, and marriage records. Their life was so private that it has left barely a trace. However, the confrontations of their menfolk do suggest that the accusations about divisions between Hong Kong women are somewhat superficial, for such divisions are often likely to have stemmed from the male confrontations. Even that potential feeder of divisiveness — gossip — usually attributed to women, was as much a feature of men's lives in Hong Kong as, indeed, it is elsewhere. This is hardly suprising, given that knowledge is power and gossip is knowledge. Edward Cree and Lord Saltoun have already proved themselves rivals to any of the women whose records survive; now, Alfred Weatherhead, a civil servant between 1856 and 1859, writes a throw-away sentence which becomes a give-away, for women did not smoke in public:

Nearly all the houses are built with verandahs, where inmates pass much of their leisure time — especially at early morn, or in the cool of the evening, enjoying the 'fragrant weed', and be-guiling the time with the current local gossip, shortened in colonial parlance into "gup".[14]

It is noticeable that the scandal of the late 1850s concerned administrative circles, those that can be equated with the taipans, or leading merchants, in social terms. But middle-class Europeans were by no means the only ones who contributed to the expansion of the new colony.

CHAPTER EIGHT

MARY ANN KINGSMILL, POLICEMAN'S WIFE

As early as February 1842, wives of officers who formed part of the expeditionary force began to live on Hong Kong Island. Soldiers' wives must have started to arrive on the troop ships at the same time, but there is no evidence of their presence until May 1843. Then, the evidence does not suggest comfort, security or happiness. Edward Cree, the eternal tittle-tattler, writes on 17 May 1843, 'Another bit of gossip is that Lt Rogers of the 18th has arrived from Trincomolee with the pretty little wife of a Sergeant of the 90th Regiment, who came out with us in the *Rattlesnake*, and lots of similar accounts of married ladies.'[1] In August Cree continues the story:

Nearly a hundred of the wives of the 55th Soldiers arrived from Calcutta. I was on shore ... we met many of the ladies on the road rather the worse for liquor. Among these, we met that poor wretched Mrs Loyd, who had been deserted by that blackguard Rogers, who has gone to England and left her to her fate. Jones, the Colonial Surgeon told me he had called to see her and found her suffering from delirium tremens. When we brought her out from England in the *Rattlesnake* she was a pretty, modest young woman. Now what a wreck she is, owing to that fellow Rogers.[2]

And Cree adds his own footnote: 'Less than a year after this I was told she was found dead on the side of the road at Hong Kong after going through the greatest degradation.'
Not every soldier's wife or sweetheart who wanted to

accompany her man to Hong Kong could do so. Very little material written by soldiers (as opposed to officers who wrote prolifically) exists, but the reminiscences of James Bodell, published as *A Soldier's View of Empire* (1982), give a heart-rending description of the process of choice and its consequences.

Bodell came out to China from Ireland with the 59th Regiment in 1849. He had a sweetheart, Winny, and when the time came to leave to join his regiment, he arrived at the station: 'Here a difficulty arose I did not expect, as no women were allowed in the Train but Married Women on the strength of the Reg.'[3] In fact, by subterfuge, Winny was got onto the train and the two spent some time together but James's regiment was soon chosen for foreign service, embarking at Cork for an unknown destination. James wrote of 8 June 1849,

When we arrived at the quay, and as we were told off in Companies to go on board of the Steamer, I shall never forget that day. I could not keep Winny off my neck. I was so bothered I forgot to unfix my bayonet. The Colonel was standing one Side of the gangway, and through Winny clinging to me, my bayonet went straight to the Colonel's Chest. He let [out] a roar ... brought me to my senses, and Winny was gently requested to leave to the Shore. This was the last time I touched Winny. After getting on Board, we stopped at the quay some twenty minutes, and the sight was something awful. Women and children screaming, young girls fainting, others half mad in a frenzied Condition. I assure you Women with 3, 4 & 6 children each was left behind. Poor things it was a sad Sight to see them. Some of them expected shortly to bring another into the World ... The four days we lay at anchor was even worse than leaving the quay in Cork. All day long boats crowded with Women and Children, Winny amongst them, pulling around the Ship ... I forgot to mention several men deserted and one man shot himself in Cork Barracks before they would leave their Wives and families.[4]

Perhaps Winny was better off not coming to Hong Kong. John Ouchterlony, a member of the 1840 expeditionary force, writes of how by October 1843 the 98th Regiment had lost

160 men and how another hundred of the 430 then in hospital would be dead by the end of the year. He continues,

'This unfortunate regiment had suffered much on their voyage from England in the *Belleisle* ... from the heat and confinement of the orlop deck, as they mustered 720, with 60 artillerymen, stores, guns, arms, provisions etc and 100 women and children. The latter were left at Hong Kong when the expedition proceeded to the north.'[5]

And as for what met them on shore, the grave-stones of the women of the 98th Regiment in Stanley cemetery, now obliterated but fortunately preserved on record before World War II, hint at the story: Between July 1843 and October 1844, seven women and eight children were buried there.

One must, however, be careful about drawing conclusions concerning other ranks from those figures alone; in September 1843 Cree wrote, 'Went with Lt Bailey ... to see some friends of his at Mt Pleasant Barracks. Found them anything but pleasant at present, two young officers we went to see are both dying of fever. As we went up we met a funeral of one of the wives & her child.'[6] Further, one must not assume that it was only the army, housed in barracks, that was affected. Malaria was particularly rife in the summer of 1843, it was assumed to be because of the expelling of bad gasses during excessive quarrying. Several merchants built villas on the slopes of Happy Valley. The views were stupendous, but a year later the fine houses stood abandoned, the occupants were dead. Unfortunately Happy Valley was full of the undrained marshes that were so useful as paddy fields; mosquitoes proliferated and, while the local Chinese had some natural immunity, the new expatriate community did not.

General George D'Aguilar, in charge of the troops in Hong from December 1843, wrote a moving even poetic account of the devastation, ending,

The 'Happy Valley' was as suddenly deserted as it was inhabited. Crumbling ruins overgrown with moss and weeds attested on every side the vain labour of man when he contends with nature. And the 'Happy Valley' restored to its primeval stillness, has been converted into a cemetery . . .[7]

General D'Aguilar put in train a draining scheme which went some way towards alleviating the situation, but his own wife Eliza was never well in Hong Kong; in the hot, humid season of 1844, she moved to Macau in an attempt to restore her health but on 5 January 1845 she finally sailed for England.

Life in the barracks at Victoria, on the north side of the island, was little more salubrious than in Stanley on the south but at least there were missionary wives in Victoria to help the soldiers' wives. Henrietta Shuck describes the situation in a letter home of December 1843:

I visit them frequently, give them books, and pray with the sick among them. They are the most destitute set of human beings I ever saw. Many of them have not a second dress, or garment of any kind. I find uses for all my old clothes, and I have begged of the other ladies for theirs. Money was given me to expend for them, and I purchased a piece of coarse, but good warm cloth, and gave it to the little boys for jackets and trowsers; and their little countenances told me, that when they bowed, and said 'Thank you Ma'am,' they felt it. The great cause of their distress has been a fire, which broke out and consumed, not only their houses, (which were made of matting,) but everything they possessed. They fortunately escaped themselves with little harm to their bodies. Sickness has disabled others of them, who were not burnt out, from working; so that altogether they are in a most suffering condition in this cold weather.[8]

Those men who could leave the army, such as Bodell, did so. By 1854 he was a Sergeant and wrote:

The last few months several Sergeants had claimed or bought their discharge, one of these Sergt had run away with another Sergt Wife and cleared off as was said to Australia. The Sergt that lost his Wife was still in the Regt. Now this woman was the same Mrs Rogers that was the Wife (pretty one) of Corporal Rogers that occupied the Barrack room in Templemore Barracks in 1848 when

I had a fight with Brown for insulting her . . . When it was known she had cleared out with Sergt Barrow, Sergt Rogers applied for his discharge and in a few weeks left the Regt but did not leave Hong Kong, as we expected he would. At this time I was paying my addresses in the love line to a young Lady living in Hong Kong, and myself began to think I could do better out of the Service than in it.[9]

Bodell married Sarah Mackinray on 3 October 1854 and by 14 October they were en route for Australia.

Former soldiers who did not leave Hong Kong, often went into the police force. Some were unmarried and formed alliances with Chinese women; those that did not have a stable relationship were said to be so prone to catching venereal disease that at one time they were subject to a compulsory medical inspection.[10] Those who married Europeans in Hong Kong chose women such as Sarah Mackinray and started a new life towards the bottom of the European social pile. Before looking at the life of a police wife, what sort of woman would she have been before her marriage?

There are certainly dozens of marriages in the St John's register between soldiers and European women; some will have been soldiers' widows. Sarah Mackinray had her mother in Hong Kong, so she was perhaps a soldier's daughter. It also seems likely that in the early days there were European ladies' maids and nursemaids.

Eventually those jobs were done almost exclusively by Chinese maids or *amahs* but in the earliest days, the Chinese men who flocked to Hong Kong came for work only, with a view to returning home, and they left their families in China. There were Chinese women already on Hong Kong Island but they worked mainly in the paddy fields or on sampans on the river and in the harbour. There were also Chinese women who became prostitutes. It was said by police inspector Charles May that of the 24,000 Chinese women in Hong Kong in 1877, 80 per cent were prostitutes.[11] The *mui-tsai* or domestic slave who features later, belonged to the more affluent Chinese society that gradually developed. There were respectable working *amahs* by at least 1857,[12] following the influx of Chinese into Hong Kong caused by the Taiping Rebellion in Southern China. But who were the female servants in the 1840s and early 1850s?

In the early days of Macau there were Chinese *amahs* but families obviously also had European and American servants. Harriet Low shows that they did not always behave well. She tells the story of her maid Nancy having to leave because she was pregnant. Then on 10 February 1833 Harriet's close friend Caroline Shillaber had problems:

This morning we parted with one of our family, Caroline's English servant. She was called up yesterday and told to pack her duds, she would be off for England in the *Reliance* ... she dared ask no questions, having a guilty conscience. She has turned out very like our '*Nancy*', not exactly a 'Nancy Case' but very near. She is quite notorious here, we find by a certain gentleman. European servants will not do in this place, they seldom keep their characters — deceitful creatures.[13]

Charles Elliot, in a letter to his sister as he and Clara travelled to Portsmouth to sail to China in 1834, mentions that 'Clara and her handmaid are less tired than you might expect'.[14] This pattern of employment obviously continued in Hong Kong. Emily Kerr talked about the rooms of Eliza and the children in her new house and in April 1845 she mentions that Eliza is to get married and that she 'marries with our consent a very respectable man in her own sphere'.[15]

Mary Ann Kingsmill's background is unknown, but what is known of her death gives a hint of life for soldiers turned policemen and their families. The somewhat contradictory details set out in the *Friend of China* of 19 July 1854 and the record of the legal historian James Norton-Kyshe need tidying up, but the story goes something like this: Police Constable John Kingsmill was a bugler in the 59th Regiment. Assisted by a loan from a Parsee merchant, Franjee Jamsetjee, he purchased his freedom and took service with his patron as a watchman, his wife Mary Ann attending to

the household arrangements. Later they lived at the
Aberdeen police station and looked after it.

But it was at Stanley police station that Mary Ann
Kingsmill died on 14 July 1854, aged 29. John is said to have
become jealous of her and administered poison. The other
version has the coroner's jury returning a verdict on John
Kingsmill of wilful murder of his wife by the administration
of a blow on her head with a heavy stick. John himself died
in gaol on 18 July, aged 35. Both were addicted to drink.[16]

What neither report notes, but the register does, is the
death, a year earlier, of a two-year-old girl, Katherine
Kingsmill of the 59th Regiment. Did she die because her
parents were drunkards and neglected or abused her, or did
they take to drink following her death? Police Constable
Kingsmill's estate when he was died consisted of only
£0 13s 7½d.[17]

Once men had left the army and become policemen,
prison warders or Court ushers, and married, it looks as
though the families tended to form a little community which
must have provided sustenance especially to the women.
That had not happened in the Kingsmill case, probably
because they were isolated at Aberdeen. Details from the
birth, deaths and marriages registers concerning another
police family — the Goodings — provide more evidence of
a close-knit community.

Private Robert Goodings of the 98th Regiment married on
6 June 1844. He marked a cross in the register, instead of
his signature, but his new wife, Mary Anne Marsh, signed
her name. In October 1845, their first daughter was born;
Robert Goodings was then a 'policeman'. Exactly a year
later, a son was born. When three years later a second son
was born, Robert was a clerk in the Magistrates' office. The
baptism took place on 4 March 1850, the same day as that
of a daughter born the previous September to James Roe, a
Private in the 49th Regiment, and his wife Mary. The joint
ceremony was obviously that of friends as events will show.
A fourth child was born to the Goodings in July 1851 when
Robert was an usher in the Chief Magistrate's office, and a
fifth child in May 1854 when he was a gaoler in Victoria

Gaol. Mary Anne Goodings died in childbirth that time, and the child died a year later, on 31 May 1855.

By then, Robert Goodings, keeper of Victoria Gaol, had married Mary, the widow of his friend James Roe. Their first child was born a year later, on 23 February 1856. Six weeks after that, Robert Goodings died of dysentery, aged 33 and Robert and Mary's only child died on 9 June that year. Mary Roe Goodings had, therefore, within a year of her re-marriage, lost her second husband and their child, and was left looking after a six-year-old daughter from her first marriage and her four remaining stepchildren. At least she had a job: she had been acting matron at Victoria Gaol where Robert was chief gaoler. Three months after his death, Mary married Robert Edward Mackenzie, the new keeper of Victoria Gaol. He had been a police sergeant in 1850 and by 1859 he had become a licensed publican.

In 1853, Mary Anne and Robert Goodings had been witnesses at the wedding of Inspector of Police James Jarman to Sarah Mitton, widow. Sarah Jarman died in the Central police station on 29 January 1856, aged 26. Six months later, the widower James Jarman married Mary Gray. They had six children between 1857 and 1863, four of whom survived. In Jarman's application to retire in 1869, he wrote, 'failing health now compels me to resign — tropical climate rendered use of stimulants necessary'.[18] The reply was that the Jarmans could have one third of their passage money to England but, as Jarman's services were not 'altogether meritous', he was not entitled to a full pension.

And so the circle of frequent marriage, frequent birth and too young death, and friendship among the police continues. Robert and Mary Anne Goodings were also witnesses when John Smithers, usher of the Supreme Court, married Caroline Cakebread on 2 June 1852; Smithers, too, was a witness when James Jarman married Sarah Mitton. Caroline and John Smithers had four children — the last born when he was sexton at the Cathedral — before he died on 6 September 1859, aged 38. Caroline, with four children under six to bring up, kept the books and did clerical work at the

Cathedral until the end of that year in order to receive his salary. Then, in October 1862, with the Jarmans as witnesses, she married Robert Browne. These details, numbing in their convolution, not only give an impression of life, death and relationships, they also demonstrate that the social stratum of the police was closely allied to that of publicans, shop-keepers and milliners.

The police families kept close; the milliners and dress-makers, as will emerge from chapter 9, did the same. It was as much from inclusiveness, or mutual support and common interest within their own circles, as from being excluded by other levels of Hong Kong society. How far such exclusion was inevitable, at least in the early years, is debatable; after all, as the last chapter and its scandals showed, social mobility was considerable: Daniel Caldwell, for example, arrived in Hong Kong with little but a will to succeed. Hong Kong was made for, and by, people like that, and still is!

CHAPTER NINE

JENNIE INNES
HAS A SHOP

One of the myths of Hong Kong's caste system is the story of Jennie Innes. I call it a myth because it has been constantly repeated to prove a point. But all the facts are wrong, thus proving only that the real point has been lost.[1]

Jennie Innes, the story goes, was in 1849 the wife of James Innes, the well-known merchant and opium smuggler of the 1830s. In the early days of Hong Kong James opened a shipchandler's business in Queen's Road. Jennie herself had aspirations to be received in high society, to be invited to dine with Mr Jardine, Mr Matheson and Mr Dent, as were other merchants' wives.

James Innes had, so it is said, been snubbed even in the old East India Company days because he was tough and uncouth. He did not mind but Jennie did. In the meantime, one would have thought to the detriment of her aspirations, Jennie had opened a glove and millinery establishment, or was it a department of her husband's shipchandlers? In her shop Jennie was treated condescendingly by her clientele, and was cut by them in the street.

All that changed, apparently, when Emily Bowring, the governor's daughter, entered Jennie's shop. She listened to Jennie's 'tale of woe' and after that the aspiring socialite received an invitation to tea at Government House. What is more, 'about a month later, the Government House chair set down Miss Emily Bowring before the quarters of Captain James Innes, and Miss Bowring took tea with Jennie'.[2]

That myth, upon which rests a whole critique of Hong Kong society, demands closer examination. Firstly, James Innes was of the minor Scottish nobility; he was 'the 7th chieftain of the Innesses of Dunkinty'.[3] A. Robertson of Jardine Matheson, writing to William Jardine in 1834, described Lord Napier as speaking 'more like friend Innes than anyone I know'.[4] That is unlikely to mean simply that he had a Scottish accent; Robertson was probably Scots himself; he certainly worked with Scotsmen — he meant the accent of a particular type of well-born or well-educated Scotsman.

That Innes was tough is not in dispute: the trouble leading up to the First Opium War was exacerbated by his behaviour in particular. But he never lived in Hong Kong. He died on 1 July 1841 (when Hong Kong was settled only by soldiers), and was buried in Macau cemetery where there is nothing on his tombstone to suggest that he had a wife, nor have I come across any other mention of one.

William Jardine did not live in Hong Kong either; he left the China Coast to return to Britain in January 1839, and died in London in 1843, also a bachelor, as was common among China Coast traders, until they returned home with their fortune. James Matheson arrived in Britain just before Jardine's death and did not return to Hong Kong. There were second generation Jardines and Mathesons, including nephews, but not to be linked in the same breath with Mr (Lancelot) Dent as *the* place to dine.

There was a Mrs J. Innes, or a name that sounded much the same. She was a widow called Jane Iness and she arrived in Hong Kong from Sydney as late as 31 January 1846. She took over Edward Hall's bakery, confectioners and general store in 1847. Another advertisement, of March 1849, proclaims that 'Mrs Iness, having taken the shop and premises lately occupied by Messrs Bigham & Co, Queen's Road, will open on or before 1 April, a bread and biscuit bakery — millinery and drapery to be conducted in one of the large rooms upstairs.'[5]

On 24 July 1850, accounts owing to J. Iness were to be sent to J.F. Carruthers, Iness's store, for immediate payment. On 20 September Mr Duddell was instructed to dispose of the whole stock of trade of the well-established drapery and general store business known as Iness's Store, Queen's Road. The reason for both these moves becomes apparent: on 21 September 1850, Jane Eliza Iness, widow, married John Brigstock, widower, with witnesses John and Jane Carruthers. Brigstock was captain of a ship sailing the Hong Kong–San Francisco route.

On 9 November that year, Mrs Marsh opened showrooms on Queen's Road lately occupied by Mrs Iness. J.E. Iness, having been resident in Hong Kong in 1849, according to the *Chinese Repository*, was absent in 1850 and 1851 (when the publication ceased). She probably sailed to San Francisco with her new husband soon after their marriage.

Emily Bowring arrived in Hong Kong with her father, the Governor, three and a half years later, in April 1854. It has to be said, therefore, that there could not have been a Jennie Innes, wife of James Innes, slighted by society and rescued by Miss Bowring.

To dispose of the Jennie Innes myth is not to insist that there was no snobbery. It is certainly true that people in trade have traditionally been looked down upon, particularly in England. Take the Bowras for example. There are at least two separate Bowra families in China Coast history. Firstly there were the two brothers, William Addenbrooke and Charles Woollett Bowra. When William's wife Emily had a son in 1848, William called himself a tradesman in the register of baptisms; the jury list of 1857 called him a storekeeper. He and Emily arrived in Hong Kong on 19 June 1844. Charles seems to have been in Hong Kong as early as 1843, when he was selling flour and gunpowder. By 1844 he had a shipchandlers and in 1845 he had added general provisions and wines and spirits. With William and Emily came Rosa Bowra, an unmarried sister. Cree, undeterred by the subtle distinction between storekeeper and merchant in the Wild West days of Hong Kong, wrote on 1 December 1844:

W Bowra, a merchant of Hong Kong has lately been joined by a sister to keep house for him — a tall, handsome girl quite the belle of Hong Kong. All the young fellows are talking about her. Bowra brought her on board this afternoon to see the ship, and, I suppose the officers too. She got plenty of attention paid her and appeared highly gratified when she left. Old Harshaw or Hardjaw, as we call him, from his facility of spinning such improbable yarns, has become dreadfully smitted, but he is an Irishman.[6]

In February 1845, Miss Hickson and Miss Bowra were the 'belles of the party' on board the *Agincourt* for dinner after the regatta — the 40 women there being described as 'all the beauty and fashion of Hong Kong'.[7]

On 17 February 1846, Rosa made a good marriage, to Alfred Humphreys. In August that year C.W. Bowra & Co. and Humphreys & Co. became Bowra, Humphreys & Co. In May 1848 a second sister, Frances, arrived from London. By 21 April 1849 she had married Captain William Roper. The expanding Bowra family was obviously successful, useful and accepted in Hong Kong's variegated society.

In 1863 Edward Charles Bowra passed through Hong Kong to join the Chinese Maritime Customs — a naval civil service supplied by the British government to the Chinese, and considered rather distinguished. The first thing he saw as he went ashore was the sign 'Bowra & Co Shipchandlers & Sailmakers'. The historian of that Bowra family quotes his disquiet at seeing his family name displayed with such lack of distinction; the proprietor may have made a good deal of money at trade, but he 'was a low common sort of man suited for his business and no merchant at all.'[8]

Another reference to class comes from George Preble, the American naval officer who dined frequently at Government House with the Bowrings and was equally as friendly with Harrison and Robert De Silver and their wives, Mrs Emily Hal and Mrs Emilie Bob. Preble, if not class-conscious himself, as, indeed, Edward Cree never was — perhaps an attribute of the seafaring — nevertheless notes the problem when he writes in December 1853:

Mrs Hal is yet a bride having been married rather less than a year. Her husband was attracted by her good looks and sprightly manners when passing through England, and recalling them on his arrival in China sent back to offer his hand and heart — was accepted and she came out ... she is a contentious little body, fond of show and dress and very desirous of shining in the aristocratic circles of the colony, which her husband's occupation of shopkeeper excludes her.[9]

No doubt there was class-consciousness involved in the attitude of the former Miss Gorsuch from Liverpool herself, but what other reasons could there have been for people's reluctance to consort with her? Firstly she was married to an American and they tended to congregate in Macau, as her brother-in-law — who was American consul there — and his wife did, rather than in the British colony. Harriet Low who was able to hold her own in any society had sometimes been made to feel very aware of being an American in Macau's heyday; since then relations had not improved: when the British had to terminate their Canton trade in 1839, the Americans cashed in.

Then there is the use of the expression 'aristocratic circles'. That was an American misreading — perhaps on the part of the two De Silver men and Preble — of Hong Kong society. Socio-historians have satisfied themselves that it was middle-class people who were merchants and (more remarkably) administrators in Hong Kong.[10] From the start Hong Kong society was middle-class — no doubt with aspirations to grander things — a past perpetuated in its status today as the acme of capitalism.

Finally, there is Mrs Hal's own personality; Preble has already hinted at it — he describes her two years later, in March 1855 as 'a silly little woman who bothers her husband, and often puts me out of all patience with her,'[11]

Emily Hal and Emilie Bob De Silver, and Emily, Rosa, and Fanny Bowra do not seem to have been involved in the family businesses — perhaps out of consideration for a social position to which they aspired. But the independent businesswoman Jane Iness was not unusual. There is evidence of quite a sizeable female business community in the early days of Hong Kong, based on the dress and millinery trades. Many of the women involved were employees, but several of them owned their own business, or managed someone else's. Mrs Marsh, you will remember, took over the premises formerly occupied by Jane Iness, but before that, in September 1850, she was advertising that she had received French bonnets and scarves at her shop in Wellington Street, off Queen's Road, and in October she had dresses for sale there.

In 1852, Mary Marsh, wife of Henry Marsh, storekeeper, had a daughter. It does not appear to have held back her business expansion because in December 1854 she moved to more 'commodious' premises next to the Hong Kong Dispensary. On 1 October 1856, Mrs Marsh's business — the oldest and best established millinery business in the colony — was advertised for sale because she was leaving for Europe. Buyers were to apply to Henry Marsh.

Mary Marsh certainly went to Europe, because in September 1860 she returned with 'fashionable goods', but her shop was still going strong in 1858 and 1859. In September 1858 the impressario Albert Smith was leaving the colony after a few weeks' stay during which he provided entertainment. He was carried shoulder high to his ship and wrote, 'All the balconies at Lane & Crawfurd's, the Commercial Hotel, Mrs Marsh's Millinery Rooms etc. were crowded with people.'[12]

Then on 19 October 1859 there was a fire, which the almost contemporary historian Ernst Eitel explains, 'destroyed the Roman Catholic Church in Wellington Street, a number of European business establishments in Queen's Road and Stanley Street, viz the stores of Mrs Marsh, Mrs Rickomartz, the Victoria Exchange, the Commercial Hotel and others'.[13]

What happened to Mary Marsh after 1860 when she returned from Europe is unclear. It looks as if her business in the early 1860s was part of Marsh, Boyer & Co. but in the 1862 *Directory* there is an M. Marsh with 'absent' against the name; in 1863 she is not named at all, and 'absent' is against Henry Marsh's name. By 1867 (there is a gap in the directories between 1863 and 1867) there is only a firm called Alexandre Boyer with no women working in it. In

1868 there is an advertisement which announces that
Alexandre Boyer has 'lately engaged the services of Madame
Marie, lately with Messrs H Marsh & Co., prepared to
execute orders'.[14] Is that our Mary in Gallic guise, or did she
die in the early 1860s away from Hong Kong?

Over the years, Mrs Marsh, Mrs Bonnett (formerly her
manageress Susanna Adams), Miss Rosa Novra, the Misses
Garrett and Mrs Rickomartz all had establishments employing young women. The only information about them is
their names in business directories, the records of their
marriages in St John's register and their signatures as witnesses at the weddings of their sister milliners. What their
life was like can only be surmised.

When you came out onto Queen's Road in Central into
the tropical deluge of July or the unbearable heat and humidity of August you might be reeled into by a phalanx of
drunken sailors straying from the dozens of public houses
that lined that street further westwards. (In 1860, there were
26 European inns in Queen's Road West alone).[15] Hong
Kong was dominated by the armed services and the services
they sought until after the end of the Second Opium War
in 1860; even after that there was a strong naval and
military presence though the army authorities apparently
made some effort to keep soldiers out of the central commercial area.

Then, particularly in the narrow streets that led up from
Queen's Road, there was Chinese life. Although European
women kept away from Chinese areas, they could not have
avoided seeing and sensing the culture which surrounded
them and which must have seemed particularly alien to
young women with no access to its language. There were
men with queues carrying heavy loads each end of poles
slung across their shoulders, while in the harbour boat-
women plied sampans, their babys strapped to their backs;
very infrequently, a woman with bound feet hobbled quickly
from her sedan chair to her house. There was extraordinary
food hanging up, and the smells to go with it, loud noises
of many kinds including hawkers' cries and the explosion
of firecrackers without which no festival was complete.

Houses leaned higgledy piggledy against each other and hung out over the narrow streets, the squalor relieved by plants and flowers, red and gold street signs, and colourful processions.

The European buildings, though, by the mid-1850s were gracious or, as Alfred Weatherhead expressed it, 'They are mostly large and handsome, and in size and architectural design would do no discredit to Pall Mall or Belgravia.'[16]

What the milliners did with their leisure time it is difficult to suggest; the lack of security would not have encouraged women to walk out of town on their own. They probably went to the parade ground to listen to the band playing, and between five and seven o'clock there was the promenade — if you were in a carriage, the five mile length along Queen's Road and out eastwards to Shaukiwan. Then there were letters home to write and George Preble enjoyed the Victoria Library, though Weatherhead said residents could not be bothered to use it. Otherwise, they must have kept each other company, swapping clothes, deeply interested in fashion.

They must have lived together, though I can find no evidence for it. The young men who came out to work for the big trading houses lived together. As the women lay in bed sweltering and sleepless, the mosquitoes whining overhead, the cockroaches scuttling across the floor, perhaps they gossiped about the clients they had seen that day in their hats and dresses, and discussed their dreams, or their prickly heat, or boils in their hair, which came with heat and humidity.

I cannot believe that their work was always pleasant. Firstly, if the experience of their sisters in Britain was anything to go by, there was a seasonal pressure that made unreasonably heavy demands.[17] But, whereas in Britain the cold would increase the misery, in Hong Kong it was the opposite. Imagine trying to hold the needle when your hands were sweating, day after day; and the trials of preventing dresses and hats and delicate fabrics from getting damp and spotted in the humid months of January to September. Gas did not reach Hong Kong until 1865, kerosene even later, so all heating to dry the air would probably have been with coal or wood. For cooling themselves they depended on human-driven *punkahs*. Water still had to be fetched in buckets — though there were Chinese 'coolies' to do that.

The young women probably lived to get married. In Britain, from where they had come to this very foreign place, between the years 1851 and 1871 there was a 72 percent rise in the surplus of single women to single men.[18] Certainly there were a lot of weddings among the milliners and seldom did they continue in their previous jobs after marriage. It looks as though the couples may have left the colony after they married, for there is no spate of ex-millinery baptisms.

Most of the women seem to have prospered as well in business as the men. One assumes that they got some satisfaction from running their businesses; they certainly formed a circle of mutual support. There were one or two exceptions to that prosperity; Mrs Rickomartz is the saddest. On 30 September 1849, Henrietta Ambrook married Adonia Rickomartz. The witnesses were the cream of the religious community and their relatives. The reason for that is to be found in Adonia Rickomartz's signature in the marriage register. It is in Japanese script and he is said to be one of those shipwrecked Japanese sailors whom Charles Gutzlaff and other missionaries, including Mrs King, had tried to return to Japan in 1837.[19]

In 1851, when the Rickomartz's first child was born, Adonia's employment was given as 'servant'. By 1857, when their fourth child was born, he was a printer, and by 1859, and the fifth child, Lucy, he was a compositor. Meanwhile, on 14 May 1858, Henrietta had started a milliners and haberdashers on Queen's Road with Mrs Jurgens. On 15 September the following year, the 'interest and responsibility' of Mrs Jurgens ceased in the firm and Henrietta was set to continue on her own.

A month later was the fire that also destroyed Mary Marsh's millinery rooms. On the 26th, Henrietta Rickomartz held a sale of millinery and haberdashery saved, slightly damaged, from the fire. It looks as if she, at least, then left for Shanghai because a firm, Rickomartz and Hurst, Milliners, came into being. But there was to be no future: on 23 May 1860, two-year-old Lucy died in Hong Kong; on 2 July, 27-year-old Henrietta died in Shanghai; and on 23 September, aged 39, Adonia Rickomartz died in Hong Kong. What happened is impossible to deduce. If they had all been in Hong Kong, it is possible to imagine some contagious disease that carried the three of them off.

The Rickomartz children were now orphans: Maria, aged nine, Louisa, eight, Henrietta Elizabeth, six and little Edward, only a year old. Once again, the missionaries who had taken an interest in the family from the start, came to its aid. In February 1868, eight years after the triple death, an engraving appeared in the *Female Missionary Intelligencer* depicting missionary schoolteacher Miss Oxlad with some of her scholars — two of them were Louisa and Bessie Rickomartz; they had been confirmed at the Cathedral the previous month. What is more, Louisa, at least, was to repay both the missionaries and society for the care she had received: in 1869 a Chinese girls' day school in the city was opened, to be run by Miss Rickomartz. In August 1872, she married Thomas Hewitt, a telegraph clerk, with all the religious and education community in attendance.

It is an opportune moment to look once again at that community, and another kind of working women. Missionary wives and single missionary teachers have the added distinction of being involved with the local Chinese community; indeed, totally, if paternalistically, committed to its care and improvement.

CHAPTER TEN

SACRIFICE, SCANDAL,
AND SCHOOLS

'It is very difficult for me [to find time to write],' wrote Mary Legge on 22 May 1850, 'what with our own family duties and the domestic care of both boys and girls, in all thirty eight young men and children and our almost constant stream of missionary visitors'.[1] Mary, wife of the LMS missionary James Legge, was replying to a letter from the Society in London to her husband, in which its secretary Mr Tidman had asked, 'Can nothing be done to establish a Female Boarding School in the Colony'. Mary was already teaching several girls, she reminded Tidman, and had been since the missionary family moved from Malacca to Hong Kong in 1843. What was needed was money, for buildings and a teacher, not will or energy.

It was this very commitment and enthusiasm, with little backing, that was often too much for missionary wives. By October 1852, aged 36, Mary Legge was dead. The missionary doctor Benjamin Hobson, writing to Tidman, described her death in intricate detail; but, in brief, a recurring bout of diarrhoea and bilious vomiting had so weakened her that when her sixth confinement began a month early she had not the strength to see the birth through. The child arrived stillborn and the mother failed to survive the night. Two of Mary's three surviving daughters and her husband were at her deathbed, as were Mrs Hobson and Mrs Chalmers, a newly arrived missionary wife.

There was a high mortality rate among missionary wives in the early days of Hong Kong. The first to die was

Theodosia Dean, who had arrived in Macau in 1837 as the single missionary Miss Barker, aged 17. She died of smallpox in March 1843, aged 23.

Theodosia was staying with the missionary wife Henrietta Shuck in March 1843 and not long before Henrietta described her own precarious health, and then the ill health of her daughter Henrietta. The arrival of the Deans, then of a Chinese lad who had been baptized in the United States, and another missionary added to her workload. Then her daughter Jane caught chickenpox and soon after that, Mecha, one of the little girls who was part of the family, had a high fever which was diagnosed as smallpox. Theodosia caught it too, but for her it was fatal. Henrietta wrote of her death, 'I feel her loss, for she was kind enough to take the charge of my children and pupils two hours every day, and give them instruction. They were making astonishing progress, and the arrangement greatly relieved me.'[2]

Henrietta had also arrived on the China Coast as hardly more than a girl. Miss Hall married the missionary J. Lewis Shuck in 1835 when she was not quite 18; within weeks they were on their way from the United States to China. During a stay in Singapore Henrietta had their first son and three weeks later they made the 19-day journey to Macau, arriving in September 1836. Within two months she had taken in two little Chinese boys, and her school was started. Meanwhile, she and Lewis were learning the language for four hours a day. By May the following year she had adopted a young Chinese girl who had been sold into slavery and had been found in a starved condition by an American who bought her and presented her to Henrietta. In October that year Henrietta gave birth to a second son. She had turned 20 the previous day.

By the end of 1838, after boasting of good health in her letters, she was taken gravely ill and was nursed by Caroline Squire and Charlotte King. She was expected to die. She recovered but her letters from then on were interspersed with recurrences of ill health — when they were not full of exhortations to her siblings to follow her state of grace. Henrietta was a very evangelical young women.

Her school continued apace, her son Lewis, aged two and a half, being one of the pupils. By February 1839 she had nine boys in the house and was expecting six more. But from the beginning in Macau, Henrietta had been interested in the education of girls rather than boys and in order to persuade parents to send their daughters to her against Chinese custom, she insisted that for every boy she took in, a girl must be sent as well. She and Charlotte King, who also spoke Cantonese, would travel two or three times a week to a nearby village and talk to the women about everything that concerned them, with the education of daughters as their true mission.

In Hong Kong, where the Shucks settled in March 1842, Henrietta's efforts began to be effective. A few months after Theodosia Barker Dean's death, when her workload had increased, she wrote in her journal for her sister, 'Three days ago a very gratifying incident occurred. Two Chinese Gentlemen brought their daughters to me, and one of them a neice also, and placed them under my care, and yesterday, another came, so that I have now six girls, making all to-gether, including my own, thirty two children.'[3]

Henrietta had not been well since that first serious illness in Macau. She continued to have children — her fourth was born in 1843 — on top of her domestic and teaching duties, and those of a missionary wife, such as visiting soldiers' wives. The only burden she did not take on was the demands of 'fashionable society' — 'We have invitations to balls and to parties,' she wrote, 'which of course we do not accept'.[4]

And so came the time for Henrietta's fifth confinement. By then, only Lydia Hale Devan and her husband, the American missionary Thomas Devan, were staying with the Shucks, as Henrietta wrote thankfully; besides, Lydia was 'a sweet sister. We seem to be agreed on all points, and I pray and believe that we shall be assistants to each other. When I am laid by, which will be, I expect in a few days, she will be able to aid me very much.'[5] But Henrietta Shuck, aged 27, did not survive that confinement; she died on 27 November 1844. Lydia Devan died in Canton two years later.

In 1854 two young missionary wives fully committed to mission work died within months of each other, and a third was widowed. Augustine Lechler married in Hong Kong in 1854; her husband Rudolphe was a member of the Basle Mission. Soon after their marriage he set off to visit his congregations on the mainland, not taking Augustine because travelling there was unsafe. She contracted diarrhoea while he was away and died on 26 April, aged 31.[6] Alvine, wife of William Lobscheid of the Chinese Evangelization Society, died on 6 August at the height of the hot wet season, aged 32. She had said in a letter in January that she had been very ill from Hong Kong fever the previous October.[7] She was in Hong Kong not much more than a year.

Between the dates of the deaths of those two missionary wives, Theodor Hamberg, another Basle Missionary died, leaving his widow Louise and two children. Augustine Lechler was no longer there to help Louise through that time. Her friend, Mary Legge, who had been at her wedding in 1851, was also dead. Rebecca Hobson, another witness, had gone to Canton. Louise left for home in Sweden on 10 July but her elder son died onboard ship before they arrived. The following year her second son died of cholera, and she died four days after him.

The missionaries Lechler, Lobscheid and Legge were to marry again. So was the Colonial Chaplain J. Irwin after his first wife, Mary, died in 1857, aged 35; but his second wife, Emma, died in 1864, aged 31, leaving two young children. Lewis Shuck also married again; but his second wife Lizzie died in childbirth in Shanghai in 1851, and he married a third time.

Louise Hamberg and Augustine Lechler had helped their husbands lay the foundations of their Mission's Hakka work. In the months before she died, Alvine Lobscheid looked after the Chinese girls left behind when two LMS missionaries moved to Amoy. She also taught them English for an hour every day. When Mary Legge died, Helen Chalmers took charge of all her Chinese girls. John Chalmers wrote to Tidman that it was not 'Without some fear on her part as well as on mine, that it will be too great an undertaking for her, having so little experience and so little knowledge of the language as she has. But it was very undesirable to send them away.'[8] Mary Legge's daughters, Eliza and Mary Isabella, were to pick up her teaching mantle from 1859 but to cast it aside on marriage not long afterwards.

The above gives the impression of a tightly-knit Protestant missionary community, not even divided by nationality or dogma, rallying round generously in times of trouble and attempting to provide continuity for Chinese children with love and compassion. That is not the whole picture.

In November 1845, James Legge himself was so ill with dysentery that he left for England with his family and three Chinese boys whose education he hoped to further there. The family did not return to Hong Kong until July 1848. Mrs Legge had, as we know, her own pupils and those girls had been left behind in the charge of a Chinese Christian, a missionary teacher brought by the LMS from Malacca, known in the correspondence concerning this matter as Chin-shen.[9] LMS missionary William Gillespie wrote to Tidman on 27 February 1847 fulminating against the state of affairs that had arisen.

Four months earlier Mrs Cleland, wife of the Reverend J. Cleland, had relieved Chin-shen of the girls because the money left behind by Legge for their support had run out. Since then Mrs Cleland had paid for their keep. The reason for the letter now was that $100 had just been received from the LMS by Chin-shen; Gillespie put it to Tidman:

What is it but saying — we can trust Chin-shen with the disposal of this money but not the missionaries. Mrs Cleland may engage in the work of instructing these children, but cannot be entrusted with the funds for their support. Could any Christian lady brook to apply to a native, however estimable and trustworthy as Chin-shen certainly is, for the monthly pittance for the support of these children — thus exalting one whom we have been sent to teach and be an example to, above the missionaries themselves in point of trustworthiness.[10]

Gillespie's letter was a long one, and he soon turned his attack, obliquely, on Legge's methods:

I cannot conclude without expressing my decided conviction, and that of my brother Mr Cleland that all Chinese girls maintained and educated by the private contribution of Christian friends in England, ought to be connected with the institution in the same way that the boys are — and that no one individual ought to have control over them so as to withdraw them or dismiss them from the institution ere their education has been completed . . . and that henceforth it be not in the power of any individual to divert such funds to the education or support of boys — which proposal in the case of those 3 boys now in England I felt bound to resist . . .

But if Legge's behaviour was high-handed, the behaviour of the third Mrs Gutzlaff was nothing short of scandalous. In 1843, Charles Gutzlaff had become Chinese Secretary to the government of Hong Kong. Little is heard of Mary Wanstall Gutzlaff — the second Mrs Gutzlaff who was so prominent in Macau with her pioneer girls' school — during the years that followed, but at some stage she had gone to Singapore to try and regain her health, unsuccessfully; she died there in April 1849. That September, Gutzlaff visited Europe and returned in January 1851 married to another English woman, Dorothy Gabriel. Gutzlaff died on 9 August that year.

The LMS papers are politely brief and discreet about what happened next. Legge wrote to Tidman in February 1852 enclosing extracts from the funeral oration preached by the acting chaplain, the Reverend Dr Moncrieff, and then re-marked that Moncrieff was to return to England by the same mail as his own letter on account of advances he had made to the widow so soon after her husband's death.

The Church Missionary Society (CMS) papers, on the other hand, show in some detail the tremendous upset that had occurred, so much so that George Smith, Bishop of Victoria, had had printed two of the letters which he wrote to the recalcitrant Dorothy Gutzlaff. Unfortunately, only the Bishop's letters survive, not Dorothy's 'disappointing' replies. Happily, however, he does quote from one of them, in which she apparently wrote: 'The time for even your giving an opinion from impartial personal investigation is gone;

and whatsoever report be sent, it will probably be received, as on a former occasion, as only one side of the question'.[11]

So far, only differences between the late Dr Gutzlaff's Chinese Union (a 'native' Christian agency) and other German missionaries had been at issue, and the Bishop had tried to stay aloof. But Moncrieff, during the funeral oration that he delivered in the Bishop's absence, had taken Charles Gutzlaff's side against those who had opposed him. He had also sent a copy off for publication in Europe without letting the Bishop see it.

Worse was to come: the Bishop, in his letter of 2 September 1851, added that the acting chaplain's motives were likely to be called into question 'by your acknowledgement that you were seeking to win the widow as your future wife'. He continued: 'The very day after the sermon was preached, and only two days after my poor friend G's death, you supposed you had sufficiently made your way and secured your ground, to pen your first written advances to her'.[12]

He did not then know the half of it! But in his written account to the CMS of 26 February 1852, he added further incriminating evidence:

About this date [October] Dr Moncrieff and Mrs Gutzlaff were seen at the same time by Rev J Johnston American Baptist Missionary, Mrs Johnston and Mr Foord purser of HM steamship *Sphynx* embracing each other and the lady reclining on the bosom of Dr Moncrieff. Mr Johnston (who resides in the house opposite to Mrs Gutzlaff) asserts that he and his wife repeatedly witnessed such familiarities afterwards.[13]

On being taxed, Dr Moncrieff admitted that he and Dorothy Gutzlaff had been engaged since 6 October. Dorothy seems to have prevaricated about her engagement, but the Bishop saw through it:

Either they were engaged less than two months after Dr Gutzlaff's death, or at that early period they practised familiarities which, taking place between unengaged persons, deserve such reprobation as the Bishop would feel himself bound to accompany with the suspension of his licence in the case of any clergyman so offending against the rules of moral propriety.

Dr Moncrieff left for England by the same mail as the Bishop's report. At the beginning of February it seems that Dorothy Gutzlaff must have written to the Bishop saying that she was about to leave and could they not shake hands. His reply of 2 February started:

I beg to say how satisfactory it would be also to my mind if, before you leave China, I could again cherish those feelings towards you and hold that friendly intercourse with you which (I regret to say) your recent course in connexion with one of my clergy before this community has interrupted.[14]

It continued in much the same vein, as his letters were wont, for some pages. From the Bishop's letter it would appear that Dorothy was ready to leave almost immediately, but 18 months later, on 20 February 1853, the rich enigmatic widow of the eccentric missionary married John McGregor Augustus Thomas Croft in St John's Cathedral.

George Smith was pompous and self-righteous long before he became Bishop of Victoria aged 35 in 1850. When he travelled through China between 1844 and 1848 looking at mission possibilities and wrote a book about it, he dismissed Hong Kong for its 'frequent spectacle of European irreligion', as well as the debased nature of its Chinese population.[15] His wife, Lydia, daughter of A. Brandram, the secretary of the British and Foreign Bible Society, may well have been a different sort of person. It was her determination to make the idea of properly organized education for Chinese girls a reality that was to open up opportunities over the years both for single British women as workers of pride and distinction, and for the advancement of Hong Kong's young women.

Scandal of a rather different kind from that which entangled Dorothy Gutzlaff and the Diocese of Victoria and involving a woman with even more determination than

Lydia Smith, surrounded the introduction of Roman Catholic education by Italian nuns in Caine Road — education which still continues today.

Emily Bowring, it is said, wore a hair shirt under her society gowns during her father's governship of Hong Kong. She certainly carried out benevolent work in the community — such as visiting soldiers' wives in the barracks — rather more assiduously than she attended society functions, though she did her best, regarding the latter, to be a dutiful daughter. With less regard for her father's feelings and position, she also daily attended mass, which was apparently common knowledge and the subject of gossip.

On 5 May 1859, Sir John Bowring finally left Hong Kong for England. As the Canossian records tell it, Sir John, not finding Emily at Government House as his party left for the ship, assumed that she had gone ahead. He did not find her on the docks either, and when the final warning came, the anchor weighed, he left without her.

Nothing was there to be done at that moment, except to leave his beloved daughter in the hands of God knows who ... and later, under a wave of bitter sorrow, write threatening letters to friends, acquaintances, newspapers begging to retrace for him his lost treasure ... his beloved daughter ... in vain.[16]

I find it hard to believe that Emily had not given him any warning, however oblique, or that he would have left without ascertaining that she was purposely missing. Surely at least there was a letter waiting to be handed to him when it was too late to go after her, or a message delivered by her sister once they had weighed anchor.

Emily meanwhile had taken refuge with a prominent and controversial Portuguese family — the D'Almada e Castro — in Caine Road. There she stayed for 11 months awaiting the arrival of the first Canossian nuns from Italy, invited to come to Hong Kong by the Italian Roman Catholic mission to teach, nurse, and look after orphans.

Ironically, John Bowring had been keenly involved in Hong Kong's developing education system and his Inspector of Schools, William Lobscheid, wrote of how in 1857, 'Miss Bowring and Miss Emily Bowring accompanied his excellency on the visit to the principal schools in Victoria and did not shrink from going into those miserable places, where the schools were held'.[17]

Six Canossian sisters arrived on 12 April 1860; they knew Emily was there waiting for them. After the first meeting between the nuns and their future companion, the latter remarked to 12-year-old Anita D'Almada e Castro, 'The habit is not very attractive, but the sisters, especially the Superior [M. Cupis] are saintly.'[18] Matilda Sharp, who went to see Emily at the convent six years later, noted

She is about thirty I suppose; was dressed in a large black silk mobcap with a huge flapping bunch of bows at the top, a short limp faded coarse odd stuff gown, a large apron and a three-cornered old black silk shawl. Yet she was very sweet and had a happy smile and looked at peace with God and man — but still what a life![19]

Emily was accepted into the mission under the name Sister Aloysia Bowring. Almost immediately, with Aloysia giving essential assistance, the mission set up three girls' schools in Caine Road: an English one with 22 girls under Sister Aloysia, a Portuguese one under Sister Giovannina, and a Chinese one under Sisters Rachele and Madalena Fan. French sisters had been in Hong Kong since 1848, mainly involved in looking after foundlings. In 1860 they revived former schools, including one for 30 girls in Spring Gardens, under Sister Benjamin. However, the two missions, French and Italian, were always to be totally separate.

Aloysia Bowring, because of her background, her dedication and the fact that she was the only one of them who could speak English, was something of a phenomenon in the Canossian Mission. A charming vignette is drawn by Mother Lucia Cupis in a letter of May 1860 to the mother house:

If you should see us, dear Mother, you would laugh a little; we only know how to speak Portuguese passably, because it is very easy, and here we have English, Portuguese, Malayan, Chinese and Irish girls. They all speak their own language and we try to make ourselves understood with the deaf-mute signs. Sometimes it happened that one speaks Irish, another plays the interpreter by repeating it in English to Novice Bowring, who in turn repeats it in French to Sister Stella, and Sister Stella will repeat it to me in Italian.[20]

But Aloysia and her Italian co-workers were as vulnerable to Hong Kong's climate and diseases and to overwork as their married counterparts in the outside world. Smallpox, cholera and tuberculosis had their day in the convent. Aloysia took on the extra workload that became inevitable and did not succumb, but 1870 was a year particularly noted for sickness. Soon Sister Aloysia was in the grip of a raging fever. She died on 20 August, aged 37. She was the sixth Canossian sister to be buried in Happy Valley in ten years and her father, to commemorate her life, paid for an enclosure to be built around their graves.

At least when one of the Canossian sisters died there was a continuity in education for the children, and this professionalism is what the Female Education Society teachers would also provide.

III
GOOD WOMEN, QUEEN'S WOMEN, AND BIG LADIES

CHAPTER ELEVEN

MISS BAXTER AND
AGENTS IN THE FIELD

'It must be gratifying to Mrs Smith,' wrote William Lobscheid, Inspector of Schools, in 1859, 'on her departure for her native land, to have been the principal means of the establishing of the first Girls' Day School on this island. To her, to the ladies who visited the Government School at Stanley in December last, and particularly to Mrs Cleverly, Mrs Bridges, and other ladies who have engaged to supply Mrs Smith's place, I beg here publicly to offer my sincere gratitude.'[1]

Lobscheid's first purpose in the eulogy that ended the preface to his little book on education of the Chinese, was probably self-serving. He was obviously a volatile man, having joined and left both the Rhenish Missionary Society, and the Chinese Evangelization Society in less than ten years, and his time as Inspector was one of some upheaval in Hong Kong's embryo education system. Many wiles were used by him and several others, religious and secular, conformist and Nonconformist, in an effort to make the system viable and universally acceptable.

Out of all this manoeuvring, the coming and going of schools, mainly involving education for boys, came Mrs Smith's Diocesan Native Female Training School (DNFTS). It was not the school in Stanley referred to above, nor the one attached to the CMS's St Paul's College, with which Mrs Smith, as wife of the Bishop of Victoria, had also been involved. It was a new venture.

The importance of highlighting Mrs Cleverly and Mrs

Bridges's involvement is that wives of Hong Kong's administrators and professionals were to be on the committee in Hong Kong which was to govern and raise funds for the school. In Britain, sometimes well-born, and always well-meaning women, usually married, were to sit on the committee of the Female Education Society (FES) that was to provide and maintain the teachers. The teachers themselves were to be single missionary women, pledged to remain thus. They were called, rather strikingly, 'Agents in the Field'.

The inter-relations between those three different groups of women are somewhat obscured by published material about the education establishments that were to evolve; just occasionally it is possible to see, mainly from the unpublished administrative records, what went on behind the scenes. But I think it is as well to be aware, as the years go by, of the underlying tension created by different responsibilities, experience, and status.

The first example of uneasy relations between the missionary women in the field and the FES committee in England had occurred 20 years earlier; indeed, there had been no links between London and the China Coast since then. Mary Gutzlaff's school in Macau, which quite early in its life concentrated on looking after blind girls, was under the auspices of the Morrison Education Society and the LMS. But in 1837 Mary was desperate for help so that she could expand her intake, and she encouraged her little pupils to write to the FES. The FES was then a fairly new organization, independent though attached to the CMS — with both Robert Morrison and Charles Gutzlaff contributing from the China Coast to its creation in 1832.

The FES responded by sending out 17-year-old Theodosia Barker. Although very young, Theodosia was not unqualified. She was highly educated and had even started to learn Chinese before she left Britain from the Professor of Chinese at London University. She was to become proficient in both the spoken and written languages. But there was another side to her, one which must have some bearing on what was to follow. As the periodical of the FES, the *Female Missionary*

Intelligencer, shows in an appreciation published after her death, 'her youthful and interesting appearance, associated with some peculiar circumstances in her early life, drew forth much tenderness towards her'.[2] She remained in poor health. On her arrival in Macau at the end of 1837 she moved in with the Gutzlaffs.

What happened next can only be guessed at, but on 4 June 1839 there was a meeting of the FES committee in Bloomsbury Square in London. The result of it was a quite remarkable letter sent from the committee to Charles Gutzlaff about his wife. From it the reader learns that, without consultation, or even notice, Mary Gutzlaff had sent two blind Chinese girls to England to be educated by the FES. It can hardly be said that the committee members were speechless at her behaviour because the letter is very full, but they were beside themselves. They could not, and would not, take any responsibility for the girls.

There was more to it than that, however: it was not the first time that Mrs Gutzlaff had acted oddly and now everything had to be aired. The letter hinted at the 'treatment' Theodosia Barker had received at the hands of Mrs Gutzlaff. It was

such as to compel her to seek another home, and that when she had settled to accept Mrs King's kind offer of shelter, most undue influence was used to persuade her to marry Mr Dean, contrary to the known regulations of the Society, as a more agreeable expedient to Mrs Gutzlaff than her remaining at Macao under another roof.[3]

The letter ended, lest there be any misunderstanding:

It has been the wish of the Committee to pass as lightly as possible over these painful circumstances, for which they had hoped some excuse might be found in Mrs Gutzlaff's state of health, but the arrival of her letter proving the necessity for a clear expression of their sentiments, they beg that it may be distinctly understood that all connexion between the Society and Mrs Gutzlaff is at an end, and that any efforts which they may hereafter make for China will be quite separate from Mrs Gutzlaff and her school.

The final irony was that by the time that letter arrived in Macau — if it ever did — the British population there, including Mary Gutzlaff and her blind girls, had fled.[4]

Much had changed, the committee obviously hoped, 20 years later. The DNFTS opened formally in March 1860 in new premises provided by the government in Albany Terrace under a temporary teacher, Miss Wilson. It had started well; on 28 November 1859 the Reverend J. Beach wrote to Mrs Smith,

We had an examination of your little Chinese girls' school the other day, Lady Robinson cheerfully accepting my invitation to her to come and distribute the prizes; and 5 or 6 other ladies were present, notwithstanding the conflicting attractions of a picnic to Stanley on the same day. About twenty of the little creatures came, and a very pretty sight it was to see them so clean and happy. I only wish you could have been here.[5]

Nea Robinson was the wife of the Governor, Sir Hercules Robinson, and she had been in Hong Kong only since September. She was quickly roped in to be patroness of the school. Mrs Cleverly had obviously become a pillar of the establishment since vying with Miss Hickson for the hand of the man who became Chief Surveyor, and she worked hard to raise money. One of the means for doing this was for well-wishers in Britain to send goods out through the FES for sale at bazaars in Hong Kong.

By the time of its only surviving Annual Report, the school was catering for 'a somewhat superior class of native females', because they were to occupy positions of 'influence and usefulness' and they were to become teachers themselves.[6] It seems that the inspiration for the Training School may well have come from the school in Stanley mentioned earlier. That was set up following a petition for a school, particularly for girls, from the local inhabitants but it had to be staffed by 'heathen' teachers — a man and wife.[7]

A further insight is given into the class of girls at the DNFTS by a letter written by an unnamed temporary teacher to Mrs Smith, in which, talking of the distance that had to be walked to her house, she explained, 'The walk itself was a hindrance to the small footed children, and in wet weather they could not come at all.'[8] Small footed is what expatriates called women and girls with bound feet, and suggests children of those the same letter called 'respectable Chinese.' In fact, their fathers were mainly teachers themselves.

Where Miss Wilson, the school's first teacher, came from is not clear, but she was successful. A woman missionary wrote to the FES committee on 24 July 1860, that she seemed 'to bring the girls on fast ... and they love her'.[9] And Miss Wilson herself wrote, 'Although I have not been well lately, things have gone very nicely. I think the children the best in the world.'[10]

Miss Wilson continues by saying that the day of 'Miss B's arrival, Mrs Irwin brought her to see me'. Mrs Irwin was the Colonial Chaplain's second wife, Emma, and a member of the School's committee; Miss B must be Miss Baxter, the legendary Hong Kong teacher, deemed by the colony's historian G.B. Endacott to be the only woman worth discussing in *A Biographical Sketch-book of Hong Kong.*[11]

Miss Baxter is a slightly enigmatic figure. She was not treated the same as the others who were sent out by the FES. They were, to all intents and purposes, indentured for five years to the Society; and they were treated rather as governesses were at that time — not so much as of a lower order, but as having fallen on hard times so that they were expected to be grateful and biddable. Indeed, among the questions asked of an 'agent's' referees was, 'is she mild, courteous and humble in her demeanour?'.[12] Details of former employment are scarce but, by 1903, at least two missionary teachers had originally been governesses, a third a nursemaid, and a fourth a milliner.[13]

Harriet Baxter was obviously from a different milieu. She was the second surviving daughter of Robert Baxter Esquire of Doncaster and Queen's Square, Westminster. He was not a clergyman, and he was obviously rich, but Bishop Smith described him as a 'Christian layman' and, as such, local clergymen used to meet over monthly missionary teas in his

Doncaster house when Harriet was young. George Smith was among them.[14]

For many years, even as a child, Harriet longed to be a missionary in China. Then, in 1859, when she was 30, Mrs Smith discussed the girls school project in her father's house. Harriet held back from offering herself as the desired teacher, assuming that someone would come forward through the FES. When they did not, she told her friend Lydia Smith that she would go, but paying her own way and unconnected to any society.

She left England in April 1860 and was involved in the same shipwreck off Ceylon as Lord Elgin, the British Ambassador on his way out to China to settle the latest imbroglio — the Second Opium War that was to result in Hong Kong expanding to include the Kowloon peninsula. On arriving in Hong Kong, Harriet found that the temporary teacher, Miss Wilson, was well-established and a more permanent one, Miss Eaton, had been recruited so she struck out on her own.[15]

Although Harriet's commitment was to the Chinese, she discovered that the children, particularly the orphans, of British soldiers, and those of mixed race, had no educational opportunities except those offered by the Roman Catholic missions. Harriet may have been loving and noble but she could not tolerate that. So she set up various schools, funding them herself, through her family. An independent Chinese girls' boarding school, a school for European orphans and children of mixed race, and a boys' day school all appeared over the next few years.

But that was only the start. She was a friend to soldiers' wives, and a friend to Chinese families, and when Lydia Smith needed her help she went with her into the back streets of Victoria visiting the lodging houses of European and American sailors. On a visit to Canton she travelled to a Chinese village 15 miles away and stayed there for two days, accompanied only by a Chinese Christian woman; and there, at the request of the villagers, she set up a day school. By that time she spoke colloquial Cantonese, from mixing constantly with Chinese women. As Ernst Eitel, who knew her and married her close colleague Mary Ann Eaton, put it, 'She made her home in Hong Kong the home of every friendless, fatherless, motherless, suffering, outcast woman or child, without distinction of nationality, creed or social rank.'[16]

In spite of all that love and compassion so willingly given, it is probably fair to suggest that Harriet Baxter was not always approachable by all Europeans. Eitel remarks,

No doubt there was little sympathy in her with sentimental ailings and sickly religionism and some people thought her character somewhat stern and hard; but her feelings were too deep and true to have any patience with fictitious sentimentalism; and she was too well-acquainted with the multitude of real sufferers in this world, to waste her time on imaginary sorrows.[17]

Bishop Smith wrote similarly of her:

Among the European community she had many friends who valued her uncompromising honesty, her Christian boldness, her willingness to risk offence when sense of duty compelled her to utter words of rebuke, her determination to call things by their right names, her courageous resistence to worldly compliance with fashionable customs injurious in their influence on Christian character, and her willingness to reprove others under the promptings of real affection and interest in their spiritual well-being.[18]

The young woman who had been recruited to do the job Harriet Baxter thought she was going to do, 23-year-old Mary Ann Eaton, did not reach Hong Kong until January 1863,[19] but it is her name, rather than her predecessor Miss Wilson's, that is always associated with the school. I think Miss Wilson may have served longer and more robustly, even though her health suffered in the job.[20] Miss Baxter was never headmistress of the Diocesan School, as is sometimes suggested,[21] although she was associated with it in many ways, and her influence was undoubtedly greater than Miss Eaton's.

In a letter Mrs Irwin wrote to Mrs Smith in July 1861, she reported, for example, how 'On Sunday morning the girls [of the School] attend my little school in the Cathedral, when Miss Baxter is kind enough to teach them.'[22] In July 1863, the DNFTS moved to a new building in Western Bonham Road, the money for which had been raised locally. Bishop Smith and the Acting Governor, W.T. Mercer, presided, and both their wives and Miss Baxter (all three of whom were committee members) attended, together with other European women. There were now 30 Chinese girls boarding there, learning Chinese and English reading, writing, plain needle-work, geography, Bible reading, 'and more especially a training in the religious truths and moral habits of the Christian faith'.[23]

Then there was the marriage to a Chinese catechist of Lydia, the school's oldest pupil, obviously christened after Mrs Smith. The day of her wedding in November 1864, Miss Eaton was not well enough to go to the house of the bride, so Miss Baxter went instead and accompanied the bride's chair the two miles to the Cathedral. There she supported the bride, 'as the smallness of her feet rendered it painful for her to stand a long time. Miss Eaton was near to her, as well as some members of the School committee ... The Hon Lady Robinson ... stopped to speak to the bride at the Church door, but was unable to be present'.[24] After the ceremony, there was a Chinese entertainment, organized by the committee, in the Bishop's dining room at St Paul's College, and then they all moved to the drawing room where Mrs Stringer, wife of the Colonial Chaplain, played the piano and sang. Lydia and her new husband stayed there for a couple of days until they left for his new job in Foochow.

The function envisaged for the Training School, of pro-viding suitable marriage partners, was starting well. Indeed, so successful was the school that Miss Eaton asked for another assistant. Miss Baxter, too, needed help. She could get it more easily, perhaps, because her sister Nona was on the FES committee. In May 1863 Nona Baxter gave the London committee full details of her sister's work and her plans for the future and asked them to send Harriet an assistant, if she guaranteed to raise the sum required. The committee was delighted. By July, Nona had 'appropriated £150 from the legacy of Mrs Freeman at her own disposal', and the committee acted.[25] By December 1863, Nona had raised the money to send Miss Oxlad and Miss Waterworth to Hong Kong.

Some of the FES agents disappear swiftly from sight. Miss Waterworth is one of them; she married a Mr Mellish and had to repay her fare; the same thing happened to Emily de la Cour, who apparently set out with Miss Eaton to teach at the DNFTS but seems to have been commandeered briefly by Miss Baxter before marrying John Gullick on 3 September 1864. She had to pay a penalty for not giving six months' notice. Miss Oxlad was to be another matter: she was to stay in Hong Kong for 12 years and then move on to Japan. It is to her sharp eye — she also painted, though her paintings seem to be lost — and facile pen that we owe some idea of what life was like for those young single missionary women, and what their feelings were, outside their work. From her vantage point in Staunton Street, she wrote a long and lyrical piece of which one of the most striking aspects for those who live in Hong Kong today is the silence:

The only sound borne upwards to us from the little world at our feet are the quarter-chimes of the clock-tower, the barking of numerous dogs, the occasional rap of the watchman as he goes his rounds, and the half-hour bells from the ships, with now and then the cheery voices of sailors, as they haul away at the ropes at the turn of the tide.[26]

Staunton Street today, following progressive reclamations of land, is rather too far away to think, even in the quietest moment, of hearing voices from the sea.

In the month that Miss Oxlad's piece appeared in the *Female Missionary Intelligencer*, December 1864, there occurred an event that was not only to threaten Miss Eaton's grip on the DNFTS — demanding more help than ever from Miss Baxter — but it was also to undermine the very existence of the school. The periodical gave a muted, apparently factual account on 1 April 1865:

A letter was read from Miss Eaton, Hong Kong, giving an account of a murderous attack made upon her by six Chinese thieves, on the evening of Sunday, December 4th on her way home from Church, by which she had been greatly alarmed, and her nerves much affected. A letter from Miss Baxter on the same subject was also read.[27]

But in the administration book of the FES in London a more detailed account was given of subsequent actions to a meeting of 9 February 1865; it confirmed the above facts and then continued:

She further states that early next morning she gave notice of the outrage to the local Committee, and to the police, and requested permission from the former to give holidays at once, instead of at Christmas, in order to give her the rest and quiet she needed to recover herself; but that no answer was received, nor any measures taken for her protection; that on the following Thursday, the parents of the elder girls insisted upon their returning home, being too frightened to allow them to remain any longer, and that, on the younger ones asking leave to go, she gave them permission to do so. She enclosed a letter from Mrs Stringer, secretary of the local Committee, informing her that she was dismissed on account of this alleged want of judgement and disregard of the School. It further appeared that this step had been taken, not in a meeting of the Committee, but by means of a circular sent to the different members for their signature. A letter from Miss H Baxter, and extracts from her journal, bearing on the subject, were also read. It was resolved, to express to Miss Eaton the deep sympathy of the Committee under the trying circumstances in which she had been placed, and to assure her that, if she be compelled to leave the Diocesan School, they will be prepared to maintain her in some other suitable sphere of missionary work, such as will probably be found at Canton, or at Pekin. They also wish her to take Miss Baxter's advice respecting her future proceedings.[28]

Miss Baxter's letter and extracts from her journal do not appear to have survived, but they obviously fully supported Miss Eaton, for the London committee's work was not yet done:

It was further resolved that the Committee of the Diocesan School be informed that this Committee have received the tidings conveyed in Miss Eaton's letter with much sorrow, as well as surprise, and that the dismissal of Miss Eaton, in the manner described, is a matter the legality of which is very doubtful. This Committee also desire to record their decided opinion that Miss Eaton has not met with that Christian forbearance and womanly sympathy from the local Committee, for which her trying circumstances so loudly called. It appears that four days were permitted to elapse without any steps being taken for her protection, or any answer given to her application, and the Committee consider that if, in the nervous excitement naturally caused by such suspense, she acted hastily, she did not merit the terms employed in Mrs Stringer's letter. They further consider that they have not themselves been treated with that Christian courtesy which they had a right to expect from a kindred committee, in the treatment that their agent has experienced, and in her being dismissed without previous communication with them.[29]

The minutes of the relevant Hong Kong committee meeting still, happily, exist, and they help to give a rounded picture of an incident which exemplifies the uneasy interaction between the three groups of women involved in the educaton of Chinese girls at that time:

December 8th, 1864. Miss Eaton, having previous to this meeting been attacked by Chinamen on her way to the School, and having written a note to the Secretary begging that her holiday might at once be given and saying that she could not remain longer at the School, this meeting was called to consider whether Miss Eaton's holidays should be given and what should be arranged for the protection of the School. It was agreed that Miss Eaton should be granted her holiday at once, she being so unwell from the effects of the late fright; but that the girls should not go away at present. Miss Baxter, promised to send Mrs Ainsworth from her School for the present. A letter was written to the Governor begging from him protection for the School. It was also agreed to subscribe a sum of money to be presented from the Committee to Miss Eaton's Chair-bearers for their good behaviour on the night of the attack.

December 8th and 17th 1864. Two meetings were called to

discuss the action of Miss Eaton, who, on being granted her own holiday, dismissed the pupils on her own initiative, thereby calling down the anger of the Committee on her head and her own dismissal. Her case was taken up by the Rev. Dr Irwin, who should have been consulted about her dismissal. Finally she was taken back, after having written a letter of apology to the Committee. Several Members of the Committee resigned.[30]

At this point, it is worth noting that signs of friction between Miss Eaton and the committee could already be detected soon after her arrival. A letter from Mrs Irwin was read to the school's Hong Kong committee on 1 July 1863:

Miss Eaton seems to have grave doubts as to the utility of teaching the girl pupils English and does not feel that their progress justifies the time spent over it. She does not find they understand her sufficiently to receive lessons in grammar or geography. My opinion is, that the study of English must exercise and open the mind to an extent which learning Chinese, in the manner in which it is universally taught, never could do and the girls thus instructed are more likely to prove intelligent and helpful wives to educated boys.[31]

After expanding her argument, Emma Irwin concludes with the remark, 'I think it would be a great relief to Miss Eaton to know that the Committee are not looking for very great things, though, after all, much must and should be left to her own discretion.'

It would also be false to suggest that the committee were not interested in the security of the school and its occupants. As early as August 1863, after several alarms at night over break-ins, it was decided that a watchman should be employed.[32]

It might be, then, that the seeds of the ruckus were sown months before. But if its effects were to be far-reaching, they were temporarily obscured and then exacerbated by what happened six months later. On 30 June 1865, Harriet Baxter died of Hong Kong fever. It took her ten days to die, during which she was mostly delirious. 'Better to die in China,' she murmured, than to 'return to England'.[33] To her friends and colleagues — such as Matilda Sharp and Miss Oxlad, who had taken it in turns to watch over her — her death was devastating. For her pupils and schools it was obviously equally so. Miss Oxlad wrote of Miss Baxter's orphans:

From the hour we returned from her funeral to the present time, it has been a continued season of anxious planning and considering what could be done to prevent her work from dying with her. I feel that a great responsibility has devolved upon me, and that whatever arrangement is made, I am quite ready to do all I can to take care of these children whom Miss Baxter has left in my charge. I feel certain in some ways funds will be raised sufficient to carry on something of what she left.[34]

And in the same issue of the *Female Missionary Intelligencer*, Miss Oxlad's mother, noting that the present number under her daughter's care was 13, aged between two and 12, with one baby, continued, 'Perhaps you will allow me to make known to your readers that I have commenced a subscription to purchase material for articles of dress for them . . .'[35]

Harriet's family, who had always been behind her, acted immediately. As soon as news of her death was received, her sister Nona arranged for £50 to be sent to Miss Oxlad 'To set her free from pecuniary anxiety respecting her support for the ensuing six months, and to enable her to have a change, if she requires it, as well as to afford time for the (Baxter) family to complete their plans for the future maintenance of the school.'[36] Further sums were also agreed upon by the committee.

Miss Baxter's death certainly caused a hiccup in the well-being of the lively and very personal institutions she had set up but every care was taken to minimize the damage and they were eventually to flourish. It was the Diocesan Native Female' Training School that was to founder, once Miss Baxter was no longer there to give moral and practical support to Mary Ann Eaton, and once its Hong Kong committee had lost its way.

Following Mary Ann's brush with Chinese footpads, she

failed to recover her equilibrium. She now carried a pistol and it is said that one evening in Bonham Road she failed to recognize an acquaintance who approached her chair and nearly pulled the trigger.[37] Meanwhile, she was receiving some solace from Ernst Eitel who had come out with the Basle Mission in 1862.

Marriage was much frowned upon by the FES and they made few concessions to it but Mary Ann Eaton was always treated more gently than anyone else. In May 1865 she wrote saying that she was engaged to Mr Eitel but that they would not marry until her five years with the FES was up. Very honourable, opined the committee. But on 30 October, Mary Ann wrote again and the committee's minutes sympathetically recorded that:

As her nerves have not recovered the shock she had received the previous December, she is no longer equal to her duties, and will not, therefore, be able to fulfil her term of five years, as she had earnestly desired to do. She therefore requests permission of the Committee to resign her situation at the end of 6 months from the date of her letter, as she requires rest and change before another hot season begins.

The committee not only accepted her resignation but 'in consideration of the exceptional circumstances in which she has been placed, they will remit the sum that would be due in virtue of her pledge'.[38]

Considering how other young women had been treated, though not necessarily in Hong Kong, that was indeed accommodation by the FES.[39] So, in January 1866 Miss Eaton married Mr Eitel (he at that time leaving the Basle Mission for the LMS) and left the School.[40]

Miss Oxlad took over the DNFTS when Miss Eaton left, with the agreement of the Hong Kong committee, the FES and the Baxter family. Indeed, Nona Baxter had put forward the idea of an amalgamation of the Diocesan School and Harriet's orphan school when Miss Eaton's departure was mooted. A Miss Rendle[41] helped her as matron for a while. But the School was failing, both from lack of money and lack of pupils. That seems to have started as early as 1865 for in July that year the Hong Kong committee records cryptically note, 'The teaching of English not be compulsory as several cases of girls being offered for sale at a high price, (A Wong £500) on the recommendation of speaking English had occurred.'[42]

The *Female Missionary Intelligencer* is even less forthcoming; it notes in June 1869 that,

Miss Oxlad has continued her faithful and unwearied labours of love in the Diocesan Native Female Training School and has completed her five years of service. Local circumstances, which she could neither have anticipated or prevented, and the constant changes going on among European residents in the Colony, have caused many difficulties in keeping up the school.[43]

That note to readers hid much that had been going on for two years. As far as one can interpret the limited material, pupils stopped coming because the reputation of the school deteriorated. It is said that the well-mannered English-speaking girls found favour as the mistresses of European men. Eitel talks elliptically of 'the results of an English education upon Chinese girls drafted from families undermined by the peculiar temptations of Hong Kong'.[44] And Dr Frederick Stewart, School Inspector in 1867, says in his report that to the 'melancholy results which in nearly every instance have followed from teaching Chinese girls English, I need not more particularly allude'.[45]

As rumours spread, so money stopped flowing; members of the committee left the colony, as European members of Hong Kong committees have always done. By 1867, the previously all-female committee seems dominated by men, men such as Mr Mellish, husband of the former, short-term 'agent' Miss Waterworth. In November, Bishop Alford, who had taken over from George Smith, was called upon to help and did not respond. In December the committee dissolved itself. At an extraordinary general meeting of the friends of the school on 8 January 1868, a temporary expedient was agreed upon, allowing the school to limp on under Miss Oxlad.

By 1870 the school no longer existed; it was called the Diocesan Home and Orphanage and was under Mr and Mrs Arthur who had been running the Garrison School. It fairly quickly became a boys' school and in 1902 called itself the Diocesan Boys' School. There, women teachers, in the minority, came and went. That school still flourishes.

Meanwhile, Miss Eaton who, one feels, did not have the spine of some of her colleagues, had moved with her husband Ernst Eitel to Canton. There, with the help of the ever-patient FES, she set up a girls' boarding school in 1868. This time she was steering clear of the superior sort of girl. No habits were to be fostered and nothing whatever taught that 'would lift the girls above their own social rank, and thereby unfit them for a happy and contented life amidst those menial labours in the fields and in their homes, which they will have to perform on their return to the bosom of their families'.[46] Indeed, no English was to be taught at all!

By February 1870 the Eitels were back in Hong Kong and by 1871 Eitel was persuading the LMS that his family, including his partially-paralysed daughter Theodora, should be returned temporarily to England. Once again it was proved that marriage, sick children, family responsibilities, and a husband who moved when he pleased were difficult to combine with running a school.

With the closing of the DNFTS it looked as if Mrs Smith's dream of continuity and progress in female Chinese education through the employment of single, unencumbered women, had come to nothing. But in the meantime, in 1869, Miss Oxlad had resuscitated the Baxter Vernacular Schools, with the help of Harriet's family, and while she was away on home leave, Louisa Rickomartz, a former pupil, ably held the fort, proving that something had come, at least, of teacher training. And when Miss Oxlad came back revitalized and was later joined by Miss Johnstone, the schools grew from strength to strength.

CHAPTER TWELVE

NETWORKS

*T*hree sorts of European, apart from missionaries, tended to come to Hong Kong; indeed, they still do. Those who were passing through and could not wait to get to the 'real China'; those who came on something like a fixed contract, from three to five years, and hoped to move on to better things; and those who came to settle, make their home, and their fortune.

From 1860 and the ratification of the Treaty of Tientsin, not only was the Kowloon peninsula (south of Boundary Street) now part of the British colony but, the Allied forces having been able to get as far as Peking and burn down the Summer Palace, China had no option but to open itself up to foreigners. The naval and military officers, who produced a plethora of vivid 'China Books', were followed now mostly by missionaries. But increasingly other travellers, including women, ventured further afield, passing through Hong Kong on their way. The Austrian Ida Pfeiffer has already been mentioned. She was much the earliest, in 1847, and, while what she wrote about Canton may today seem like travelling to be taken in one's stride, she was a pioneer then, particularly for women.

Lady Brassey visited the colony in 1877, and Isabella Bird and Constance Gordon Cumming both arrived in December 1878. Their accounts add some superficial images to the Hong Kong of that period, and also give the strong impression that Victoria itself was not particularly attractive to the traveller. It was too British, not at all Chinese, apart from the women manœuvring their sampans and the odd colour-

ful procession. The keen travellers headed up the Pearl River
and Hong Kong was merely a stepping stone where they
had some useful letters of introduction. The only things
worth praising were the effect of the harbour and the Peak
under a clear blue winter sky and a gentle sun, and the
hospitality of people who appeared to have endless money
and servants. Travelling to Canton there was the frisson of
pirates and the exoticism of China, until so recently inac-
cessible. There they could visit Chinese houses — usually
of the rich — where banquets were laid on and sometimes
a visit to the women of the household, as well as a hideous
prison and places of public execution.

Apart from the missionaries, most expatriate women in
Hong Kong had little opportunity for meeting Chinese
women, except their *amahs* (ladies maids and nannies). As
a result, life was necessarily confined to European mores
and pastimes. Millicent McClatchie, passing through Hong
Kong in 1895 on her way to stay with her sister and consular brother-in-law in China, described the situation
squarely: 'It is only the "griffins", as foreigners who have
been out less than a year are called, who will come out with
sleight-hammer assertions regarding the natives and their
customs. And don't they get laughed at for doing so.'[1]

Men, whether in business or administration, had increasing occasions to meet and deal with Chinese men, even
on a semi-social level, but Lady Brassey describes how wives
were excluded, a situation which often still obtains today,
by no means only in Chinese circles. She and her husband,
a Member of Parliament and substantial business man, were
sailing round the world in their large yacht, the *Sunbeam*.
The journey was quite a feat and they were often royally
received and, indeed, they entertained royally, receiving two
hundred on the *Sunbeam* in Hong Kong one evening. A
group of Chinese business men wished to mark the voyage
and Thomas Brassey was invited to a banquet. But the chief
host had to express regret to Annie Brassey that 'their
manners and customs did not permit them to ask ladies, as
they were particularly anxious to invite me, and only abandoned the idea of doing so after considerable discussion'.[2]

Those women who were not passing through or had not come as missionaries with work to do, had, therefore, to make their own lives as wives, and they did. Three women in particular — Matilda Sharp, Louisa Coxon, and Mabel Cantlie — allow us to build up a picture of the life of middle-class married women between 1860 and 1900. All three left some sort of a mark, not only because two of them left a written record. Their lives were not quite as superficial as Isabella Bird suggests when she wrote:

Victoria is, or should be, well known, so I will not describe its cliques, its boundless hospitalities, its extravagances in living, its quarrels, its gaieties, its picnics, balls, regattas, races, dinner parties, lawn tennis parties, amateur theatricals, afternoon teas, and all its other modes of creating a whirl which passes for pleasure or occupation.[3]

Isabella especially blamed the Governor between 1877 and 1882, Sir John Pope Hennessy, for the proliferation of cliques. He was a forceful, opinionated man whose liberal attitude towards the Chinese went against the instincts and interests of the conservative business community. His policies, so everyone said, had led to an influx of riff-raff, an upsurge in crime and too much leniency in punishment so that life and property were as unsafe as ever. Pope Hennessy was also a Roman Catholic and Isabella Bird, who was staying with Bishop and Mrs Burdon, after bewailing the crime situation in a letter of 9 January 1879, continued:

I hope the Governor will be recalled. Pleasant as it is to a stranger, I believe that half the people don't speak to the other half — none of the missionaries except 2 are on speaking terms — those of the CMS and Bishop Burdon are on just speaking terms and no more. Dr Eitel of the London Missionary Society has just left the mission to become the Governor's secretary and is helping to advance Roman Catholicism. The Governor is only on *official* speaking terms with members of the executive council and not with the Chief Justice at all and is believed to be as much as a personally ... [illegible] and ambitious man can be anybody's tool, the tool of the Portuguese Bishop Raimondi. I now think that the reason for his attention to me is that he wishes to appear on friendly terms with the English Bishop . . .[4]

I think in many ways Isabella is more conscious of Hong Kong's cliques and quarrels than were those getting on with their lives there, particularly in those letters to her sister, such as the above, which were not published in *The Golden Chersonese*, presumably for reasons of discretion. There was obviously, in some circles, an unease in relations between the predominantly Protestant expatriate population, and the minority Roman Catholics (the majority of whom were Portuguese from Macau, and French and Italian missionaries). A glimpse of that has already been seen from Harriet Baxter and the reaction to Emily Bowring's attendance at mass. However, Matilda Sharp who was a church-going, pious woman, in the way that Victorian women of that era were, wrote of attending Miss Baxter during her last illness, of visiting Emily Bowring in her convent, but not of the religious and government cliques and feuds. The extravagant was for the fleeting visitor alert for impressions and incidents to delight the sensations, and for those caught up in the disharmony. Most of the European community of two thousand or so (as against a Chinese population of 125,000) were not any more involved in upsets than the average person in a small community is today.

Matilda Sharp's life, particularly her 35 years in Hong Kong, has been lovingly reconstructed, through her letters home, by Joyce Smith who works today at the hospital that bears Matilda's name. So I propose here not to describe her life in detail but to draw on her letters, so far as possible those Joyce did not quote from, to give a more general impression, sometimes by contrast, of women's life in Hong Kong.

Matilda was a schoolteacher in Suffolk, one of a large family of orphaned daughters, when, aged 26, she met Granville Sharp in 1855. By December 1858 she had travelled to Bombay, married Granville who worked for a bank there, and come with him to Hong Kong to start a new life. In 1860 Granville set up as a bills and bullion broker and later dealt in land. Over the years, Matilda's letters show the uncertainty of Hong Kong's economic expansion and the effect it had on those connected with business. There was money to be made in Hong Kong but there was also money to be lost and by no means every middle-class family was as constantly rich and extravagant as Isabella Bird's description suggests.

The Granville Sharps did eventually move to a pleasant house in the exclusive Peak district in 1878, and certainly at his death in 1899, six years after Matilda's, his estate was able to endow a hospital to be named after her. But often during those early years she was glad that her widowed sister Lucilla had come out in 1865 and married Granville's solicitor cousin, Edmund; the families were not always prosperous at the same time but they supported each other as necessary; often they shared a house.

A letter from Lucilla shows that Pope Hennessy's humane treatment of criminals was not disparaged only by visitors:

Our new Governor is causing a stir. He has even forgiven criminals again and again, and no sooner was this known by the rascals on the mainland than they all came swarming over. Burglaries have been a nightly occurrence and there were scenes of violence of all kinds ... [5]

But, as early as 1865, long before Pope Hennessy's arrival, Lucilla wrote home, 'I have learned to load Matilda's revolver. I see that she carries it with her whenever we go for a walk or ride, quite as a matter of course.'[6] And they were burgled twice in 1866.

Matilda's interest in the education of Chinese girls has already been mentioned; she was on the committee of the Diocesan Native Female Training School. She did also make an effort to learn Cantonese, and she did venture into parts of Hong Kong that, she suggests, most European women avoided. She tells how she took a friend to shops in the Chinese quarter in 1867, though her interest was not necessarily that of contact with the Chinese: 'It is not quite the thing,' she wrote, 'for ladies to go to these but I am interested more and more as English shops are so expensive.'[7]

That same year Matilda wrote that she and Lou (Lucilla) were still learning Chinese, and continued:

I seldom speak anything else and insist on the servants speaking Chinese to me. I really feel we are getting on a little and it is so interesting to go shopping. The other day I was very indignant about the impoliteness of a shopkeeper. I spoke to him in Chinese and he would answer in English. At last I said, 'I wish you to speak Chinese to me. I want to learn.' He smiled and touched his ear, 'Too muchee trouble pain ee give my ear to hear you speak Chinese. You just now begin. Want a little more learn then I can speak.' I said, 'If you don't speak Chinese, I don't buy.' They do not like us learning as it gives them such an advantage over us if we have difficulty understanding what they say, or not to make yourself understood by them.[8]

That Matilda persevered, with a language which even today, with all the modern learning techniques, continues to defeat expatriates, and without the motivation of missionary women, conveys a strong impression of her character.

Matilda is the only first hand source I know for how European women dressed at home, particularly during the impossibly hot months. On 10 August 1866, she writes that, 'You cannot come out and no one comes to you until sunset. [It is] not living but vegetating.' So, on days like that, until 5 p.m., she and Lou would either wear a 'cool and comfortable Chinese short dress and trousers', or a loose flannel chemise with loose buff linen trousers and a loose jacket, 'all beautifully light and cool', together with thin, loose-thread and open-worked Chinese slippers with no sides or heels.

Matilda has already said that English shops were expensive and it is quite obvious that women married to men whose business fortunes fluctuated were as economical as such women would be today. In the 1870s Matilda had a sewing machine and made clothes for herself and others, 'I made three frocks before lunch for a motherless child who goes home by mail today,'[9] she wrote. But in the 1860s, she employed a Chinese tailor. She wrote on 31 May 1866 how he came every day at 8 a.m. 'Lou and I are employing him for a week or two in getting ready our winter things.' He worked from 8 until 4 p.m. and they paid him 20 pence a day. 'He fits very nicely,' Matilda wrote, 'and makes a dress beautifully. Our *amah* can help him sew.' He was producing, for example, 'pantelettes in magenta flannel, so much nicer than skirts'. Their family may have suspected that Lou and Matty were going troppo!

It is less clear if the Sharp women's Chinese tailor ran up the fashionable dresses that went over the crinoline hoops of the day. I suspect that Mrs Marsh and her like may occasionally have been resorted to. Matilda did not care for the crinoline, particularly in the hot weather; in August 1866 she wrote, 'Crinoline and stays are unbearable.' 'Why?' she asked in another letter, 'do our dresses extend so wide and sweep the floor besides?'[10] In May 1867 they went to Government House and were 'amazed to notice the small crinolines, the length of skirt of the latter I dislike but the small crinoline is a great comfort'.[11] As for millinery: 'Lou has just made herself and me a new bonnet and several tasty and pretty caps — a finish and style to our morning toilette.'[12]

Matilda did not fill her days with fashionable clothes. She loved her garden and got great peace and satisfaction from it; and it is to people like her that we owe the colourful tropical impression of Hong Kong today. She liked to read, anything, from the Bible to Pushkin, Trollope and Anderson's Tales in German, and to play the piano. When asked by a member of her family if she found it lonely when Granville was away on business or working long hours before Lucilla arrived, she demurred, 'Far from it. The days are not long enough.'[13]

She had her house to run, of course, with its regulation number of Chinese servants — all men, except the *amah* who attended to her personal needs. There was more to it than one might suppose. On one occasion, for example, the household went on strike for more wages and she and Granville, determined not to give way, did 'house pidgin'.[14] But Matilda's greatest preoccupation, I think, was to do her duty towards her friends, neighbours and the community. The latter may have been gradually widening to include

Chinese but so far, for women like Matilda, it was only Chinese girls in need of education. More obviously in need of her attention were other European women.

Matilda was childless, as was Lucilla, and never sorry to come home after the exertions of someone else's children; but she was always willing to look after a friend's offspring if she was ill or about to be confined or even when a woman died.

Miss Johnstone, who arrived with the FES in 1874, tells how in 1880 she spent a week's holiday with Matilda on the Peak. 'It was a delightful change,' wrote Margaret Johnstone, 'nine degrees cooler than where we live'. She also notes that Matilda had known Miss Baxter well and 'she is very good and kind to me'.[15] It was not all one way: Matilda notes how the second Mrs Legge, Hannah, 'Had kindly come to enquire how I was, she thought I looked poorly on Sunday.'[16]

Hannah Legge was to leave for England soon after, in 1865, in poor health. She had been in Hong Kong since 1859 but did not, apparently, take to the life as her husband's first wife, Mary, had done, although her letters show that she tried to do her duty.[17] That Matilda was friendly with Mrs Legge (LMS), as well as Mrs Burdon (CMS), Miss Johnstone (FES), Miss Baxter and Emily Bowring, adds to the evidence that the religious divisions in society described by Isabella Bird may not have affected the women quite as much as they did the men. Although Matilda was religious, she was not narrow. She remarked in 1877 of two lads who had come out with a clergyman, that they 'are strictly fed on Bible meat and are rather in danger of growing into little prigs.'[18] Perhaps by 1879 religion was more overt and religious differences had hardened because of the arrival of a Roman Catholic Governor.

Matilda's religious convictions inspired her to be as ready to help the 'needy' as her own circle. At first that category was mainly army wives. Like Henrietta Shuck, Emily Bowring and Harriet Baxter before her, Matilda Sharp went out of her way to relate to those women who ended up in Hong Kong married to ordinary soldiers; after all, the private's lot was universally acknowledged to be poor. It was, even in Matilda's day, only a few years since Florence Nightingale had found the army organization in such a deplorable state during the Crimean War of 1854–5.

The depths of an army wife's life are described by Matilda in a letter of December 1875:

I saw a sad sight yesterday at the barracks: a poor woman with black and bruised mouth where her husband had hit her with a poker when drunk. He was lying in bed fast asleep, drunk. She is only twenty three and a pretty young woman. I felt so sorry for her. Last Christmas he was a sergeant but lost his stripes and was downgraded to a private through drunkenness. I have heard many English women marry Chinese in Australia but they are gentle, industrious and sober husbands and that the women prefer them to the drunken Englishmen and Irish in the colonies.[19]

There are lighter moments, such as Matilda describes at the beginning of that same letter:

I went to the barracks yesterday to have thirty women and children to tea with me on Tuesday next, the 28th. They were hugely delighted. Granville will have a steam launch that will take them from a wharf close by and bring them here to be closer to us.

Tonight Mrs Burdon and two friends will dine with us and I shall get wisdom from them about my tea; they are famous for such large parties. I think of borrowing from my neighbours several swings and rocking horses to put them in my garden. Then I shall have large dishes of stewed apples and rice pudding and things they don't generally have at such parties, such as meat patties. At this time of year they get plenty of cakes.

Matilda was by no means the only one who felt a duty to her European 'sisters' in distress. In 1889 the Hong Kong Ladies Benevolent Society was formed, with the purpose of introducing method and organization into the charitable works which had started at least as early as those recorded by Emily Kerr in 1844. Help in cases of 'sickness, want, poverty or distress' was directed towards men, as well as women and children, but not Chinese or Portuguese, and dispensed, with the aid of subscriptions and donations, by a committee of 'benevolent ladies'. Matilda Sharp was involved, though she is not named as a member of the early committee. By 1904, the Hong Kong Benevolent Society, as it later became known, had dealt with 1,000 cases.

Louisa Coxon was, I suspect, a rather different type from Matilda Sharp, though she was a life member of the Ladies Benevolent Society and had, thus, the right to recommend cases for consideration. Louisa is best known for being the chief agitator behind the setting up of the Ladies Recreation Club, suggesting that if she was more enthusiastic about recreation than benevolence, it was recreation in a positive, outward-looking way.

The best introduction to her must be the description of her on her way to the races. Among the frivolous activities dismissed by the seriously adventurous Isabella Bird were 'races'. They were a Hong Kong passion before there was a Hong Kong — there was a British East India Company race-course in Macau — and they still are a passion today. From the beginning it was a pastime, perhaps the only one, in which both the British and Chinese shared an undisguised delight. The races, which took place for three days around Chinese New Year, were the highlight of everyone's Hong Kong social calendar. Constance Gordon Cumming, passing through, but a friend of 'olden days', was staying with Louisa Coxon at that time in February 1879 and wrote:

Mrs Coxon, being one of the very few people here who cares for the exertion of driving a pony instead of being carried by men, drove me out cheerily each morning in her little pony-carriage, which, I think, was the only wheeled vehicle in that vast assemblage. Everyone else went in chairs, borne by two, three, or four men.[20]

That same year, Louisa Coxon took to the stage. Until then men had played the parts of women in Hong Kong's amateur theatricals. She used the stage name Mrs Hockey, for it was still not entirely respectable. 'Mrs Bernard' hid, it seems, Mrs Ayres, the wife of the Colonial Surgeon, and

'Madame Chervau' was probably Christine Vaucher, the wife of a silk merchant.[21] It was Mrs Bernard who received most of the plaudits, but the three women had broken a tradition that previously barred women from a lot of fun.

Louisa's husband was Atwell Coxon, who started as an accountant with the Chartered Mercantile Bank of India but became a bill and bullion broker, like Granville Sharp. He was an apparently clubbable and community-spirited sort of a man; at various times, from at least 1862, he was on the Hong Kong Club Committee and that of the Rifle Club, captain of the voluntary fire brigade, and worshipful master of the Zetland Masonic Lodge. Louisa obviously had to find her own amusement and must have decided at a certain point that her husband, whose stage name was Hockey, was doing something with the Amateur Dramatics Society from which there was no need for her to be excluded.

She did not stop there. In 1883, she and at least eighteen other women (whose names have been lost) decided that they needed somewhere of their own where they could meet and play tennis and indulge in other healthy activities. They wrote to the Acting Colonial Secretary asking for a piece of land for the purpose. He was supportive, though other male administrators through whose hands the letter passed were dismissively waggish.[22] Nevertheless, the request was granted and in 1884 the Ladies Recreation Club was opened by Diamantina Bowen, wife of the Governor, Sir George Bowen. Lady Bowen, born an Ionian Countess, was renowned for her good works in the colonies where her husband was governor and one can picture her pleasure at opening the women's club.

The LRC as it is affectionately known today, was not just a place for women to meet: Louisa Coxon and her sisters obviously appreciated the need for physical activity for women. Mrs Archibald Little who arrived in China in 1887, wrote of her introduction to European women in China that they,

Live tightly girt, and *gant de sueded*, just as if they were going to drive out in a carriage and take a turn in Hyde Park with the thermometer in the sixties. Now, as for months together here the thermometer seems to be in the nineties, this simply means that for months together the ladies here take next to no exercise, and in some cases none. No small proportion of them neither play lawn tennis, nor ride. Meanwhile the men are walking, rowing, bathing, shooting, playing cricket, tennis, etc., and hence, I imagine, the rosy cheeks of one and the pale weariness of the others.[23]

In Hong Kong, particularly after 1884, there was no longer any excuse, at least for middle-class married women living on the Island. Indeed, it is fair to assume that it worked; a Chinese woman, Madame Wei Tao-ming, visiting Hong Kong for the first time in 1906, wrote:

I saw my first white man. I was agape. The men seemed very strange, with their light hair and their loud free mannerisms. But the women, walking arm in arm with them, on their big feet, talking and laughing with an equal lack of shyness, stupefied me. On the whole I thought they were incredibly odd but still something about their bodily freedom stirred responsive chords in me.[24]

As well as the physical freedom that was a cause for envy, that description shows the lack of contact between Chinese and Western women. It is confirmed by a visit that Kitty Pope Hennessy, the Governor's wife, made to Canton in November 1878. The couple visited a former high official and his family, and Kitty was questioned intently by the women about foreign women; they explained to her that she was the first one they had ever met.[25]

In Hong Kong it was to be some years before middle-class Chinese women had any sort of relationship with their foreign 'sisters'. There was, however, at least one exceptional family. James Stewart Lockhart and his wife, Edith, not only entertained Chinese men in their house — which was unusual enough in itself — but, according to his biographer, Shiona Airlie, they also entertained the wife of one of them.

Stewart Lockhart had come out to Hong Kong as one of the first cadets, young administrators earmarked for special training, in 1878. He put off marriage as long as possible but eventually, when he was 30, he succumbed to a locally-born young woman, daughter of bullion broker Alfred Hancock and his Sheffield-born wife, Harriet. James married Edith in 1889 when she was 18, and when he was already Assistant Colonial Secretary.

He continued to rise successfully in the Civil Service and by 1895 he was Colonial Secretary with increasing responsibilities, particularly after the British leased the New Territories from China in 1898. The cadets all spoke Cantonese, that was one of the purposes of the system, and thus Stewart Lockhart was able not only to forge closer links with Hong Kong's rapidly-growing Chinese intellectual and mercantile elite, but also better to understand their culture. He was, indeed, passionate about things Chinese, a scholarly interest which Edith did not apparently share. She did, however, make a capable and welcoming hostess in their fine house, Ardsheal, on Plantation Road on the Peak.

Wei Yuk, an unofficial member of the Legislative Council, had been educated in Scotland — so the link with Stewart Lockhart may have been as much Scottish as Chinese; that education, too, would have made it more natural for Wei Yuk to consider taking his wife with him to visit the Lockharts. What is more, his wife's father was missionary educated and had travelled abroad. The visits were frequent and Stewart Lockhart was asked to be godfather to young Wei Lock. Unfortunately, nothing exists to describe the relationship between Edith and Mrs Wei.

The close ties between European women are emphasized when Mabel Cantlie notes the death at home in January 1889 of Edith Hancock's newborn brother and her visit to console Edith's mother who already had eight children. Mabel's diaries will be used in this chapter as confirmation of the pattern of mutual support already suggested by Matilda Sharp's letters.

Dr James and Mabel Cantlie had arrived in Hong Kong in July 1887, planning to stay indefinitely. His ill health, not helped by overwork, persuaded them to leave in 1896. Mabel, who was 26 when she arrived, kept a diary during those nine years, of which, unfortunately, only four exercise books (1889–91 and 1893) are accessible. They are not detailed like Matilda Sharp's letters, but really little more than engagement diaries, rather wooden and sparse; they do, nevertheless, give some impression of Mabel's life.

Her granddaughter, Jean Cantlie Stewart, drew on the diaries for her biography *The Quality of Mercy: The Lives of Sir James and Lady Cantlie* (1983), but the Hong Kong period was, necessarily, only part of Dr Cantlie's distinguished career, in which his wife played no small supporting role. Her medical help will start the chapter on women and medicine. During World War I she had an acknowledged contribution of her own to make, particularly with the Red Cross. As early as 1910 she was the first Commandant of the first women's VAD (Volunteer Nursing Detachment) which was to provide such invaluable war service. At the end of 1919 she was awarded an OBE. Cantlie himself is best known in Hong Kong for his part in setting up the Medical School, long before there was a university; his work during the plague of 1894; and his untiring research into many tropical diseases. He has a small niche in China's history, too, for rescuing Sun Yat-sen, China's first President, and one of the first students of the Medical School, when he was kidnapped in London and held in the Chinese Embassy in 1896.

Some of Mabel's visits to women were in connection with James's profession as a doctor, but often they were just to bring comfort — acts of sisterhood which came to her naturally. When Mrs Hirst, with whom Mabel usually went singing, was 'out of spirits', the Cantlies took her with them to see a patient. Both Mrs Judd and Mrs Dalrymple had babies in 1889, and there was Mabel calling regularly. Mrs Holliday, with whom Mabel often painted, was recovering from dysentery — off went Mabel to visit her. But it was when Annie Dennys, wife of solicitor Henry Lardner Dennys, had a baby on 21 July 1889 and did not recover that Mabel really put herself out. The families were obviously close. Mabel noted that James, or Hamish as she called her Scottish husband, was tending Annie during the night of their fifth wedding anniversary. During the day

Annie's other children — there were three of them all under six — were with Mabel, as well as her own two young sons. Annie died on the night of 1 August and immediately Mabel took the bereft children home with her and in the days that followed comforted the widower, oversaw the household and packed up Annie's clothes. A few days later, she was preparing clothes to send the Dennys children home to England. Then there was the christening of the baby who had survived, and Mabel was deputy godmother. She packed the children's clothes while also visiting Mrs Hirst who was not well, and then took the children on board the *Shanghai*, and went to see Mrs Hirst again on her way home.

Mabel rarely notes emotions in her diary but as she said goodbye to the Dennys children she recorded, 'I feel it so as my own will soon be away from me now.'[26] On 14 February 1890 she wrote, 'I packed up the children's toys and my heart ached sadly all the time. My little darlings, how I will miss them.' Keith, their eldest, was only five, and Colin barely three when this heartbreaking decision was made, slightly earlier than was usual, but then the Cantlies were rather familiar with the diseases that carried off little children in Hong Kong.

What they went through had been the lot of parents since at least Julia Baynes's time in the 1820s. It was not just the breaking up of the family, but the rendering of the wife, already barred from any paid work or public expression, more potentially unfulfilled than ever. Wives sometimes went with their children home to Britain. Often that was obviously pure maternal duty, at other times it was an excuse for a marriage that was not happy to come to a graceful conclusion in the days when divorce was still not something to contemplate.

Fortunately for Mabel she had her husband's relentless medical work to throw herself into, and her responsibility, which she obviously felt keenly, towards other women. Sometimes her visits were connected with public humiliation or tragedy. In 1890 Robert Fraser-Smith, the outspoken founder and editor of *The Hong Kong Telegraph*, was found guilty of libel and sentenced to two months imprisonment by the Chief Justice. On 13 December Mabel wrote, 'I went to see poor Mrs Fraser-Smith . . . it is so sad poor thing to hear her story of the unkindness of people here.' A few days before, pirates had attacked the steamer *Namoa* and killed the captain. The day Mabel visited Mrs Fraser-Smith, she also called on the captain's wife, Mrs Pocock. A few months later, Daniel Edmund Caldwell, son of Daniel Richard and Mary Ayow, who had become a lawyer, ran away when he lost a great deal of money; off went Mabel to comfort Miss Caldwell.

Not all was duty in Mabel's life; there was recreation, too. She talks of a cricket match, a ladies team organized by Mrs Keswick, wife of the Jardine Matheson taipan, against a men's team — 'left handed and with broom sticks'.[27] There was walking — once fifteen miles — and one wonders what this Victorian woman wore, and what shoes. Then there was tennis. Mabel gave tennis parties of her own; she played tennis at Government House with Lady Des Voeux, and at the Ladies' Recreation Club, noting on one occasion, 'Mrs Palmer played 1st round of championship against Mrs Coxon'.[28] The following day: 'I played my round at tennis against Mrs Bottomley and won 3 to 6, 4 to 6. I am rather off play just now so did not as well as I should.' The next day it seems that Mrs Palmer may have overdone it against Mrs Coxon: 'Went and saw Mary Palmer in the afternoon as she was rather seedy and Hamish had been to see her.'

There was the theatre, too. Adelina Patti passed through Hong Kong and Mabel not only heard her sing 'beautifully' but had the thrill of lunching with her as well. Other performances were more mixed. On 17 February 1890, Mabel noted, 'I went to Mrs Coxon's theatricals,' but she did not comment on the quality. In June 1893, however, she wrote, 'We all went to a concert at Mrs Coxons which was a poor affair as far as singing goes.' Of course, Mabel, as a singer herself, was likely to be critical. Two weeks later, another such concert was 'fairly good'. Nettie Hancock, Edith Stewart Lockhart's sister, played the violin.

James Cantlie, not content with his medical innovations and burdens, was also a founding member of the Hong

Kong Literary Society and often gave talks; just as often, he failed to go because of some emergency. Mabel attended regularly because women were allowed to be honorary members for half the subscription fee. The wags, encouraged by a columnist in the *China Mail*, were as dismissive of their presence as they had been of Louisa Coxon's request for a piece of land:

That certain curmudgeons object to the admission of ladies, and think that their presence would kill the budding hopes of future Gladstones and Brights of this great nation. That if the dear and fair ones are limited to having their 'say' at home and not during the meetings, there should be no objection to their presence as honorary members[29]

The 'Odd Volumes' Society was less radical. On 2 March 1893 Mabel noted that Hamish gave the presidential address which was a 'great success' and 'attracted a large audience.' But Hamish must have told her because she added, 'I did not go as ladies were not admitted.'

It should be said that the position of British women in Hong Kong, particularly married women, lagged behind that of their sisters at home. In Britain, the Married Women's Property Act, for example, was passed in 1882, allowing a woman to acquire, hold and dispose of property, and to sue as an individual in her own right. The law was not amended to allow that in Hong Kong until 1906, nor could a married woman enter into a valid contract.

In her increasing involvement with her husband's medical work, Mabel was not discriminated against; she was needed too much. In the early 1890s medical care in Hong Kong was making progress. Within a few years there would be several private hospitals (in addition to the civil, naval and military hospitals) bevies of nurses, both public and private, and, in 1903, the first European woman doctor.

The hospital set up in memory of Matilda Sharp was part of the advance. Mabel recorded Matilda's death on 22 August 1893 and added: 'Hamish went through a wonderful scene with her old husband. He is going to cremate his wife tomorrow.' It was the first cremation in Hong Kong, at Matilda's request. Mabel noted, 'Hamish had to go down and watch the fire and it was a gruesome sight.' The sometimes gruesome sights of the next chapter were not, apparently, a subject for Mabel or Matilda's pen.

CHAPTER THIRTEEN

QUEEN'S WOMEN

*I*t is unlikely that Matilda Sharp, for all her sympathetic and independent inclinations, visited Francisca Berger in the Civil Hospital on 24 October 1883. Matilda may have known the name, if she read the newspapers carefully. In January that year the *Daily Press* had an item about Francisca on a charge of assaulting a male servant to whom she owed $48. The following day, surprisingly, the paper corrected itself. It was the servant, a female *amah*, who not only owed the money to Francisca, but also abused her, thus provoking the slap.[1] Thirteen years earlier, Francisca Berger, connected it was said with the San Francisco troupe of singers, had been taken to court for owing S. Emamoodeen two months' house rent.[2] And the year before that, in 1869, there was a case concerning a promissory note of $449 given by Francisca in Singapore in 1868 to L. Davidson. Francisca had 'run away' from Singapore.[3]

By 25 October 1883, Francisca was dead, murdered by her lover. The *Daily Press* described her as a prostitute and within a month her estate of clothing and jewellery was being auctioned by the Official Administrator.[4] Uncommonly, Francisca was given a proper burial service, although no one bothered to get her name right — in the burial record she is Francisca Beyer, single, of Gage Street.

When Alice Windsor, single woman, of Gage Street, died three years earlier, aged 24, no one gave her a burial service; the same applied to Chubby Douglas of the same street who died a year after Alice, and to Florence Gladstone in 1887. She died in Hollywood Road and was only 17. Caucasian prostitutes, particularly if they were British, were pariahs in Hong Kong — in public, anyway. There was more to it than simply being a 'fallen woman', as they would be in Britain; in the imperial context they were letting down the side of whites in the eyes of non-whites.

What was Francisca's proper name, and where did she come from? The answer, if there is one, is relevant to particular waves of prostitutes arriving in China, originally from Europe, and opens up general as well as particular questions about prostitution. Looking at her name casually, and the date of her first appearance in Singapore, one might suppose her to be a Polish Catholic fleeing the repression of the Russians after the Polish insurrection of 1863. The Russian Governor General, Fedor Berg, encouraged prostitution in Warsaw as a means of repression, and Francisca might have even taken his name in the way that Alice Gladstone, Florence Windsor and Pearl Cleveland chose tongue-in-cheek soubriquets. Names were often changed, for obvious reasons; Hazel Stone, for example, was known also as Helen Scott and Mary Ellen Morrisey.

But Francisca was given a burial service by a Protestant pastor, the Basle missionary Rudolphe Lechler, and that rules out, too, the possibility of her being part of a wave of Jewish prostitutes escaping pogroms and their results which was to reach its peak in Hong Kong in the late 1880s. Several prostitutes in the history of Jewish prostitution were called Berger.[5]

It is tempting to imagine that Francisca might have simply taken her name from the San Francisco troupe of singers; but what is more likely is that she came originally from a German-speaking principality in the area of Central Europe undergoing the upheavals that were to lead to the unified state of Germany. She and her lover, John Drewes, a river pilot, spoke German to each other, and he is known to have come from Hanover and to have been formally called Theodore Wilhelm Drewes.

When in 1870 Francisca was charged with owing rent, it was for a place in Tank Lane. She must have been very broke and desperate when she arrived in Hong Kong because Tank Lane was not within the central area to which, since 1867, European prostitutes had been informally confined — that bounded by Hollywood Road, Wyndham Street, Wellington Street and Graham Street — where today one can buy fine Chinese antiques. The Lascars (Indian seamen) boarded near Tank Lane, and beyond it lived Chinese prostitutes servicing Chinese clients. Not long before Francisca was murdered, however, she had been living in more select Upper Wyndham Street and had just moved in with Kitty Waters and Sally Clarke, the 'madame' who rented the property in Gage Street.

There is some evidence that the life of European prostitutes was not always the degradation and humiliation that it was in many parts of the world, that, indeed, some of them led lives similar to that of the demi-mondaine in Paris. Certainly the evidence before the coroner's court when Francisca Berger was murdered shows an attempt by Sally and Kitty to convey a scene that might, in some respects, have been replicated in ordinary European homes in Hong Kong.[6]

The brief details of the shooting, as reported by them, were that Drewes came to the house in Gage Street quite late in the evening to see Francisca, spent some time with the three women — as had been his wont during the two weeks that Francisca had been living there — then went away (to his own house in Pottinger Street round the corner). He came back later — which was not surprising — but then shot Francisca in the neck and himself in the mouth. Before the shooting, Sally Clarke was playing the piano and Francisca was singing. There was, apparently, no scene, no shouting, just talking, eating sandwiches, playing the piano and singing. There was beer but no drunkenness. (Beer was what prostitutes drank, and got drunk on, among themselves; they served wine and champagne, as well as cigars, to clients). The conversation was mostly in English because Francisca did not like her 'sisters' to feel excluded.

But Francisca was murdered; her life was not usual. How did her life of debt, court cases, running away, and violent death fit in with that of her sisters in prostitution, bearing in mind that one of European prostitution's most interesting features in Hong Kong is how separate it was from Chinese prostitution? (The latter will be elaborated upon in later chapters as the concern of European women of a different kind).

Some of the history is obvious. In 1845 there were 595 Europeans — 455 men, 90 women, and 50 children — in Hong Kong.[7] By 1872, the ratio was much the same: there were 3,264 European men and only 699 women[8]. These were semi-permanent residents; the figures do not include soldiers or Royal Navy sailors or merchant seamen. The Chinese population moved similarly — though with a great increase in population following the Taiping Rebellion in Southern China in the 1850s; then, for the first time, respectable Chinese women were brought to the safety of Hong Kong. In 1872, there were 78,484 Chinese men and 22,837 women;[9] and five sixths of the 24,387 Chinese women in the 1876 census were said, by police magistrates, to be prostitutes.[10] In 1880, the barrister J.J. Francis suggested that there were 18–20,000 prostitutes, compared with 4–5,000 respectable women.[11]

Thus arose several strands of prostitution each with its own different area: Chinese prostitutes for Chinese clients in the west of Victoria; Chinese prostitutes for soldiers and sailors and such permanent European residents as policemen, all of the women being confined to Wanchai towards the east, as were Japanese women used by the merchant service and warrant officers; and European or American prostitutes for middle-class Europeans in Central. Ironically, any Chinese women going with Europeans (or even worse with Indians or Lascars) were at the bottom of the sociological heap as far as the Chinese were concerned, while at the same time Europeans did not allow Chinese men to go with European prostitutes. Those sociological nuances reflected and were reflected by the law, particularly as it concerned keeping prostitutes used by sailors and soldiers free from venereal disease.

Venereal disease among soldiers and sailors was by no means a problem only in Hong Kong, but in 1857 the colonial government took its own action; it instituted a system of registration and inspection of brothels, of compulsory examination and punishment for communicating venereal disease. A lock hospital came into existence.

In Britain a similar system in 18 garrison towns and naval dockyard towns was introduced in 1864 and refined under the Contagious Diseases Acts of 1866 and 1869. Hong Kong was brought into line with the law in England and Wales in 1867; in reality it meant little change, except that the police were given wider powers, and licensing was placed under the Registrar General who designated localities where prostitutes were to live. These were those areas described above: Wanchai, Central and Taipingshan. Prostitutes were to be inspected weekly at the lock hospital and given a certificate of good health. In practice, over time, that law applied only to Chinese prostitutes servicing the European soldiers and sailors the authorities were so anxious to protect. Chinese prostitutes in the Chinese area were left, as happened so often where Chinese custom affecting only the Chinese was concerned, much to their own devices.[12]

European prostitutes were too expensive for soldiers and sailors; they, too, therefore were not regulated in the same way. They remained the responsibility of the police rather than the Registrar General, but they did choose to have weekly inspections. These were often carried out in their own homes by the doctors in private practice who did the same at the lock hospital.

A Chief Inspector of Brothels was appointed to ensure the licensing and registering of brothels and each brothel keeper had to pay $4 per month tax.[13] The women thus registered, with their names up outside the brothel — which also had a large number displayed — were known colloquially as 'Big Numbers' but officially as 'Queen's Women'. That implies that a tax to the colonial treasury was a tax to Queen Victoria, thus making them 'Queen's Women', but in fact the word 'quean' comes from the Old English 'cwene' and means 'ill-behaved woman', a nice play on words that probably would not have amused Victoria.

In the 1870s and 1880s in England, the Contagious

Diseases Acts came under increasing pressure to be abolished from a number of groups spearheaded by that of the Christian feminist Josephine Butler. In Britain, plain-clothes policemen could swear before a magistrate that a particular woman was a common prostitute. The magistrate could then order the woman to be subject to periodic examination; resistance meant imprisonment.

Josephine Butler's father, John Grey, had been active in the anti-slavery campaign; an aunt was educated and politically assertive, and her husband was a sympathetic clergyman. She was primed to be a social reformer. By 1886, the Acts had been repealed, Josephine Butler and her cohorts having convinced the government on several levels — moral, political, and scientific — that they led to the harassment and regulation of often completely innocent women and failed to achieve their aim. Not only was enforced examination 'symbolic rape', but working-class women were obviously more likely to be picked upon and perhaps even driven into prostitution by the very nature of the regulations — which took their reputation away from them and kept them under the eye of the police. What is more, the double standard applied against women in favour of men was unacceptable; 'You cannot,' added Josephine, 'hold *us* in honour so long as you drag our sisters in the mire'.[14] But in some ways more telling was proof that the medical rationale was unsound: the requisite medical information was not available at that time for either adequate diagnosis or treatment of venereal disease.[15]

The Acts having been repealed in Britain, the Colonial Office was compelled to instruct its colonial dependencies to repeal their Acts, too. The law had already been under attack in Hong Kong. In 1877, soon after Sir John Pope Hennessy arrived as Governor, a case came to light which brought the abuses of the whole system to public attention. It emerged that policemen brought out from England to try and create a decent police force, some of them married with their wives in the colony, were expected to act as *agents provocateurs* — to go with Chinese women who were not licensed as prostitutes to prove that they were breaking the law. On the occasion in question, two women trying to escape the trap fell to their deaths. Pope Hennessy instituted an enquiry, but his governorship came to an unhappy end before he could take action on it.

Now that Hong Kong was instructed to take action, the authorities found ways of not doing so; they still believed that the regulation of Chinese prostitutes to protect British sailors and soldiers was essential. Among the arguments that they used was that none of the prostitutes, including the Europeans, wanted the regulations, and particularly the regular inspection, to be abolished. Indeed, there were petitions sent to London in 1888 not only from the 42 Chinese and Japanese brothel keepers concerned, but also by a list of 25 'European' prostitutes, asking for the status quo to be maintained.[16] That highlights the difference in more general attitudes between the colony and Britain. In Britain, there was an increasing awareness of injustice, whereas, the majority of people, Chinese and expatriate, including prostitutes, came to Hong Kong only to make money.

European prostitution was increasingly overt and causing concern, at least in some quarters, though not for the sake of the prostitutes themselves. In the 1870s, 'females of a certain class' were accustomed to drive out in their carriages, a fashionable recreation in Hong Kong, along the Shaukiwan Road beyond Happy Valley and the race course. They were obviously displaying their wares because it became so objectionable that it was forbidden.

Then driving became unfashionable, so it no longer mattered if 'undesirable females' drove or not. By 1893, the situation was much worse, or the moral climate was less accomodating. *The Hong Kong Telegraph* reflected the change. On 10 March, the blunt fulmination against overt prostitution and the unlicensed selling of alcohol, must have brought a blush to many a cheek, even if the middle-class women concerned, such as Mabel Cantlie, had not been embarrassed or threatened by the blatant displays of prostitution in question. These took place in a shop ostensibly

dealing in 'small wares' on Queens Road right beside a hotel
frequented by, among others, 'missionary ladies'. 'The atmosphere reeked of prostitution.'

What is more, while those women flouted their 'gorgeous
equipage' (presumably sedan chairs and not charms) there
was many a man who failed 'financially, physically, men-
tally and morally'. Indeed, in Hong Kong 'the women who
hold their heads highest, who loftily monopolise the right
of way and crowd everybody else out, these are of the class
that in any civilised country dare not show itself.'

Who were those women? It is in tracking down the
prostitutes' petition of 1888 and its list of names that one
comes across a phenomenon, at first surprising, in the
history of Hong Kong's prostitution. Apart from four rather
oddly interspersed Chinese names, there are 21 names that
are nearly all very obviously Jewish. What is more, it is
quite likely that the list constituted nearly the full com-
plement of expatriate prostitutes in Hong Kong at that time.
There were never very many: in 1877 there were 17 known
to the police;[17] in 1907, there were 40;[18] and in 1930 there
were 17 according to the governor in May and 21 according
to a League of Nations questionnaire in November.[19]

Where had the Jewish prostitutes come from, and why?
The most simple answer is that they were part of the
European dispersal that followed the pogroms instigated by
Alexander III of Russia when he came to the throne on the
murder of his father in 1881. Other events creating pressures
leading to economic misery, weakening of family and
religious ties, persecution and migration, included the
Hungarian revolution of 1848 and the lifting, in 1856 and
1860, of residential restrictions on Jews; the banishing from
Moscow in 1891 of 20,000 Jews; the pogroms in Kishinev
(Moldavia) of 1892; and the starvation in Galicia and
Bukovina of 5,000 Jews annually between 1880 and 1914.
Particularly relevant to the appearance of Russian Jewish
women in Shanghai after 1905 was the Russo-Japanese war.
The Russian Revolution of 1917 provided a further agent of
migration.

In *Prostitution and Prejudice: The Jewish Fight Against White*

Slavery, 1870–1839, Edward J. Bristow tells the whole tragic story of human — particularly female — degradation, exploitation and misery. Although some women travelled independently, mostly they were procured and trafficked often through false marriages. They arrived in China from Europe — particularly after the opening of the Suez Canal in 1869 — via Alexandria, Cairo or Port Said, Bombay, Singapore, Saigon, Hong Kong and Shanghai. From Shanghai, two minor routes took them to Harbin in Manchuria or the Philippines.

From a diatribe in a Hong Kong newspaper, one learns that in 1888, for example, Graham Street was one of the most 'disreputable rookeries' in the colony. There, 'unsexed women' included Austrians, Russians, Italians and Levantines, as well as an 'attendant army of scoundrelly pimps and loafers'.[20] By 1930, the League of Nations questionnaire on trafficking had elicited the Hong Kong prostitutes' countries of origin as, France 11, USA 3, Australia 3, Russia 1, Lithuania 1, Latvia 1, and Mauritius 1.[21] By then sociological means were beginning to provide what is now the basis for historical fact but earlier anxiety about trafficking tended to produce more generalized material such as *The White Slave Market* (1912).

One of the authors, Mrs Archibald Mackirdy, was the founder of shelters for women and girls in London. Her co-author, W. N. Willis, who researched and wrote the chapter on Hong Kong, was an Australian Member of Parliament. His conclusion was that Hong Kong was

Simply alive with continental bars and open brothels, principally kept by foreign prostitutes — Roumanians, Polish and Russian Jewesses, and different Southern European races. These women are generally in the charge of their Russian, Polish, or Roumanian masters — men of the lowest and most brutal type of 'pimp' — many of them escaped criminals who are 'wanted' in their own countries.[22]

The cold figures of the League of Nations questionnaire, and the passionate denunciation of *The White Slave Market* leave the seeker after individual women somewhat at a loss.

It is possible, however, taking that 1888 list of 21 Jewish names, to reconstruct the lives of one or two of them from the local papers; though it is only from their moments of formalized trouble that one can do more than imagine them. Two of the names are C. and A. Goldstein. The *China Mail* reports that on 12 May 1887 those two — with their names spelt Goldstine — of 34 Cochrane Street, were charged with behaving in an indecent manner. Then there is a Mary Goldenberg, signed only with an X, and an S. Goldenberg. Are they the same as, or related to, Bertha and Isabella Goldenberg? One cannot be sure, but in 1883, Isabella, of 31 Cochrane Street, was in court.

Some time previously, she had had a difference with Kate Docking, which had been brought to court. They had been good friends since then until, that is, the end of January when Kate Docking and Lizzie Cox of 21 Cochrane Street came to Miss Goldenberg's house, and Miss Docking wanted her to drink some gin. She declined, and words followed. Kate Docking, it is said, hit Isabella in the mouth and on the ear. Lizzie Cox took no part. Kate was fined $5, Lizzie was discharged.[23] In November 1885, Bertha Goldenberg, mistress of a licensed brothel, accused John Johnston of having kicked her about and broken a door in her house. He was fined $2 and ordered to pay 50 cents amends to Bertha.[24]

Another strand is also suggested by *The Hong Kong Telegraph* of 1893. The newspaper maintained that there must have been 345 'unclassified' American women in China — meaning, quite obviously, prostitutes. It is certainly true that there were moral clean-ups in the big cities of the United States, particularly in New York, causing the closing of brothels and the dislocation and flight elsewhere of inmates.

In the early years of the twentieth century, the United States authorities were embarrassed about the situation in Shanghai, where even prostitutes who were not their citizens claimed to be 'American Girls' because it was classier.[25] Under the claims of extraterritoriality, they opened a court there in which an American judge got rid of them all by 1907 and many of them flocked to Hong Kong. Some of

them then married down-and-out European nationals and
drifted back to Shanghai where they were now outside the
jurisdiction of the court. But it meant that in 1905 and 1907
there was an unprecedented number of prostitutes in Hong
Kong. In 1905 there were 36 Americans and in 1907, 40
Europeans, of whom 23 were American and only one
British.[26]

The United States authorities assumed that there were so
few British prostitutes because the colonial government had
some magic formula or law for expelling them, and they
wanted to use it. But Sir Frederic Lugard, in reporting to
London, maintained that 'their presence is rare simply
because such women do not come to Hong Kong to ply the
trade of prostitution'. Nor would he use the law unless
prostitutes broke it by living more than two to a house,
disgracing their nationality 'by receiving asiatics, by public
solicitation, or other scandalous procedure'.[27]

Of all the American prostitutes in Hong Kong, Eva (born
Nellie) Saunders, who arrived in 1888, stands out. Through
her court cases, she gives the most detailed information,
apart from the case of Francisca Berger, of the life of a
'European' prostitute. In 1890, she hired the services of a
firm of solicitors when her 'protector' committed suicide and
the Official Receiver advertised the sale of his furniture at
44 Lyndhurst Terrace. As Eva argued, the furniture belonged
to her.

Both Eva and Francisca are examples of prostitutes with
'protectors' — a category distinct from a Chinese woman
known as a 'protected woman'. When a 'protector' became
a 'pimp' or procurer of clients, a man who lived off a prostitute's earnings and controlled her, presumably depended
on circumstances. In Britain, by the end of the century,
pimps were mostly foreign as, indeed, were many of the
prostitutes. That type of man flourished largely as a result
of reforms. When the traditional brothel came under attack,
as it did in Britain and, therefore, as it was supposed to do
in Hong Kong, towards the end of the century, prostitutes
had a housing problem. Partly to solve it, they took premises with men posing as their husbands who not only

helped secure accommodation but also protected them from robbery and violence and gave them companionship.

How far John Drewes, Francisca Berger's 'friend' and murderer, or the man whom Eva Saunders said she 'formed an intimate acquaintanceship with' on the 'third or fourth time' she met him, fall into the broad category is open to speculation. The inquest when Francisca was murdered could establish no motive. Kitty and Sally very carefully denied that other men came to the house that night while Drewes was there, though there had been an earlier visitor. In the same way, they denied that he had been drinking heavily, though it was established from another witness that he had recently become a heavy drinker and also that he had assaulted Francisca on more than one occasion previously.[28] But something as powerful as jealousy must have prompted John Drewes to go and get his gun. Francisca was his woman, but not his woman.

As far as Eva was concerned, her 'protector', Mr Apcar, was a young Armenian stockbroker and clerk employed in the trading firm of a relative. Eva recounts how from February 1889 until the time of his death, 'I was almost kept entirely by him' and that he paid her cash for her services.[29] She lived 'under his protection'. But she was not exclusively his; she had come to Hong Kong 'to make money,' not to seek a relationship. She accepted his paying the rent on Lyndhurst Terrace because she was in debt at the time, but she paid, she claimed, the household expenses.

Apcar became jealous of her other clients and there were disputes about money. He went with other women but, in keeping an account of the money he spent on Eva, he put the money he paid to other women against her name. What was more, she believed that he was 'going to places where a man visiting European women ought not to go'. Having lost money in the stockmarket crash of 1889, and in a tangle with his personal relationships, Apcar committed suicide in September 1890.

Eva won her court case but was left paying her costs. She was then involved in another case when her lawyer sued her for payment. She undertook her own defence — which was that she had paid $350 in settlement; a sum her lawyer said was only a retainer — and lost, after altercations with the judge which must have provided sly amusement to both professions and the general newspaper-reading public.[30]

Although the increasing debt of a prostitute towards her protector was often used as a control by the man on the woman, in this case Eva managed to hold her own. But there is more to Eva Saunders' litigiousness: when taken in conjunction with a similar propensity on the part of her 'sisters', it suggests that in Hong Kong many were able to fend for themselves; they were exploited (as well as exploiting) in many ways, but not downtrodden.

It looks as if Francisca and Eva came to Hong Kong as prostitutes, perhaps women already hardened by experience, whatever had initially driven them to the life. There were, however, women forced by their circumstances to resort to prostitution for the first time in Hong Kong itself. Bridget Montagu is an example. She had married a Portuguese shopkeeper in San Francisco and accompanied him to Hong Kong. When he abandoned her, she went to live with an Irish barman from the Crown and Anchor tavern in Queen's Road. When he was sentenced to two months' imprisonment for drunkenness, she took lodgings with a young Portuguese widow, Maria Rosa, from Macau, who had formerly lived with a policeman. Both women, now lacking men, or protectors, and any other means of earning a living, became full-time prostitutes. But they were unlicensed and in 1873 they were charged with running a clandestine brothel. Bridget, then aged 23, was sentenced to a fine of $50, or one month's imprisonment, and required to undergo medical examination for six months. She paid her fine and returned to working as an independent prostitute. She was known, thereafter, to have had a lover who was a beachcomber, a man, therefore, at the bottom of the male social heap, but then she disappeared from Hong Kong.[31]

Bridget's case highlights three other general points. At least in 1873, regular inspection was not always a matter of choice for European prostitutes — it could be enforced. Registration was as compulsory for European prostitutes as for Chinese; though presumably if you knew the system you could make your way round it. The fact that there were unlicensed women like Bridget also shows that the official numbers of European prostitutes are not reliable.

It was possible for a woman to pull herself out of Hollywood Road or Lyndhurst Terrace. One way might be to benefit from a grateful client's will. Hazel Stone, alias Helen Scott, under her name of Mary Ellen Morrisey, was a beneficiary under the 1919 will of solicitor Victor Deacon. She received four parts of his estate — his wife six parts, Fanny Pearce, spinster, seven parts, and his nephew seven parts.[32] Hazel had first arrived from Shanghai in 1883 and lived in Lyndhurst Terrace and Wyndham Street where she was a ratepayer, presumably the madame. That supposition is reinforced by her travelling back from San Fransisco in 1896 in the company of three other single women.[33] She is not heard of again after the bequest of 1920 which may have allowed her to retire.

There is no evidence of respectable working women being coerced or inveigled into prostitution in Hong Kong. At one time in my research I wondered if I was being naive about the bevy of milliners described in Chapter 9, but I think not; I believe them to have been genuine working women in establishments that were not fronts for prostitution. But I think that their wages and working conditions must have been satisfactory because in other parts of the world their industry was a source for procurers. It is certainly true that shops could be a front for brothels; there was one opened in D'Aguilar Street in 1897 by Mrs May Yorkee, a prostitute whose German 'husband' Schwaln was her pimp.[34] What is likely is that owners and manageresses of millinery establishments made some effort to keep their businesses respectable; not to do so would have been to lose custom, women in business being vulnerable simply because they were in business and therefore threateningly independent.[35]

What is in some ways surprising is that the apparently unacceptable situation in Queen's Road and elsewhere, and regular, sometimes lurid court cases, leave not a ripple in the letters and diaries of Matilda Sharp and Mabel Cantlie. They were women who cared about the lives of other women; and they were out and about perhaps more than most; Mabel, as the next chapter shows, was also involved in medical matters. Not only that, her husband was called to Mr Apcar when he was found shot.[36] Even if one looks at the cases handled by the Hong Kong Ladies Benevolent Society, there is no information. In 1906, there was an English woman 'with a somewhat chequered career' who was granted a passage to Saigon where she had 'the promise of a good employment'.[37] Saigon was a stopping-off place for prostitutes and the implication is that she had been there before. But she was of 'good education' which hardly fits the image of Hong Kong's European prostitutes.

There is just one whiff of concern but, because it comes from Mackirdy and Willis's *The Slave Market*, so long on passion, so short on fact, it has proved impossible to follow up the claim that: 'At Hong Kong things were extremely bad until the advent of Sir Frederick Lugard and his good and clever wife ... This lady has done a great amount of good in a quiet, unostentatious fashion by cleaning some of the immoral dens of Hong Kong.'[38]

There is one woman who looks as if she provided the solace to her fallen sisters that these middle-class women failed to give. Bella Emerson, who may just have been the mythical tart with the heart of gold, had arrived from San Fransisco in about 1875, aged 26, and rented various properties over the years in Hollywood Road and Graham Street from Chinese landlords. When she died in 1892, aged 43, after 17 years in the colony, she had gained a reputation for 'good works' and ' charitable instincts' practically 'without limit'. It is said that she exercised an 'open-handed munificence' towards the 'destitute and deserving' which made her a household name. In which houses, the newspaper does not spell out, though it does suggest that it is not the newspaper's 'business to deal with a career that would furnish materials for a modern romance'.[39] But is her apparent behaviour enough to give any impression of that of a madame towards the inmates of her house? Relations between prostitutes generally seem to have been influenced as much by alcohol as sisterhood. How respectable working-class, as opposed to middle-class, women interracted with them is without evidence but the fear of having their own reputation tainted was probably important.

It was only Chinese prostitutes who were to engage the attention and concern of European women in Hong Kong in a way that is documented — first in the provision by missionary women, supported by benevolent ladies, of refuges and homes similar to those which proliferated in Britain; later in the campaigning against licensed prostitution. That campaign was not to defend sailors and soldiers, but to put an end to the degradation through slavery of young Chinese girls.

By a gentle irony, the first woman doctor in Hong Kong should have arrived to take care of those Chinese prostitutes. For some years the Colonial Office strove to bring Hong Kong into line with the reformist law in Britain created under the pressure of public opinion. Hong Kong managed, by agreeing and re-enacting to suit itself, to go its own way. One of the innovations recommended in 1898 was the appointment of a 'lady doctor' to look after women suffering from venereal disease. The main argument was that in Ceylon a woman doctor had helped to overcome the reluctance of women to go to hospital. A Hong Kong Official replied that 'considering that the most pure and most virtuous women in European countries' went to men doctors 'I in no way believe that Chinese prostitutes have a stronger feeling of delicacy on this subject.'[40]

London persisted, and such a doctor would also have the power to visit brothels. Hong Kong held fast, for Chinese society was without the castes of the Subcontinent, the hot summer months would be 'too trying' for an 'English lady' visiting brothels and, as Sir Henry Blake added in January 1900, 'for many years past the female venereal wards have been in charge of a very capable matron'.[41] While it is true that from 1884 Mrs Jane Ackers built up experience in this field, she retired in February 1902, depriving the system of her capability and leaving it still without a woman doctor. To strengthen the irony, the next chapter will show how pleased Lady Blake was when a woman doctor was finally appointed, but not by the government, and not to treat venereal disease.

CHAPTER FOURTEEN

LADY DOCTOR MRS HICKLING

*T*here were Western doctors in Canton and Macau from the early days of the East India Company, but when Dr James Cantlie arrived in Hong Kong in 1887 he had no nurse to help him in his private practice and there were no trained nurses in the Government Civil Hospital run by the Colonial Surgeon.

Mabel Cantlie was totally untrained, but she would walk miles with her husband to visit patients and give what assistance she could; she would even help him to bring patients back to Hong Kong from Macau. She visited a leper colony with him several times; and she helped him with experiments, studying botany to be more effective. She perfected her French to translate foreign medical articles, and typed his own articles and books. When her children had gone home to Scotland in June 1889 — even though she had another son in 1892 — she often worked in his laboratory.

Soon after his arrival Cantlie realized the need for private nursing in Hong Kong. In 1889 he asked Maude Ingall, a trained nurse, to come out. She lived with the Cantlies — that is, when she was not away on a case, which was most of the time. Later, in 1893, Maude's brother was to marry Mabel's sister, Lilla Barclay Brown, but even before that she was treated very much as one of the family, a friend to Mabel and an invaluable help to James.

Even with that additional medical assistance, European mortality continued to be a frightening feature of Hong

Kong. On 22 May 1890, Mabel wrote, 'We had a dreadful night last night as Mrs Goodman, wife of the new Attorney General and Hamish's [James's] patient died suddenly of dysentery.' Sometimes there was nothing Hamish could do, as in 1894, when the Governor's wife, Felicia Robinson, having recently given birth to her sixth child in ten years, died of sprue, which was undiagnosed; Mabel wrote, 'I fear they have called Hamish too late.'[1]

But Maude Ingall's presence did impinge on Government House. Sir William Robinson's predecessor, Sir William Des Voeux, was often ill and his wife Marion had a baby in November 1889. Maude saw her through the confinement and cared for her after the birth, though James Cantlie delivered the baby. As a result, Des Voeux set himself the task of organizing government nursing in the colony, particularly for the Government (Civil) Hospital. He describes in his memoirs the problems he had, firstly because marriageable women quickly married and secondly because the Roman Catholic sisters hired were not sufficiently trained and were not willing to do everything required. In November 1890, fully trained nurses were more successfully brought from England.[2] Mabel and Maude did their best to welcome Miss Eastmond and five sisters from a London teaching hospital, calling on them often.

In March 1890, Cantlie had opened his own home hospital on the Peak in a private house, Mabel doing most of the furnishing and organization. Maude Ingall became its first matron. On the surface it was an important innovation and had much success. It was not officially registered but it received something of a seal of approval when Lady Des Voeux visited it in April 1891, although relations between the two families were not as warm as they had been; Mabel noted in her diary on ll December 1889, 'We are much annoyed just now that the governor is being treated by [Dr] Jordan on the quiet.'

There were other personal strains, as Mabel's diary records. Firstly, Maude's love life was rather up and down following her appointment and it obviously affected her work. Mabel wrote on 13 March 1891, 'Went and had a long talk with Maude who is very unhappy. She does not please Hamish in the way she treats the patients. I am deeply sorry.'

Assistance was sought for Maude both from Britain and the Government Civil Hospital. Miss Mary Thompson there offered to send for her sister. Eventually Maude left and Sister Annie Thompson took charge, but not altogether satisfactorily. 'We regret to find,' wrote Mabel, 'that Sister Annie has been doing things we do not approve of and Hamish almost sent her home today.'[3] A few months later she added, 'We find that Sister Annie has been ever since she came taking her money from the hospital all the time she was [there] thereby swindling us thoroughly.'[4] Sister Mary, meanwhile, was having trouble with a boyfriend whom Mabel thought was Sister Annie's intended, and a married woman took over the running of the hospital.

Gossip over the affairs of the heart of nurses was to be a constant refrain in Hong Kong — a place always short of personable young women. The hospital bearing Matilda Sharp's name opened in January 1907. Its Medical Superintendent, Dr James Sanders, had arrived the previous September, and his sister Edith, a nurse trained at the London Hospital, came in December as its first Matron, bringing with her two nurses. By 1908 Edith had married James Smith, Chief Manager of the Hongkong and Shanghai Bank, and Isabel Slade, wife of the barrister Marcus Slade, wrote to the recent Governor, Sir Matthew Nathan, 'I suppose you have heard all our gossip from Hong Kong of the past few months. How the beautiful nurse from the Sharps hospital, who has no heart for gaiety and who lived solely for her work and the gospel made a secret marriage (which we all talked of for two months previously) with Mr J.M. Smith.'[5]

Mary Mellor, first matron of the War Memorial Nursing Home in 1932, married, in 1940, the chairman of her hospital (and the Matilda Hospital), Sir Vandeleur Greyburn who was also Chief Manager of the Hongkong and Shanghai Bank.

All that seems rather trivial in relation to what was to happen in Hong Kong in 1894 and the part that nurses were to play; but nurses were to be both trivial and heroic in Hong Kong for at least the next fifty years. They were, after all, human, not angels, and were by no means popular with everyone, for they could be superior. The gossip writer 'Veronica',writing in the *Hong Kong Weekly*, addressed letters to various individuals whom she wished to satirize; in 1907 she published them as a book. One of them began

Dear Sister Nightingale. You will probably think it a great impertinence on my part to dare to address you at all, much less to offer you advice or to give you information on any subject whatsoever. Does not the training of a hospital nurse nowadays cover a complete knowledge of the world, the flesh, and the angels?[6]

Isabel Slade had quite deliberately talked of Edith Sanders as a 'nurse' when she was a 'matron' for, as Veronica explained, it was an 'unforgivable offence' at the Government Civil Hospital to address a sister as 'nurse'.

It is worth noting that in Britain before Florence Nightingale and the Crimean War there were no trained nurses, and in the 1890s and even before World War I there were few middle-class women with jobs and few women were trained in any profession. Presumably, to be young, attractive, single, trained and earning money was to be a threat in more ways than one.

The Hong Kong Nursing Institution was to show similar signs of that tension between married and unmarried women — married committee members and unmarried professionals — that was glimpsed in missionary teaching. It was set up under the patronage of Lady Blake in 1901 to continue the private home nursing that Maude Ingall had pioneered in 1888; indeed, the nurses were to be housed in the Peak Hospital which James Cantlie had set up and where Maude was the first matron.

Nurse Gray and Nurse Hair were brought out and served between 1901 and 1902, nursing 257 and 290 days respectively. There was obviously a need for their services. Isabel Slade was on the committee, which might have had something to do with her attitude towards nurses because the succession of nurses did not always do what was expected of them, or honour their contracts. By 1905, Lady Piggott, as well as Mrs Slade, was on the committee, with Helena May, wife of the Colonial Secretary, as patroness. That may have something to do with a tension which later existed between them.

Mabel Piggott had more justification than anyone for being on the committee and speaking her mind, for she had been responsible for the setting up of the Colonial Nursing Association, based in London, in 1896. Stationed in 1895 in Mauritius, where her husband Francis was Advocate General, she noted a serious gap in colonial medical services: while the indigenous people were given some priority, Europeans, often stationed away from urban centres, were without medical help of any sort. Being Mabel Piggott, a phenomenon which will be elaborated upon later and which stemmed not only from temperament but also from her upbringing as the daughter of the Liberal Member of Parliament J.W. Johns, she discussed the matter with the governor and then wrote to Sir Edward Winfield at the Colonial Office in London, as well as to friends in other colonies. Soon, the Secretary of State for Colonial Affairs, Joseph Chamberlain, and his wife, were involved in the project. The first nurse sailed for Mauritius in 1896 and by 1910, 500 trained British nurses had been sent out to the colonies by the Colonial Nursing Association. Mabel Piggott was given full credit for the venture and remained associated with it until her death.

So, when in 1905, the year of Mabel's arrival in the colony where her husband had just been appointed Chief Justice, the Hong Kong Nursing Institution was in financial and organizational difficulties, it is not hard to picture the committee meetings. The practical difficulties were solved by turning the private Institution into the Hong Kong Branch of the Colonial Nursing Association, so as to obtain reliable nurses, and putting it in the hands of the Government Civil Medical Department as far as funding was concerned. By the end of that year, Mabel Piggott was honorary secretary. In an undated note to the Governor, to thank him for a book he had sent her, Mabel told him that the latest nurse had sent in her resignation, though all kinds of urgent calls awaited her. 'I shall send in mine,' added Mabel, 'If I can't mend matters'.[7] At the public meetings of subscribers in 1904 where those upsets and changes began to be discussed — meetings which were still taking place three years later — it is the men associated with the Institution whom the press reports suggest made the running, and perhaps they did, in public.[8]

Whatever the shortcoming of nurses, and the politicking associated with their services, their worth was proved in the spring of 1894 when bubonic plague hit Hong Kong. It was not known then, and not for some time afterwards, that it was carried by the fleas resident on rats, and panic hit the colony. At least three thousand Chinese died and thousands more fled. Eleven Europeans contracted the plague and two died, a mortality rate of 18.2 per cent, whereas the Chinese mortality rate was 93 per cent. Miss Eastmond, matron of the Civil Hospital, and her nurses had been in Hong Kong for only three years and the adjustment must have been enormous, but Dr Lowson of the hospital wrote in his report:

If ever this Colony has had reason to congratulate itself it was when we were able to procure well-trained British nurses. I think the greatest compliment that I can pay these ladies is to say that had it not been for their presence there could have been no well-run epidemic hospital during last Summer . . .[9]

In 1887, the Alice Memorial Hospital had been set up and there an Italian nursing nun died of plague in 1894, infected, as Lowson described it, by 'excessive zeal'. In another plague epidemic in 1898 two Civil Hospital nurses — Elizabeth Higgin and Emma Ireland — died. There are windows in St John's Cathedral to commemorate their eight years service. Two other Civil Hospital nurses, Miss Barr and Miss Batchelor, distinguished themselves during the Boxer rebellion of 1900 when they were lent to the British naval authorities in China.[10]

The Alice Memorial Hospital was founded by Dr Ho Kai (under the auspices of the LMS) to commemorate his English wife Alice. He had married in England, where he was studying medicine in 1881, when Alice was 31, seven years his senior. He came back to Hong Kong, bringing Alice, in 1882 but by 1884 she was dead, apparently of a broken heart over the death of a newly-born daughter.[11] The result of Alice Ho's death and of her husband's love for her was the hospital in Hollywood Road which was to grow and produce several different branches and develop the training of nurses, particularly Chinese women, in Hong Kong.

In 1891, 45-year-old Mrs Helen Stevens, a trained LMS nurse, was appointed its Matron, or 'Lady Superintendent', replacing a Chinese woman, Mrs Kwok, whom she much admired but who was not trained. She stayed 11 years — until the year before her death in 1903. Even though she was learning Cantonese, Helen's first weeks were daunting, as she described:

In the male wards no woman's foot had ever trod. I entered tremblingly — at first only to take pulses and look around, and it gave me no comfort to be told that patients would not know whether I was a man or a woman. I may as well say at once that nursing has never obtained a footing in our male wards, nor, as far as I can see, ever will.[12]

The Alice Memorial Hospital was so crowded that in 1893 the Nethersole, named after its benefactor's sister Susan Nethersole, was opened in Bonham Road (where a later building of the hospital still stands) to be a centre for women and children. Now Helen Stevens, with space to breathe, began to think of proper hospital rules and from that grew a nurses' training programme for young Chinese women.

Ah Kwai, mission educated and resolved not to marry, was the first probationer. She and her companions had problems for, as Helen wrote,

In China caring for the sick is — or was — looked upon with the utmost abhorrence by the heathen, and even by many of the native Christians; and much that was cruel and false was said about my dear girl. Many and bitter were the tears shed by her and for her and the hospital work was heavy upon myself because my helpers were in many ways most helpless. I had taught them that whatever they wanted, and whenever, I was at their beck and call, and I am glad to say they never spared to send for me by day and night.[13]

Ah Kwai's susceptibilities were considered too delicate for her to nurse during the plague but Miss Davies, an LMS teacher, and Miss Jones of the CMS nursed there with the Italian sisters. Helen Stevens ran the hospital through that difficult time and the plague years that followed. Miss Langdon took over from her in 1902.

Now a maternity hospital was needed, and that, too, was conjured up — the Alice Memorial Maternity Hospital. Lady Blake, the governor's wife, laying the foundation stone in 1903, remarked, 'I hear with great pleasure that a Lady Doctor is going to preside over it, for I know myself what a comfort it is when there is a lady doctor to consult for women and children.'[14]

Alice Sibree was probably Hong Kong's first woman doctor, though London had earlier recommended the employment of one to be in charge of women prostitutes, and the first doctor in China, the missionary Dr Coombs, reached China in 1877. The advancement of women doctors in Britain had, because of the obstacles placed in their way, been relatively slow. An exceptional woman, Elizabeth Garrett Anderson, got onto the medical register by necessarily roundabout means by 1865, but London University did not accept women for degrees in medicine until 1878. By 1900 there were 110 women doctors.

Alice Deborah Sibree was an obviously exceptional woman and was to devote herself to medicine, particularly for women patients, in Hong Kong until her death there in 1928. She was 27 when she arrived, having studied at the

London School of Medicine for Women and had special training in obstetrics and gynaecology, particularly at the Rotunda Lying in Hospital.[15] The LMS brought her out and she came from a well-established and talented LMS family. Her father was James Sibree, a missionary in Madagascar for 50 years, and her mother Deborah, née Richardson, taught the wives of students there.

Alice learned Cantonese even before she took up her post in 1904 when the hospital opened — a practice followed by her successors. She was not only an obstetrician but also helped to train the nurses in midwifery — a training which had not been formalized in Britain until 1902. 55 trainees started in 1905. Later, Alice was in charge of government midwives — many of whom she had trained. Gradually the profession of nursing came to be looked upon as honourable in the Chinese community.

In 1909 Alice went on leave to Britain and while there she resigned. Whether she did so because there had been tension between her and a male colleague, Dr Gibson, or because she had decided to marry, is not known. But while she was away she married Charles Hickling, pastor of the Union Church in Hong Kong and a widower. Alice was now 34, and Hickling 19 years her senior. On their return she became involved in many aspects of Hong Kong's social welfare, as well as medical care, some of which will show up in due course.

Her place at the Alice Maternity Hospital was taken by Dr Eleanor Perkins, a 28-year-old medical missionary who had studied medicine at the Royal Free in London. In 1913 Eleanor imitated her predecessor when she resigned and returned to England to marry the Superintendent of her hospital, and a widower, Dr I.E. Mitchell. Six years later the Mitchells returned to the hospital and stayed until 1925. Dr Annie Sydenham took over then and continued that distinguished train of women missionary doctors. Her main goal and success was to develop antenatal and postnatal care and she was to stay in Hong Kong for three decades. Margaret Watson, the first medical social worker in Hong Kong, describes her as a doctor of 'great courage and great dedication'. The two of them were to work together on the distribution of milk and scarce extra food in Stanley internment camp.[16]

Meanwhile, in 1913, Dr Alice Sibree Hickling, who had left the LMS, went to work, under the auspices of the government, at a maternity home in Wanchai operated by the Chinese Public Dispensary Movement. She was regarded by the government as something of a stalking horse, so that they played some part in what was otherwise a purely Chinese funded and run organization. In 1916 she was appointed Government Supervisor of midwives. In 1922, when the Movement opened a maternity hospital for poorer women, the Tsan Yuk, in Western District, Alice was put in charge of that; 10,000 babies were born there in 11 years. A government memorandum, justifying various policies to the Colonial Office, praised Alice for having raised standards without raising opposition.[17]

She started an infant welfare clinic at Tsan Yuk in 1923, and a training school for midwives. That year, as a result of her sensitivity in practising Western medicine in Chinese operated establishments which the Chinese were happier to attend, she was appointed Assistant Medical Officer in Charge of Native Hospitals. In 1925, the gynaecology wards and theatre were opened at Tsan Yuk, 1,400 women being treated over the next eight years. An outpatient department was also opened, and the following year, a VD clinic. The latter was undoubtedly Alice's innovation and followed a short visit to the colony in 1920 by Mrs Neville-Rolfe, General Secretary of the National Council for Combating Venereal Diseases, whom Alice helped and supported.

Alice Hickling retired from the Tsan Yuk Hospital in 1927, though she remained in government service, as Visiting Lady Medical Officer, until her death a year later. In that capacity she was followed by Dr Iliff, Dr Ariel McElney and then by Dr Agnes Dovey. Dr Dovey's title in 1928 was Assistant Visiting Medical Officer to Chinese Hospitals, and in 1940, Lady Visiting Medical Officer. In 1938, she and Dr

Louise Hunter, also a Lady Medical Officer, were to be among the first group of women, including a Chinese, Ellen Li, appointed Justices of the Peace.

Figures for 1904 and 1940 show the progress of women nurses and doctors in the Government Service. In 1904 there were two nurses; in 1940, eight doctors, two of them Chinese, and 75 nurses. In 1925 a woman Medical Officer, Dr Ethel Minett, with experience of school work in England, was appointed to a new position in the Hong Kong School Medical Service. Ethel, 44 when she arrived in Hong Kong, had also practised in British Guiana, with her husband, Dr Ewart Minett. In 1928, when Lady Clementi, the Governor's wife, was asked for help in linking together women interested in social and welfare work, Penelope Clementi wrote back, knowing that Ethel Minett was visiting London, that they should contact her; not only was she Medical Officer of Schools in the colony, but she was, besides, 'In touch with almost all women's interests here. She is a particularly able woman.'[18] She has also been described as, 'a wonderful little woman, short and fat with sparkling eyes who did everything so thoroughly'.[19]

In 1933, when the Tsan Yuk was preparing to be handed over to the government, and a gathering was held, the Secretary for Chinese Affairs, A.E. Wood, said of Alice Sibree Hickling, 'Her name will always live in Hong Kong'.[20] I'm not sure that it has; a reminder of her life and work, and that of the other women involved in medicine in Hong Kong, is timely.

CHAPTER FIFTEEN

MISS EYRE
PROVIDES A REFUGE

*F*rom the time that missionaries had any connection with China, they reported back descriptions of the poor treatment of Chinese women and, as a result of that, the fate of many girl babies. That distressing phenomenon was a most potent persuader of missionary women and benevolent ladies to work to bring relief.

Asile de la Sainte Enfance

The first group to answer the call in Hong Kong was four French convent sisters who arrived in September 1848 at the behest of the Apostolic Prefect of Hong Kong, Bishop Focard; indeed, their leader, Sister Alphonsine, was the Bishop's sister.[1] The home for abandoned children — L'Asile de la Sainte Enfance (Home of the Holy Childhood) — already held 170 children but because Focard's plea had been made while he was on leave in France, there was no accommodation to greet the sisters and they lived under such conditions that their health deteriorated. On 13 October 1850, 37-year-old Sister Alphonsine died of cerebral fever and her co-founder of the Paul de Chartres convent mission to Hong Kong, 33-year-old Sister Gabrielle Joubin, died two weeks later. Two weeks after that, three more sisters arrived to face what was hardly a warm welcome.

At the beginning, money was so short that the purchase of baby girls had to be curtailed. That was rectified by early

1850 and negotiations with likely women could be resumed, for not only did the home take in traditional foundlings — those brought to them — it also purchased little girls who might otherwise have a less happy fate. One of the alternatives to death was to be sold as a *mui tsai* or, as Europeans called them, 'slave girl' — a term which will be elaborated upon later. Every woman who brought in an abandoned child was rewarded with one franc or $1, while those women who helped the sister care for the children were paid $8 per month.

As a result of the two sisters' deaths, and with more funds available, conditions were improved. A house was rented in Johnston Road, Wanchai and a sanitarium was set up in Macau where the sisters could go and rest and recuperate.

In 1899, when the refuge had been going for 50 years, there were 400 inmates, most of them babies and little girls, but there were also some *mui tsai* seeking refuge from cruelty and there was even the odd European child. Mary Anne Mitchell's daughter, Kate, died there in 1856. There was also an elderly European woman left without family after one of the plague visitations (which continued until the 1920s). By 1899, Mother Felice had been in Hong Kong for 10 years, and her deputy, Sister Louise, 11.[2]

Berlin Foundling Home

Soon after the French sisters arrived, the appeals that Charles Gutzlaff made to missions in Germany when he was in Berlin in 1851 started to have some effect. The Reverend Mr and Mrs Neuman arrived later that year, separate from the Berlin Missionary Society; they were under the auspices of the Berlin Women's Missionary Society for China, formed in 1849.

The Neumans took a house near Morrison Hill to set up a Foundling Hospital. Their head nurse, who must have come at the same time, was Fraulein Lisette Nagel. The Home, known as the Berlin Foundling Home, moved several times because of health problems, and ended up at West

Point with other similar organizations, in specially built accommodation. Europeans in Hong Kong referred to those who worked at the home, and the womens committee in Germany (which never appeared in Hong Kong and had some connection with the Female Education Society in London) as the 'Berlin Ladies'.

Usually the Home was headed by a husband and wife. The Neumans returned to Germany rather soon because of his ill health, leaving Lisette Nagel temporarily in charge; and they were replaced by the Reverend Mr and Mrs Ladendorf, the latter called the matron, while Fraulein Nagel was head nurse and Fraulein Heidsick was school mistress (1862). Fraulein Heidsick was replaced by Fraulein Süp who in 1866 was teaching 22 girls — though that does not accurately reflect the numbers in the Home.

A newspaper-inspired history in the 1930s wrote cynically of the Neumans in 1850 that 'these good people were extremely surprised not to find large numbers of dear children perishing in the streets'. It went on to suggest that they managed to acquire 12 girls from one to six years old by sending to the mainland. That same piece says that there were 16 children in 1860 and 52 in their new home in 1866.[3] According to the annual report, there were 162 children in 1902, and 192 in 1904.

Babies up to the age of two were cared for outside by wet nurses and *amahs*, paid for by the society; then they would be looked after by older girls in the home; at six they would attend the school and at 14 or 15 they would leave it. Staff turnover was low: Fraulein Mathilde Grotefend was there for nearly 20 years, and Fraulein Borbein for 15.

Not surprisingly, Matilda Sharp interested herself in the work of the Home and the social well-being of its women staff; in November 1865, she invited two of them to tea. She questioned them closely and reported home her findings. Asked if they had foundlings left on their doorstep, she was told that it was fairly uncommon because it was illegal. The French nuns were obviously delightfully unaware that they were breaking the law when they paid for foundlings. Six weeks previously, however, a parcel had been found which contained a dead baby — the parents being unable or unwilling to pay for its funeral. Asked if abandoned babies were ever boys, the answer was a firm, 'No, never'. Matilda had noted that she had not heard crying when she visited the Home; apparently the babies only cried when they first arrived in the strange home from the comfort of their wet nurse.[4]

Hildesheim Home for the Blind

Abandoned baby girls were not the only problem: the selling of blind Chinese girls into 'slavery' was a particularly painful phenomenon for European women to face. Mrs Gutzlaff, you may remember, had run a school for blind girls in Macau in the 1830s. Four young women were sent to England, including Agnes Gutzlaff, and Mrs Gutzlaff took Fanny and Jessie Gutzlaff with her to Philidelphia — they were still in the Institution for the Blind there in 1917.[5]

In 1890 the Hildesheim Mission for the Blind, supported by another Berlin women's committee, grew out of the Berlin Foundling Mission. But in 1899 beriberi broke out in the home and the girls were sent to Macau. In 1901, the Hong Kong government gave the mission land in Kowloon, between Hunghom and Kowloon City, and a new home was built, part of which was the Blindheim Industrial School. There were 20 girls there. That area is today part of the urban sprawl of Kowloon; then it must have seemed like being in rural China for the European women who worked there. Another branch opened on the Island in 1914.

By 1904 there were 40 blind girls, aged between one and 23 in the original home and the local European community fully supported it. In 1903, for example, the Ministering Children's League — one of the proliferating benevolent ladies committees — raised $1,000 through a sale, and Helena May, presented the money with her husband, the Colonial Secretary and Acting Governor. Subscriptions and donations were paid by Miss Johnstone who ran the CMS school Fairlea, Mrs Hoare, the Bishop's wife, Miss Hamper, superintendent of the Victoria Home and Orphanage, and Mrs Hamilton Sharp, Granville Sharp's sister-in-law.

More money was constantly needed, as Fraulein Johanne Reiecke and Fraulein Postler, who were in charge of the institution then, pointed out: sometimes blind 'slaves' who were prostitutes ran to them for help. How could they keep them with their more innocent charges? A separate home must be built. Then there was the typhoon damage of 1904 — somehow a new building, housing 80 girls was built.[6]

Victoria Home and Orphanage

There seems to have been little bad blood between the various Protestant missions of whatever nationality; indeed, they worked closely together and symbolized that by an ecumenical service held in the Cathedral in 1897 at which Chinese Christians, men and women, converted by the FES, CMS, the LMS, and the Basle and Berlin Missions worshipped together. Nevertheless, the CMS obviously felt that there was a need, once the Diocesan Home and Orphanage (formerly the Diocesan Female Training School) had become the Diocesan Boys School, for a CMS orphanage.

The Victoria Home and Orphanage was set up in 1881, also at West Point, by the Reverend John Ost and Mary Ost, who was Bishop Burdon's niece. There, rescued 'slaves' and Chinese and Eurasian orphans were cared for. Mary Ost had a daughter in 1881, and another three years later; how they fitted into the setting, the life and the work, one can only imagine. Miss Agnes Hamper, aged 36 and an honorary CMS missionary, took over in 1892; by then those for whom the Home was a refuge included orphans, destitute children, rescued 'slaves', and penitentiary girls. In 1902 the home moved to Kowloon.

Perhaps because of the move, though Miss Hamper does not suggest that, the girls were often unruly. She quotes from her diary, in the annual report for 1903, constant entries such as 'so and so very naughty', or 'so and so gave way to violent temper', and 'had to whip so and so'.

Sometimes the girls left; sometimes they were asked to leave.[7] There was a two-way traffic between the Victoria Home and the Po Leung Kuk, a Chinese committee set up in 1878 to assist in the suppression of kidnapping and traffic in human beings, and the home that went with it where girls sold into prostitution could find refuge. It was not a refuge for ill-treated *mui tsai* ('domestic slaves') as such, though Miss Hamper's home was.

It was hardly surprising, given the treatment that the *mui tsai* and prostitutes had received outside, that some of them were difficult to deal with. Neither can a Christian environment have been comfortable for all of them. Later that same year, however, Miss Hamper noted, 'All the girls much better behaved.' Sometimes girls were suitable to be sent to Miss Johnstone's school at Fairlea.

In 1904 Miss Hamper left because of ill health, and her assistant, 33-year-old Rose Bachelor went on leave. Miss Annie Storr, formerly a milliner, Miss Sarah Hollis, a nurse-maid, and Miss Edith Houlder took over. The Victoria Home was helped by Mrs May and the Ministering Children's League as well; and in later years Mrs May's daughters were also involved. By 1907, there were 78 children in the Home. In 1926, typically for Hong Kong, the hill the Home was on was to be levelled for development and the institution was divided between Taipo Orphanage and Heep Yunn School.

The Eyre Refuge

Miss Lucy Eyre was one of those who helped to subsidize the Hildesheim Blind Home. She was originally, from 1889, one of Miss Johnstone's assistants at Fairlea, but like Miss Baxter she paid for herself and was not indentured to the FES, and gradually she began to make her own mark. One of her projects was the Hong Kong Refuge for Chinese Women and Girls — that is, 'fallen females' — which she set up on the Island just off Pokfulam Road, towards the end of 1904. Its committee was suitably ecumenical and not a refuge for benevolent ladies. It consisted of Lucy Eyre as

1 Elizabeth Fearon. Wife of a Country Trader in Macau 1826–1838.

2 Harriet Low. Painted in Macau in 1833 when she was 24, by Chinnery.

3 Emily Bowring. The Governor's daughter, 1858.

4 Matilda Sharp. Portrait of 1875 found in Matilda Hospital 100 years later.

5 Kitty Pope Hennessy. Governor's wife in Hong Kong 1877–1882.

6 Mabel Cantlie. Doctor's wife who kept a diary in Hong Kong 1889–1896.

7 Helen Stevens. Matron of Alice Memorial Hospital 1891–1902, and her nurses.

8 Dr Alice Sibree Hickling, Hong Kong 1903–1928.

9 Mabel Piggott. Wife of the Chief Justice 1905–1912.

10 Flora Shaw Lugard and Sir Frederick Lugard, Governor 1907–1912.

11 Helena May and family *c.*1910 (before Sir Francis was Governor 1912–1919).

12 Sybil Neville–Rolfe.
General Secretary of the
National Council for
Combating Venereal Diseases.

13 Alicia Little. Campaigner against
bound feet, 1900.

14 Penelope Clementi.
    Married in Hong Kong
    1911, Governor's wife
    1925–1930.

15 Nan Severn. A Big Lady
    1921–1925.

16 Clara Haslewood, 1914.

17 Stella Benson.
Novelist and
campaigner
1920–1932:
portrait c.1931.

18 Gladys Forster and her youngest daughter, Hong Kong early 1930s.

19 Phyllis Harrop. In charge of
'wayward girls' 1938–41
(with two repectable friends).

20 Hilda Selwyn-Clarke (*second from right*) with Mme Sun Yat-sen (*centre*) and colleagues on a junk with trucks and supplies, 1939.

21 Agnes Smedley in Kuomingtang uniform, 1937–1940.

22 Emily Hahn and a baby
gibbon in the 1930s.

23 Freda Utley, Hilda Selwyn-Clarke, and Agnes Smedley in Hankow, 1938.

24 Hong Kong 1940 (*left to right*) Agnes Smedley, Emily Hahn, Hilda Selwyn-Clarke and her daughter Mary, and Margaret Watson.

25 Ellen Field.
    War heroine, 1941.

honorary secretary, 39-year-old Miss Ada Pitts, a CMS missionary, as honorary treasurer, and the new LMS doctor, Alice Sibree, as medical officer. Other members included Miss Johnstone, Mrs Bannister, the Archdeacon's wife, Mrs Genaehr, of the Rhenish Missionary Society, and Miss Skipton, headmistress of the newly resurrected Diocesan Girls' School.[8]

The work of the Refuge had begun in a small way in 1901. Unlike Miss Hamper of the Victoria Home who freely exchanged girls with the Po Leung Kuk, Miss Eyre and Miss Pitts saw it as a heathen place and therefore entirely unsuitable for rehabilitating the fallen. The early matron of their Refuge had been Chinese, but Miss Eyre was determined that a European superintendent was needed, and in 1904 she found Miss Freegard, through the recommendation of the YWCA training home in London, where they were in the vanguard of such work. Miss Freegard then underwent three months training under the Eastbourne Rescue Home in the south of England, not just in order to take care of the young women who came or were sent for shelter, but also to make sure that the home paid its way; it was to go into the laundry business.

'Laundry work' and prayer, pioneered in Britain in the 1880s, has been described as 'the standard redemptive regimen'.[9] By 1905 the Refuge held 25 inmates and was limping along fairly well. Miss Eyre solicited work for the inmates from wherever she could, for part of the money earned would go to the girls to help them clothe themselves — the clothes being made on the premises. Some of the girls were blind, and the Refuge hired a blind teacher from the School for the Blind in Canton run by an American woman missionary, Dr Mary Niles. The blind girls were those 'slaves' whom the Hildesheim Home could not take because they were prostitutes, though they were still hoping to build separate accommodation for them.

Miss Eyre's home was a refuge, but it also had prison-like qualities in line with similar homes in Britain. She complained that being on the main road was not only a problem as far as the laundry business was concerned, but also because it was difficult to make it secure. The inmates had to be prevented from leaving, and communication from outsiders was to be avoided, no doubt for their own good, as their 'owners' might try to force them or lure them back into vice.

After appealing for funds to help generate self-sufficiency, Miss Eyre added that a sewing machine and a harmonium would also be appreciated. Donations came not only from committee members and other FES missionaries, including Miss Carden the headmistress of St Stephen's preparatory school, as it then was, but also from Colonel C.B. Eyre in England, presumably Lucy Eyre's father. One wonders how the missionary women, with their small salaries, managed to contribute to all these various ventures. It is also noticeable that whilst Church organizations in Britain concerned themselves with all prostitutes, not only was the Refuge in Hong Kong entirely for Chinese prostitutes, but the missionary women never mention European prostitutes. It seems difficult to accept that it was because they were outcasts in European society. One has to assume that the remit of the various missions was to minister to the Chinese heathen, and that even if they had wished to extend that, their ability to raise funds locally would have been affected because of European attitudes to European prostitutes.

Miss Eyre was nothing if not determined; in 1907, two weeks after Lady Lugard arrived in the colony for her husband to take up his appointment as Governor, Miss Eyre and Miss Pitts descended upon her at Government House to discuss their Refuge, particularly its financial needs. They told Flora Lugard that their 30 young women cost about £500 a year. In convincing her of the need for the Refuge, they apparently played down the heathen–Christian aspect. Flora noted in her diary for the first few weeks of her stay (the only part of it that survives) that their 'different and better purpose' to that of the Chinese Po Leung Kuk, was that the Eyre Refuge kept an eye on its girls 'in after life' — a rather ambiguous phrase; the Chinese institution helped only girls under the legal age of 18, 'and keeps no truck with them after they leave their doors'.[10]

The following day, Flora, as ecumenically as it was necessary for her to be, visited the Italian Convent with its European and Eurasian orphanage — where the girls contributed to their keep through lace and embroidery work — and its foundling home for Chinese girls. She notes that only 5 per cent of the latter 'are reared'; [11] that must mean that the foundlings were so suffering from neglect and exposure that when they were taken in they did not survive. This makes sense of the information given by the French Convent for 1850: that when in January 111 babies 'passed away' and 26 others joined them in February 'the gates of heaven' were opened to them.[12] That presumably means they were baptized before they died, bringing home to the secular reader the sense of success felt by the nuns in what seems on the face of it a thankless task.

The Italian Convent also housed a Chinese orphanage, as opposed to a foundling home, and a refuge for 'destitute, incurable old people and girls of the unfortunate class'. As with other refuges for prostitutes, the Registrar General often sent girls to the convent; these would be girls under the legal age who needed the protection of the law.

Just over a week after her visit to the Italian Convent, Flora Lugard visited the French Convent which performed the same forms of 'cosmopolitan charity'. And the next day she visited the women's prison. Then — over a period of days — it was to the Victoria and Matilda hospitals, the wives and children of the Austin Barracks, the Victoria Barracks, those in Kowloon and those on Stonecutters Island, the Civil Hospital, the Maternity Hospital, the Fairlea Refuge and Girls' School, and the lunatic asylum. There was one European woman in prison and two in the lunatic asylum (as well as half a dozen men).

Lucy Eyre and Ada Pitts felt, as has been suggested, a strong Christian mission towards the prostitutes who came to their Refuge. They were part of a powerful movement in Britain to rescue 'fallen women' through reforming refuges but the spur to the CMS Refuge in Hong Kong was undoubtedly the strong antipathy felt by the two women towards the Chinese institution the Po Leung Kuk. How strong can be gauged from a confidential report presented to the Colonial Office in London in 1921 by a commission constisting of Mrs C. [Clive] Neville-Rolfe OBE, General Secretary of the National Council for Combating Venereal Diseases in London, and Dr R. Hallam.

Other aspects of that report and of Mrs Neville-Rolfe's work will be discussed later, but among the visits the commission made was one to the Po Leung Kuk. Alice Sibree Hickling had been its Medical Officer for two years, but no longer was; and Miss Pitts had known it for 20 years. Until two years previously she had visited it often, since then, neither she nor any other European woman had visited it at all. The reason is not suggested but may have had something to do with the anti-*mui tsai* campaign, which will be discussed later. It is important to note that the committee of the Po Leung Kuk welcomed the commission's visit and gave them every assistance, and Miss Pitts accompanied them.

What Mrs Neville-Rolfe and Dr Hallam put in their report is, however, controversial. It should perhaps be read bearing in mind the emotions raised by both the anti *mui tsai* campaign and the attitude over the years of Christian Miss Eyre and Miss Pitts to the Chinese institution for the protection of women and girls. Nevertheless both women were obviously scrupulously honest by their own lights. Miss Eyre, whose views are most outspoken, could not be accused of being anti-Chinese. Her missionary work with the FES was as self-sacrificing and her reports of work with Chinese women were as warm as that of the other FES missionaries. Dr Hickling's credentials, if you look only at her work described in the last chapter, would appear to be impeccable, and Mrs Neville-Rolfe came from a similar stable.[13]

Firstly, Sybil Neville-Rolfe and Dr Hallam saw with their own eyes conditions for the young women which they found unsatisfactory. The inmates were unsupervised, and without adequate recreational facilities. There was a suggestion of academic education — the girls were holding Chinese primers — but no proof of it; there was no teacher, and there was no suggestion of training in any craft, such as cooking. They saw a room where girls 'awaiting marriage' were kept and they seemed to have no occupation at all. According to the Report, Miss Pitts and Dr Hickling maintained, that

The home is largely used as a recruiting ground for cheap supplementary wives by members of the Committee (Many of these girls become second or third wives, for the welfare of whom the husband can only be held responsible for one year from the date of marriage).

The Committee have luncheon parties there on Sundays, and the marriageable girls attend on them. Two members of the Committee are reputed to be owners of the land on which the principal Chinese Brothels are situated, but we had not time to verify this from the land register.[14]

The Report was not published, so it may be that its accusations against the Po Leung Kuk were not known about at the time, except to the initiated. The Governor, Sir Reginald Stubbs, as will be seen later, is unlikely to have taken action on that issue.

The YWCA and the Helena May Institute

Not all Lucy Eyre's ventures involved her in such a passionate response; but it was obvious that she cared deeply for the women in the society where her mission found itself — however paternalistic, even colonial, her attitudes could be construed to be today.

The origins of Hong Kong's Young Women's Christian Association (YWCA) — part of the organization founded in London in the mid 1850s by Lady Kinnaird — are somewhat obscure and diffuse. Its present-day literature concerns itself with the Chinese organization — for Chinese women, run by Chinese Christian women — that started officially in 1920 with a full-time Chinese staff (helped from 1918 by a Canadian, Nell Elliot). It was to be a strong focus for the development of middle-class Chinese women in the 1920s and 1930s.[15] It is clear, however, that Lucy Eyre and Miss

Hamper of the CMS had set it stirring much earlier, with regular meetings for Chinese Christian women by 1893. By 1896 Lucy was writing of a European committee and the need to help Eurasian girls. But it was not until 1909 that the organization managed to find a home, in Beaconsfield Arcade. Bible and needlework classes were held there. When in 1912 it had to close and only temporary premises were found, it was obvious that something radical had to be done. It may have been during this time that the Chinese side went underground in some girls' schools, later to re-emerge.

In 1913, Miss Eyre's YWCA merged with the Hong Kong Benevolent Society, which had been set up in 1889 as a purely 'ladies' charitable committee. Out of this was born the Helena May Institute, what is today a successful women's club in charming and historical premises right in the middle of busy central Hong Kong.

The Helena May was built to answer a need, which both its parent organizations obviously felt was critical, of providing affordable, comfortable accommodation for single, European women — missionaries, nurses, teachers, doctors, the increasing number of secretaries, and travellers. It was named after Helena May not only because she was the Governor's wife but also because she was an active promoter of the project, as President of the YWCA, and as the woman whom the benefactors of the building wished to honour for her community work.[16]

Helena was well established in Hong Kong not only because her husband had been Colonial Secretary before he became Governor in 1912, but also because she was the daughter of Lieutenant-General George Digby Barker, General Officer Commanding the forces in China and Hong Kong (GOC) from 1890 to 1895. He was from time to time also Acting Governor; indeed, Helena was married from Government House in 1891, to her father's then secretary and one of the Hong Kong cadets, Henry May.

The YWCA fizzled out, perhaps because of other concerns during World War I. Nan Severn, wife of the Colonial Secretary in 1921, writing home then, gave as the reason for its demise that the rules, centralized in London, were not designed for Hong Kong conditions; referring everything back imposed administrative demands that could not be met. But, as she also explained, the Helena May — opened in September 1916 — took the place both of a women's club and the 'Y'; everything was held there, though it seems to have been a purely expatriate set-up.

Nan, assuming that it was for those with needs that she did not have, held back but was persuaded that she should use it. 'They like Peak people to use it as much as possible,' she wrote, 'as the more we use it, the more popular it is with other kind of people.'[17] An unwitting piece of condescension which will be explored more thoroughly in the next chapter.

Nan, incidentally, was among those European women who helped raise money for the resurrected Chinese YWCA, trying to erect their own hostel on Caine Road similar to the Helena May. She noted that although they had paid for a Canadian 'Lady Secretary' and were glad of help in raising money, it was an independent venture. 'They' she wrote, meaning the Chinese women behind it, 'are trying to teach the Chinese [women] to stand on their own feet and organise themselves.'[18]

The novelist Stella Benson had a more robust approach to the Helena May. She first came across it when she was a single woman in Hong Kong in 1920 teaching for a term at the Diocesan Boys' School, as part of broader travel that included China. It was heaven-sent to an impecunious novelist, though she did note that when she mentioned where she was staying, the interest of the man she was talking to rather obviously waned.[19] Stella came back in 1930 as wife of a member of the Chinese Customs Service, James O'Gorman Anderson, and was on the Helena May's Library Committee, often doing duty in the library itself. She had some astringent things to say, in her diary and in articles, both about the activities at committee meetings and the philistine behaviour of library users who often ordered books via their coolies as if they were ordering groceries. 'Please give bearer 2 books' wrote one subscriber.[20]

At her first library committee meeting, the rather radical

Stella, ready to do battle against the forces of reaction, found herself insisting that if they were throwing out Aldous Huxley's books as 'improper', it was 'surely more under-mining of innocence, if innocence *must* be considered, to accept Collette's book *Cheri*'.[21] At the next meeting she was edged into a different tack: someone had complained about *All Quiet on the Western Front*. As Stella explains her case, 'All my thunder really demanded was a definition — are we a Girls' Friendly Christian Association or a[n] Adult Library Club?'[22] She wrote a little later of the haven for 455 members, 'I remain devoted to the Helena May and should like to make it a good women's club, if not prevented by the uplifters.'[23]

Stella had seen life too much in the raw, admittedly at her own choosing, to accept easily Hong Kong's colonial way of life and attitudes. Born into the landed gentry in Shropshire, England, in 1892, she could have wafted through a middle-class English life, except for her poor health and her fine mind. She was involved in Women's Suffrage before World War I, and lived in the East End of London, writing about it in *I Pose* (1915). She had worked on the land and then lived in the United States doing menial work.

The impression of Hong Kong in the 1920s and 1930s that Stella leaves in her as yet unpublished diaries is a healthy antidote to the sometimes saccharine and pious efforts of women whose missionary status and zeal, or status that came to them through marriage, allowed them to guide the lives of other women. But, while laughing with Stella at what to us seems asking for satire, one has to assess her sometimes unreasonable prejudices against a Hong Kong expatriate society that usually kept her in the depths of despair. She is, for example, forever meeting an interesting or an open or a clever woman and defining her as very much not a 'honkongeress'. If one were to add up the number of times she wrote something similar one would deduce that she had as many compatible acquaintances as most of us have in Hong Kong or similar transient places.

People who came to Hong Kong in control of their lives — men and missionaries — came to make money or preach and practise the Gospel; Stella Benson, a sensitive, progressive and secular intellectual never really fitted in, though she was to leave her previously unsung mark on the history of Hong Kong's women. Ironically, the Helena May library which, before the War, held all Stella's novels, now holds none. The Japanese used the Institute to billet troops and stable horses, and the library did not survive, though it was later restocked and is now one of the Helena May's main attractions.

CHAPTER SIXTEEN

BIG LADIES

'All our great ladies here are nice, which is very lucky,' wrote Nan Severn, wife of the Colonial Secretary in February 1921, soon after her arrival in Hong Kong.[1] She also referred to that same group as the 'big ladies', and that is a somehow even more felicitous expression, with its physical connotations, as well as those of status. Some British women must have seemed very large to the petite Chinese.

By the Big Ladies, Nan meant a group dominated by the wives of the Governor, the Commander in Chief, the Admiral, the Bishop, the Chief Justice, the Colonial Secretary and the Attorney General. The precedence that accompanied the status was, as will be shown in the next chapter, very important, but so was a sense of social responsibility towards the community, and a feeling of solidarity with each other. Nan Severn's unpublished letters home, written between 1921 and 1925, give a strong impression of all those aspects.

Claud Severn had been Colonial Secretary since 1912, until 1920 living the life of a bachelor. It is said that he nearly married Miss Goggin, Matron at the Diocesan Boys School, where he loved to go and collect the boys and take them to sing with him in the Cathedral choir; but she died in January 1920. In February, the novelist Stella Benson, then unmarried, was taken by him to the theatre. She described the 51-year-old as 'such a clever, humorous old stoutie'.[2]

In September, Claud married Margaret Annie (Nan), only

daughter of Thomas Bullock, Professor of Chinese at Oxford, and Florence Horton Bullock. Stella, meeting Nan on 10 October 1922, when Claud was Acting Governor and Nan, therefore, first lady, wrote that she was a 'large very sweet-faced young woman with bobbed hair, doesn't say anything interesting but looks gentle and comfortable somehow'.

It is sometimes necessary to interpret Stella; for a start, she was younger than Nan. Stella in 1921 was 29, Nan was six years older. Whatever her conversation with the rather intimidating novelist, Nan had had a comparatively interesting life. Born in 1886 in Peking where her father was then in the consular service, she had been educated in Oxford and then, between 1904 and 1907, at Girton, the women's college at Cambridge. Women could not get degrees there until 1948, though they could apply for *ad eundem* degrees at Trinity College Dublin; Nan did not do so but during World War I she worked as chief clerk in the Tribunal Department of the Ministry of National Service at Oxford, and received an MBE for it. In the evening and on Sundays she worked at the Red Cross Auxiliary Hospital. For a sense of the difficulties faced by a woman going to Oxford or Cambridge then, even from her family, and of working, virtually untrained, in a Red Cross Hospital during the war, Vera Brittain's *Testament of Youth* (1933) is essential reading. Although Nan read maths at Cambridge, she also spoke fluent French which was to help her during visits to the French Convent in Hong Kong and impress Society. She was also a life-long botanist. But she did not have to learn to cook until World War II, when she was a widow living in Oxfordshire doing voluntary service. She died in 1967, aged 81.[3]

Nan's letters are not erudite or of great moment; indeed, one historian who read them hoping for political nuggets complained unfairly, I feel, of the concentration on horses. Certainly Nan had a string of racing ponies — which was very uncommon; more usual was for a wife to have one pony in her husband's stable. Nan was the first woman to have her own stable and one afternoon she won four races with three ponies. Whatever her shortcomings, and those of her letters, the latter do throw light on the life of Big Ladies. She wrote sensibly on 25 February 1921:

I find there is heaps to do here; but I am trying not to involve myself in too much work till I know the people and conditions a little better. I have just promised to be vice president of the Girl Guides which are being started and which Lady Stubbs is making herself rather responsible for. I refused to take the Peak stall at the Ministering Children's League Bazaar, but I expect I shall help with it. It means organising all the Peak activities, and obviously a newcomer doesn't know the pitfalls enough.

But Nan was already well and truly involved because two weeks earlier the Bishop held a meeting of 'a select little party of the seven leading official ladies in the colony, to try and work up a little more religious life in the colony'.[4] By March she was the principal secretary of the new Diocesan Association. Lady Kirkpatrick, the General's wife, was the military secretary, and Mrs Bowden-Smith, the Commodore's wife, whom Nan was to describe as 'very pretty and charming and a particularly nice person',[5] was the naval one. The meetings of this association, or Nan's attendance at them, became increasingly rare, but then she did start a family and that, in Hong Kong, at 35, even with servants, would have been a demanding enterprise, though less so than in the nineteenth century. Hills and heat and the combination thereof kept pregnant women rather immobile; cars were still a rarity. Lady Stubbs was producing a family at the same time, and it is quite obvious that the two women sustained each other, which was important, as the Governor's wife was often unwell.

That ill-health is reflected in Stella Benson's view of Marjory Stubbs. The Governor, in 1920, was 'a bluff, unsocietyish sort of creature' with 'fresh ideas about politics'. But, as for his wife, Stella was 'vaguely alarmed' by her: 'She had a sort of courteous shyness, and a pale non-grandeur that is attractive in an almost touching way.'[6] Stubbs obviously felt that his wife needed protecting and, considering Stella's feminism and later work on behalf of Chinese prostitutes in

Hong Kong, it is ironic that she should have written admiringly of him. When in late 1920, Sybil Neville-Rolfe, General Secretary of the National Council for Combating Venereal Diseases, arrived with a colleague on a fact finding mission, she was told that Stubbs was 'specially dubious' of the advisability of a woman speaking on such a subject. Meeting them on the day of their arrival, he confirmed that they were 'not welcome' but, in addition, he informed them that 'he would not permit Lady Stubbs to identify herself in any way with the work of the Commission'.[7] The commissioners never met her.

Stubbs had also told them that no one else would wish to be involved. That turned out to be patently untrue; they received cooperation from many sectors of the community, from the Chinese, and from the government medical department (though not from private practitioners who carried out examinations of prostitutes) and from women, including Chinese women. The Report remarks that the Governor 'did not anticipate that the educated women residents of the Colony would participate in the campaign. Fortunately, we were able to reach almost all the white women residents ... through having secured the co-operation of the leaders of each group.' As they explained, Lady Kirkpatrick, Mrs Bowden Smith, Dr Alice Hickling, the wife of the manager 'of the senior shipping firm', and the Head of the principal school for Europeans at Kowloon, 'each convened conferences of their own circles'.[8] As a result, a training school for intending speakers was arranged and 20 to 24 'of the most responsible educated women' attended a course of eight lectures at the Helena May.

Two years later, Sybil Neville-Rolfe was still in correspondence with the Colonial Office about her report, and she told W.G.A. Ormsby-Gore that just when she had been about to set up a voluntary branch of her organization which was to include, among others, Dr Hickling and Miss Pitts, Stubbs had vetoed such an enterprise, saying he would set up a small government committee.[9] I have not been able to find out how far the Big Ladies who had responded so positively persevered, but I do know that part of the success of the commission's visit can be attributed to Sybil's personality and determination.[10] Alice Sibree Hickling, for example, set up the first VD clinic and today Hong Kong is well-served by its successors.

It was as well that there was a network of such Big Ladies to support Marjory Stubbs in any of the work that she was allowed by her husband to do, because the demands for community work and representation from on high had become heavy.

The first two Governors of Hong Kong, Henry Pottinger and John Davis, were not accompanied by their wives and it was probably not until Maria Bowring moved, in 1854, into the imposing new Government House, situated in the centre of the community that was beginning to consolidate, that the position and work of governor's wife began to grow. Often the first lady was in Britain, ill — as was Lady Bonham who left in 1851, and Lady Kennedy who died in 1874 on her way home — or looking after her family, but when she was in Hong Kong, increasingly she created a separate and distinctive world and work of her own.

Little is known of Kitty Pope Hennessy, who followed Georgiana Kennedy. She was a potentially most interesting governor's wife, half Malayan and the daughter of a consular official — Henry Low — married to a man with unfashionably progressive views, including sympathy towards the Chinese, she could have made an unusual mark. But she is remembered only for the scandal which contributed to her husband's departure, and she destroyed all her own papers, as well as many of his.

Isabella Bird, after spending an evening at Government House early in January 1879, wrote of Kitty that she 'sat in a dream, spoke to no-one, and only roused herself to fire up fiercely at her husband who retorted with cold sarcasm'.[11] The following day, a recommendation that Thomas Hayller should be made Chief Justice was withdrawn. The relationship between Kitty Pope Hennessy and T.C. Hayller Q.C. has been explored as deeply as it can be by Pope Hennessy's grandson in his biography *Verandah* (1964). There is little to be gained by rehashing something so nebulous, if so inflammatory at the time.

Only once is Kitty to be seen performing duties with a grace and intelligence, tinged with a sense of humour, which could have made a positive contribution. That was when the King of Hawaii visited Hong Kong in April 1881 and twice during the same very public occasion fell heavily and obviously asleep. His minder, William Armstrong, tells how on the first occasion Kitty let her fan slip to wake him and the second time asked the band to play the Hawaiian National Anthem.

Kitty's successor was Diamentina Bowen, of whom little remains but an aura of good works. She is like Blanche Macdonnell of whom it was said by the Chief Justice in 1870, 'No lady who presided at Government House will have left the Colony more deeply or more generally regretted.'[12] Or Nea Robinson (wife of Sir Hercules) whose husband's success between 1859 and 1865 Ernst Eitel attributed to her 'extensive and beneficial influence'.[13]

About Marion Des Voeux a little more is known, because Mabel Cantlie knew her and because her husband, 22 years her senior, wrote an autobiography. She arrived in Hong Kong in March 1889, aged 23, as the hot damp season began to build up. During that summer, white ants began to invade Mountain Lodge, the governor's Peak residence, and in May there was a typhoon and the Peak tram, opened the year before, stopped running. Marion must have become pregnant immediately on arrival because she gave birth to a son in November; she now had four surviving children out of eight pregnancies.

Meanwhile, the Governor had assistance in entertaining, 'the value of which,' he writes, 'may be gathered by a remark made to me by a colonist. "[She] has the rare gift of appearing glad to receive, and thus make happy, at least for the moment, every guest who enters her house" '.[14] It seems that governors' wives had one particularly important social function. When the wife of a distinguished visitor fell asleep on Des Voeux's shoulder during dinner, Marion, quickly perceiving the state of things, got up, 'thereby causing the ladies to leave the room'. She had, however, to pretend to be absent-minded as dinner was not finished: the ice-cream was being served.[15]

Marion, like Kitty Pope Hennessy in 1882, accompanied her husband to Canton in 1889, protected from trouble by 50 Chinese troops, but she also had her own commitments; one of her major interests was the foundling homes of the French and Italian convents. Edith Blake, wife of Sir Henry, and Flora Lugard, wife of Sir Frederick, will appear later, and Flora's heavy schedule of visits during the first weeks of her stay has already been described. It was during Flora's time, in 1908, that electricity and electric fans were introduced into Government House, which must have made a considerable difference to life. Gas lighting had arrived in 1865.

Following them were two governors' wives whose commitment to the local community was combined with a love for Hong Kong born of being more than Big Ladies passing through. Helena May's young womanhood and marriage, and her involvement with the creation of the Institute that bears her name, have already been discussed, but she gave more besides when she was Colonial Secretary's wife to organizations such as the Hong Kong Ladies Benevolent Society.

As governor's wife during World War I Helena was expected to give a lead, and did. Hong Kong was far away from the centre of action but its women raised money and produced clothes. In July 1915, a 'snowball bag sale', in aid of Belgian refugees in England and the starving in Belgium, was to have been held at the Peak Club but that was found to be too small; hurriedly Helena May invited the organizers to hold the sale at Government House with tea in the ballroom. It was through Lady May that Lady Lugard, her predecessor, issued her appeal in Hong Kong for her own refugee fund in England. Indeed, Helena was often a link between organizations in Hong Kong and Britain.

One of the best known of such organizations, and the one with the widest international involvement of middle-class

women, was Queen Mary's Needlework Guild which produced, collected and distributed handmade clothes for the
War effort — for the sick and wounded. Mabel Cantlie was
involved with its inception in London when she was asked
to take some patterns to the Palace for Queen Mary to
assess. She continued her work through the Red Cross. In
Ceylon, where her husband was governor during the war,
Marjory Stubbs was Vice-president of the Guild and received
a CBE; in Hong Kong, Dr Alice Hickling was Secretary of
the Guild and received an MBE. In British Guiana, Penelope
Clementi was also involved in the Guild's work and
received an MBE.

Penelope Clementi was almost as much a part of Hong
Kong as Helena May. Between 1910 and 1912, her father
was Commodore in Charge in Hong Kong and during that
time she and Helena May and her daughters became friends.
On Christmas day 1911, aged 22, Miss Eyres became
engaged to 36-year-old Cecil Clementi, who had come out
as a cadet in 1899 and since picked up several local dialects
and languages. In 1907–8 he had walked from Central Asia
to Hong Kong.

By 1913 Cecil Clementi had been appointed Colonial
Secretary in British Guiana. There, Penelope shared his love
of walking and riding, and wrote a book — *Through British
Guiana to the Summit of Roraima* (1920). Clementi was
appointed Governor of Hong Kong in 1925 and their
youngest daughter, now Alwin Ovenell, wrote to me that
'they were coming back to a place that had already deeply
engaged their affections'.[16]

Of all the historical buildings and monuments in Hong
Kong that the developers have destroyed, it is ironic that the
Clementis' creations should have remained virtually
untouched; ironic because he was quite sure that Sir Cecil's
Ride and Lady Clementi's Ride, the bridle and walking
paths they created, would be made into roads. They have
not been, and remain perhaps more of a boon than they
were when Hong Kong was such a different, small, quiet
place.

As for Penelope Clementi's other community activities,

Alwin Ovenell writes, 'My mother had a very vital personality and was always ready to urge the cause of benevolent societies or to direct hospitality where she knew its
lack was felt.' Her naval connections led her to an interest
there, and, as a result of her hospitality, the navy responded
by giving great parties for children onboard ship. Out of her
'At Homes' grew *thé-dansants* and garden parties, and out
of them a committee for the entertainment of soldiers and
sailors from the Garrison.

Looking at her mother's diary for January 1926, Alwin
Ovenell notes a Government House party for 300 children
from the naval yard, Garrison and police, a *thé-dansant* for
the sailors, a party for the Girl Guides and Brownies, a visit
to the Chinese Maternity Hospital at Tsan Yuk (Alice
Hickling's Hospital), one to the Helena May, and one to the
Little Sisters of the Poor at Kowloon. She had also given
away prizes at the Ying Wa Girls' School and then there was
an 'At Home' at Government House for 1,000 with the bands
of HMS *Hawkins* and HMS *Hermes*.

But over all that shone the physical beauty and the
outdoor life that Hong Kong offered *par excellence*. The
Clementis left in 1929, when he was appointed Governor of
the Straits Settlements. It is not surprising, as Alwin Ovenell
writes, that 'there were tears in my mother's eyes as she left
the Colony'.

Penelope Clementi was followed by Violet Peel whose
name is remembered today by the existence of the Violet
Peel Clinic, a centre for children, which is caught up in the
never-ending road works and elevations as you approach
Central from the east. As with Marion Des Voeux, we are
left to find out about Violet Peel's activities through the
rather wooden reminiscences, unpublished in this case, of
her husband, Sir William, Governor between 1930 and 1935.
But Stella Benson sets the scene in her inimitable way:

Sir William Peel ... is a handsome stolid old man — almost
exactly like any other amiable orthodox old man controlling any
tassel of the fringe of empire — full of mild anecdote and
kindness to ladies. Lady Peel is a very simple prattling kindly

unsmiling person full of household cares — I did not see one instant's calmness in her eyes or one smile, but she was pleasant in an anxious, homely way ... After dinner Lady Peel talked to me a long time in a flurried way about white ants.[17]

Sir William writes of how he and his wife of 19 years took great interest in and paid great attention to the creation of infant welfare centres, of which the Violet Peel Clinic, paid for by Chinese philanthropy, was one. In 1929, the Society for the Protection of Children had been set up and they became joint patrons of that also. The SPC was a very popular organization to be involved with, having a large general committee of Chinese and Europeans and an equally large executive committee. Dr Agnes Dovey, Dr Louise Hunter, and Adjutant Dorothy Brazier of the Salvation Army were all involved; and the list of financial contributors in 1934 stretches for pages. It was probably a useful meeting place for British and Chinese who, until after World War II, still led almost completely separate lives.

The importance of the network of Big Ladies in personal relations is quite clear: Marjory Stubbs, for example, was the godmother of Nan Severn's daughter Claudia, and the two mothers lived in the same village in their latter years. Nan Severn and Penelope Clementi were second cousins and while Cecil Clementi was Governor of the Straits Settlement from 1929 Alwin, a year younger than Claudia, lived with the Severns.

A year after Cecil Clementi became Governor of Hong Kong, Tom Southorn was appointed his Colonial Secretary and came over from his posting in Ceylon. Bella Southorn is in some ways better known as Bella Woolf, and perhaps her volumes of pieces about Hong Kong, *Chips of China* (1930) and *Under the Mosquito Curtain* (1935) were as much known in her time for the fact that she was Virginia Woolf's sister-in-law as for their quality. She had however, been a teller of tales long before her brother Leonard married Virginia, and she had a following among children in Britain. Her Hong Kong pieces, though slight, are charming, well-written and humorous.

Bella, though small in stature, was an ideal Big Lady, ready to be involved and to lift burdens. The Clementis and the Southorns had known each other in the Colonial Service in Ceylon and Bella provided support for Penelope from within three days of her arrival, when she accompanied her to a Girl Guide meeting. Bella later became Colony Commissioner and helped develop the movement 'in a spirit of the greatest goodwill and cooperation among the races'.[18] The Southorn's house, 'the Eyrie' was not ready, so they stayed at the governor's Peak residence, Mountain Lodge. There the two families intertwined, 'Cousin Bella' who had no children, responding warmly to the needs of Penelope's children.

The intricacies of Big Lady activities and reputation are illustrated by a behind-the-scenes correspondence concerning these two women. In late 1927, Penelope Clementi was very ill. Her daughter describes it as a pelvic abscess that required an operation dangerous in those days. She was not really well enough to accompany Cecil on an official visit to Canton in March 1928 but she pushed herself. Meanwhile, a letter from the Honourable Mrs Franklin, Convenor of the British Colonies and Dependencies Committee of the National Council of Women of Great Britain had winged its way to various governors' wives, including Penelope Clementi, suggesting the creation of links between women. She was too ill to answer it, as her husband said when he did so for her, but he also said that he considered that the circumstances of Hong Kong 'make it impracticable to form in this Colony any group of women such as you have in mind'. He concluded, 'I am, therefore, taking no action on this matter.'[19] Mrs Franklin took exception to this response and wrote to a friend, one of Clementi's predecessors. She did not mention who had written the unhelpful letter and her friend wrote back that he could not think of any women's organizations in Hong Kong from his time of 1904–7, but that if she wanted anything done she should write to Lady Clementi. He added that there was another capable woman in the colony — Bella Woolf; so there should be no trouble in tracking down the sort of organization she was after.[20] Penelope Clementi, meanwhile, recovered, saw the original letter and, as a previous chapter describes, recommended the Committee to get in touch with Dr Ethel Minnet who was familiar with all Hong Kong's women's activities and was then visiting London. A quick calculation of when Penelope Clementi and Ethel Minett were in British Guiana, shows that they must have been there together and were obviously friendly.

Bella Woolf Southorn was in Hong Kong from 1926 to 1936 and was a lynchpin of its Big Lady activities, from the Police Boys' Club which her husband set up, to the International Women's Club which she founded in 1933, based on a similar organization that she had been involved in starting in Ceylon. Situated alongside the famed Hong Kong Hotel, in what is now the Landmark Building, she intended European and Chinese women to be able to meet there. Ellen Li, one of the pillars of Hong Kong's Chinese community today, still remembers meeting Phyllis Harrop, who will appear later, there for lunch in the late 1930s.[21] Maurine Grantham, governor's wife after World War II, and whose husband had served with Tom Southorn in Ceylon, wrote to Bella about its continuing usefulness and success in 1958.[22] Bella received an OBE in 1935 for 'public services in Hong Kong'.

Bella and Stella Benson, because of their link through Virginia Woolf, were thrown together. Stella and Virginia got on as well as either would with anyone who was not an intimate. They admired each other's work, but neither thought highly of Bella Woolf Southorn. Virginia, writing to Stella about *Tobit Transplanted*, Stella's novel, which she had just read, remarked, 'I should be driven desperate if I lived in a wilderness of Bellas. She sends home photographs of herself opening golf clubs from which I get my only idea of English life in China.'[23] Stella wrote typically in her diary, 'Mrs Southorn is very sharp and plain, a very flattering manner in which she makes you feel somehow that she makes it her business to be very pleasant to everybody in order to Help Her Husband's Career. It is curious she should be Leonard Woolf's sister and yet have no subtlety at all.'[24]

The two novelists were both fretful intellectuals who would die before their time. Bella, 54 in 1931 when Stella met her, was full of life, sharp gossip, fast talk, and kindliness. Her husband died in 1957 and one can tell how hard that hit her; yet Penelope Clementi's daughter can write, 'I did meet her once again, in Oxford not long before her death [in 1960] and she still had a bright perky manner, smoked at table between courses, and was ready to be full of fun.' Bella's sense of humour, at her own expense as much as at anyone else's, is well-remembered. Invited to launch a ship, a common function of Hong Kong's Big Ladies, she made a delightfully brief and appropriate speech: 'I may not have the sort of face that launched a thousand ships, but I have great pleasure ...'[25]

Bella's directness jarred with Stella who had a fluent pen, not a quick tongue. But in her often consciously-literary acidity, Stella does add an important dimension to the activities of the Big Ladies:

I went to a monstrous teaparty that Mrs Southorn was giving; by a clever ruse she managed to include both the Kowloon Decayed Gentlewomen and the Peak Flourishing Gentlewomen having asked scores of the latter (me among them) to come and 'help entertain the poor dears.' Some of the Kowloon GDs were unexpectedly grotesque looking, like the insects that wriggle away when you turn a stone over, poor darlings. There was something very poignant about their best dresses, all put on to 'come to tea at the Colonial Secretary's House' — hearts beating beneath them happily ignorant of the fact that to Mrs Southorn and to the other opulent Peakites it was a philanthropic rather than a social occasion ...[26]

Two weeks later, Bella gave a similar mixed tea party for 'Peakites' and Chinese; again Stella was asked, and commented to her diary about the 'parish tea atmosphere'.

There is a negative side to the activities of the Big Ladies or Ladies Bountiful. They meant well, but on their own terms; often they were handing out largesse *de haut en bas*. To us — and to Stella Benson — it can look both patronizing and paternalistic.

But Bella Woolf Southorn *did* mean well, as her unpublished letters to her brother show, particularly when in 1913 she was unrestrainedly critical of the manuscript of his novel *The Wise Virgins*. She wrote, 'I have good friends too whose failings I could use for stories — and make a success of them — but I should despise myself horribly if I did so. And if that's the price to pay for being a great writer, I'd sooner remain inglorious.'[27] Then, 45 years later, when she was a widow and had occasion to mention Virginia's disparaging use of her in a novel, she wrote to Leonard how she and Tom, in discussing the meaning of life, had come to the conclusion that 'the best things to do were to do your job as well as possible and to be as kind as possible'.[28] That there could be another, even less benevolent side to the Big Ladies is clear from the next chapter.

CHAPTER SEVENTEEN

AT THE COURT OF
SIR MATTHEW

A misunderstanding took place in February 1907 between Sir Matthew Nathan, Governor of Hong Kong, and Lady Piggott, wife of the Chief Justice.[1] It was of small moment in itself but it bears scrutiny because it was symptomatic of Nathan's behaviour in a particular sphere. Indeed, I believe that a new critical look at his governorship is appropriate as a result of evidence that comes to light in the train of the Mabel Piggott incident.

The Hong Kong historian G.R.Sayer ended his chapter on the period 1904–7 and Nathan's governorship, 'Nor was Hong Kong unconscious of the loss when he left and retained for many years the memory of the wisdom and compassion of her youngest and only bachelor governor.'[2] The first question to raise is one of fact — that concerning Nathan's age: he was not 32 when he arrived, as Sayer suggests, but 42.[3] Charles Elliot was 40 when he was given power over Hong Kong's destiny, Hercules Robinson 35, and Pope Hennessy and Stubbs 43. Behaviour which might just have been understandable in a 32-year-old, is less acceptable in a governor ten years older.

The fact that Nathan was a bachelor need not have had much impact — governor's wives were often absent from Hong Kong. He has, however, been included in a list of 'asexual' historical 'high achievers'[4] and it seems that he remained single because he did not care for close relations with women.[5] This need not have been significant except

that he seemed to relate well with them through an apparent propensity to gossip with them, the results of which
were unfortunate. I believe that he probably did not care for
gossip but indulged in it or encouraged it merely as
something to talk about when he was with women, because
he did not know what else to talk to them about. His
biographer writes that 'He worried that his dinner parties
were slow and he found troublesome the local ladies'
tendency to petition him' about anything they felt was their
due.[6] In an unsent draft of April 1905, he referred to Hong
Kong wives as social climbers, coining as he did so the
delightful variation 'pushful'.[7] His dislike was not apparent
to the women concerned.

The Island, a weekly magazine of the period, notes, on
Nathan's departure, that 'nothing was too small to escape
his notice'. That is obvious when one goes through his
papers and finds dozens, if not hundreds, of the least billets-
doux from Big Ladies during his governorship in Hong
Kong, and letters written to him afterwards when he had
moved on to Natal. Few other people would have bothered
to keep them, nor a note in his diary about each one
received and sent. One of the outstanding features of the
notes is their brittle determination to amuse and provide
gossip, usually of notable bitchiness. Now and then there is
a draft reply; it never picks up on the tone or content, but
is always a model of wisdom and compassion.

Also revealed is his liking for children; he was very kind
to them and there are endless notes from Big Ladies
thanking him for a present or an outing on behalf of their
young daughters; and when the daughters were older, notes
from them with thanks, but also carrying on the tradition
of sharp gossip.

Hong Kong's middle-class wives have, as H.J. Lethbridge
would have it, been 'caricatured as the sharpest peckers in
the colonial pecking order'.[8] Implicit in that description is
an obsession with precedence and patronage — the perks
of status and the possibilities for advancement. Nathan, in
his remarks about them, has confirmed that tendency. I do
not think that my own exploration, so far, has supported

that claim — there were other things going on in society at the same time that were valuable — but certainly the behaviour that Nathan managed to draw out of them would provide corroborating material.

Before pursuing the Nathan–Piggott saga, a story about preferment concerning an earlier character would usefully set the scene. It may be that manœuvring to obtain invitations to Government House was helpful in the advancement of one's husband's career, but as many, if not more, careers were made or broken in the corridors of the Colonial Office in London, and there is some evidence that those making the decisions were not always activated by the worth of the candidate; indeed, that gossip, that supposed purlieu of females, played a corrosive role.

The story of James Stewart Lockhart's exile to the wastes of Weihaiwei, a British pimple on China rather smaller and even less significant than Hong Kong, cannot be proved, but then gossip and its results rarely can. Certainly, instead of becoming governor of Hong Kong as he hoped and expected, he remained mouldering as Commissioner in Weihaiwei for the 19 years that remained of his career.

Usually when a governor went on leave, often for several months, or when there was a hiatus between governors, the Colonial Secretary became Acting Governor. Henry May did so, for example, between the departure of Sir Henry Blake in November 1903, and the arrival of Sir Matthew Nathan in July 1904. But before Blake arrived in 1898, and following the departure of Sir William Robinson in January, Stewart Lockhart might have expected to fulfil the same function. Allegedly because of the Sino-Japanese War, however, it was the General Officer Commanding (GOC), Major-General Winston Black, who was asked to administer.

Stewart Lockhart and his family blamed Black and Robinson for his lack of promotion, then and later. Edith Stewart Lockhart told the story to her daughter Mary after her husband's death, and Mary wrote it down in a notebook which her father's biographer has made use of.[9]

Stewart Lockhart, as well as being Colonial Secretary, was also Registrar of births, deaths, and marriages. Miss Black, the General's daughter, became secretly engaged to the Governor's ADC and wished to marry him without her parents knowing. Stewart Lockhart, deeming the marriage unsuitable, refused to perform it. Miss Black went to the Governor who ordered him to do so. When the General heard the story, he vowed he would ruin Stewart Lockhart's career 'somehow or other.'[10]

As the story goes, the Governor became involved because he was having an affair with Miss Black and found his ADC useful cover. The incident is, apparently, referred to in a letter from Robinson's successor, Sir Henry Blake, to Stewart Lockhart; but it is also suggested that neither Robinson nor General Black's reports to the Colonial Office ever denigrated Stewart Lockhart; the implication being that it was all done in the corridors of Whitehall. Whatever the truth of the story — and there are many holes, including the fact that Robinson was a widower from 1894, and could simply have married Miss Black himself — Stewart Lockhart and his family believed that the incident blighted his promising career; and certainly the career was blighted.

That there was backbiting and sniping and the influencing of careers of colonial officers in the Colonial Office is also apparent simply by following the progress of the career of Mabel Piggott's husband, leading up to his appointment to Hong Kong and beyond. Peter Wesley-Smith highlights the phenomenon in his article 'Sir Francis Piggott: Chief Justice in his Own Cause'. It is necessary to note how ambitious or, as Nathan might have it, how 'pushful', Francis Piggott was and, indeed, how assertive Mabel was, to lend balance to my suggestions about Sir Matthew Nathan's behaviour. Piggott, from the time he decided to enter the Colonial Service when he was a barrister of 41, and Mabel was 38, nagged the Colonial Office to appoint him governor somewhere; at a pinch he would settle for being Chief Justice in an interesting place. Scrawled on one of the Colonial Office files after one such (later) request is the remark, 'Only the most unmistakable snub is likely to have any effect on such a man — and he fully deserves to receive it.'[11]

In 1901, Mabel Piggott, obviously taking advantage of the

relationship with Mrs Chamberlain, the wife of the Secretary of State for Colonial Affairs, that she had forged through the setting up of the Colonial Nursing Association, had occasion to write to her saying, 'We are both devoted to the Far East and of all the Colonies, Hong Kong is the one we should have liked to live in.'[12] Piggott did not become Chief Justice of Hong Kong then; but he was appointed in 1904, in preference to Sir Henry Berkeley, then Attorney General, and another candidate whom the Colonial Office had put forward.

Newly knighted, his ambitions beginning to be attained, Sir Francis Piggott arrived in Hong Kong with Mabel, a woman of 50, of considerable beauty — judging by her undated photograph — and of some achievement herself. There was no house accompanying the post, so Sir Matthew Nathan invited the Piggotts, in the meantime, to live in his Peak residence, Mountain Lodge. They stayed, from 26 July 1905, for nearly a year, and when they moved they charged for the unused coal that remained. But none of that in itself is enough to explain the fact that when Nathan left the colony he and the Chief Justice were not speaking. There is an explanation, one over and above any complaints that Piggott may have had about his professional treatment.

Matthew Nathan had been Governor for a year when the Piggotts arrived. He already had his circle of Big Ladies, particularly Helena May to whose daughters he was so kind, and Emily Hatton, wife of the GOC, Major-General Villiers Hatton. The General was to leave in 1906, his relationship with Nathan, a mere Major, in tatters over a letter written by Nathan's 29-year-old Private Secretary, Richard Ponsonby. Undeterred by the friction, Emily Hatton continued her solicitude of the darkly handsome, mustachioed, bachelor Governor, making sure that his social life was up to scratch, while Helena May provided him with a ready-made family to whom he only had to be a kind uncle. Along came Mabel, often indisposed herself, endlessly caring about Nathan's health. How Helena May reacted becomes clear later; it was quite obvious, too, that Emily Hatton resented Mabel living at Mountain Lodge, where she and the General had been wont to stay for the odd night or weekend. It was quite a bit higher up and cooler than Flagstaff House. In a letter to his mother of 14 July 1906, Nathan noted that he had dined with the Piggotts but the Hattons did not come as the two wives concerned were not exactly bosom friends.[13]

In view of what was to happen in February 1907 and thereafter, it is necessary to look, too, at the relations that Mabel may have had with other women. Katherine Berkeley, whose husband, the Attorney General, was passed over in favour of Piggott for the Chief Justice position, served on the committee of the Hong Kong Ladies Benevolent Society with Helena May, Isabel Slade, wife of barrister Marcus Slade, and Eleanor Hastings, wife of solicitor George Hastings. When Mabel Piggott joined the committee of the Diocesan Girls School in 1905–6, Helena May and Isabel Slade were also members along with Eleanor Hastings's sister-in-law Dorothy, Emily Hatton, and Mrs Hoare. Meanwhile, the Hong Kong Nursing Institution was in trouble, as an earlier chapter shows. Helena May had taken over as patroness from Lady Blake, and Isabel Slade was on the committee. It is easy to see poor Mabel Piggott muscling in. She was a passionate and determined woman; she was founder of the Colonial Nursing Association; she knew what she was talking about, but she was new in Hong Kong. By the end of 1905, she was set to be the honorary secretary. By February 1907 there had been time for some resentment to build up.

It is obvious that Mabel patronized other women, particularly Helena May, her junior in years, but familiar with Hong Kong since 1890. Helena's husband Henry May was not an obviously 'pushful' man, and in regular notes to Nathan, Mabel had a tendency to put him down. In December 1906, while Nathan was away recuperating after an accident and May was Acting Governor, Mabel wrote to Nathan, 'Mrs May was enquiring of Mr May's historic speech the other day of me, and I assured her it was what the Germans call *haarstraubend* [hair-raising].'[14] And, about Isabel Slade's health, Mabel wrote, as she visited the invalid and had her children to tea, 'I fancy she has become nervous about herself, dear little woman.'[15]

It was how one amused the Governor, whom Mabel regarded so warmly that she wrote to him in April 1906, from Mountain Lodge, 'Friendship is a delightful gift of the gods, and both Frank and I hope that one begun out here at once, with you, may only grow stronger and deeper as year succeeds year.' It is possible to suggest, from how he later treated her, that Nathan did not reciprocate her feelings; it was not in him to do so.

In February 1907 the Duke of Connaught, King Edward VII's only brother, his wife, and daughter Alice, came to Hong Kong on an official visit. There were all sorts of engagements but the social highlight was obviously an intimate dinner for 45 guests at Government House on the sixth. Nathan had no wife; who should the Duke of Connaught take into dinner?

It is worth, here, looking at some examples of Hong Kong rules of precedence. Alexander Grantham, who was a mere cadet in 1925, though he was to become Governor after World War II, writes even of the inter-war years, 'In those days Hong Kong was very protocol-minded and the heads of firms and senior government officials were extremely conscious of their positions and demanded proper respect from their juniors which we dutifully gave.'[16] But the formal order of precedence — Governor, GOC, Admiral, Bishop, Chief Justice, Colonial Secretary, Attorney General — provides only a rough guide-line where wives were concerned. Certainly, seen from the top, it seemed to work more discreetly, and with warmth and courtesy. When William Des Voeux arrived as Governor in 1887, Marion did not at first accompany him. At his first reception he had 95 women to entertain and Mrs Cameron, wife of the GOC, acted as his perfect hostess, while her husband sent the regimental band. Des Voeux had earlier put a notice in the *Gazette* appraising the community of the help he was to receive.[17]

Nan Severn writes in 1921 of the delicacy displayed towards her as wife of the Colonial Secretary at her first big dinner party at Government House: 'H.E. took me in as bride in front of Lady Kirkpatrick and Mrs Bowden-Smith, the General's and Commodore's wives, who are really senior to me.'[18] But two weeks later Nan wrote, 'I was just going to dress when Lady Stubbs rang me up to say she was so overtired that she wasn't going to dine in public, and I was to act as hostess.'[19] And in June, for the King's birthday, there was a ball at Government House at which Lady Fitzpatrick was hostess, Lady Stubbs having developed dengue fever three days after the birth of a daughter in May.

On that evening of 6 February 1907, Sir Matthew Nathan, of course, took in the Duchess of Connaught; Helena May was taken in by Commodore Williams; Francis Piggott took in Mrs Williams. Mabel Piggott was taken in by General Maxwell and the Duke of Connaught took in the wife of Nathan's Private Secretary, Richard Ponsonby.

Can you imagine the frozen scene? Nathan's biographer suggests that what happened was a failure on the part of the Colonial Secretary, Henry May, to advise Nathan about protocol, and there may be an element of that in the Governor's choosing Mrs Ponsonby. But there is more to the incident than that: Mabel was expecting something else. The letter she eventually wrote to Nathan on the subject is too passionate and scrawled to make it quite clear what happened, but it must have gone something like this: Matthew Nathan had implied to Mabel, when the Royal visit was first mooted, that she would sit next to Connaught that evening. In the meantime, he had been persuaded out of it on the grounds of Mabel's 'unkindness' reported to him by people who were not her friends, such as the Ponsonbys, and since they were much more his friends than Mabel was, he had listened and changed his mind.

The Ponsonbys and other fairly junior military friends of theirs and Nathan's believed that they had been slighted on occasion by the wife of the Chief Justice. That was probably so; one can just see Mabel acting the *grande dame*. They reacted by being overtly rude to her, and so it became a vicious circle, which could have resolved itself because many of those involved were leaving the colony. But there was an opportunity to pay Mabel back. Nathan, perhaps genuinely convinced that Mabel had acted badly, was not averse to 'punishing' this overpowering woman married to a Chief Justice who was a constant thorn in his side. What is more, the Governor was comfortable with his Private Secretary's wife; he knew her well — she often accompanied him on tours and to prize-givings even when Ponsonby himself did not. With her sitting between him and the Duke of Connaught, he could turn to her when things got sticky with the Duchess and feel at ease.

A week after the dinner, Nathan wrote to Mabel saying that something she had said had been repeated to him and he would like to come and see her about it. In his diary he recorded that she was offended that the Duke had taken Mrs Ponsonby and not her into dinner and that he had to take action.[20] Mabel thought they had cleared the air at their meeting, but obviously they had not. She had gone too far, though what she had done can barely be pieced together, particularly since his diary suggests that she needed mollifying rather than berating. The day after the dinner, one of the newspapers reported that the Duchess and Princess Alice had tea with Lady Piggott at Mountain Lodge (where she was no longer living) so that they could enjoy the Peak. They travelled there in a 'specially decorated car'.[21] Did something happen between the ADC and Mabel when they reached the top? She writes of what she had told Nathan 'about the "staff" at the tram station'. And she pleads, in a letter that should never have been written, particularly not to a man such as Nathan, 'Allowing I am hot tempered and hasty *no chance* was given to allow of my recovering myself.'[22] On what occasion is not clear.

Perhaps even more pathetic than Mabel's twelve pages of self-justification, desperate hurt, and calls for fairness, followed by her temporary departure (already planned) from the colony, is her letter written between their talk and that long letter. In it she enclosed an article 'which I hope may modify your newly aggrieved doubts as to the methods and stability of the CNA [Colonial Nursing Association]. Forgive me,' she continues, 'for troubling you with this, but as I

worked for nine years to perfect every branch of the work
. . . [23] Where Francis Piggott stood in all this is only hinted
at by the fact that between Mabel's departure and Nathan's
own a few weeks later, the Chief Justice received an invitation to Government House, and refused it.

If a bundle of over-flowing letters from Mabel Piggott was
all that remained of that incident, it would hardly be worth
disinterring. But the letters that several women, and the
daughter of one of them, wrote to Nathan after he had been
posted to Natal disparage Mabel Piggott in a way that
Nathan must have encouraged, or they would not have
written thus. They also make it clear that his influence
created a milieu for his successor and his wife that was not
helpful, for all his 'compassionate' letter to Lady Lugard
when her niece died soon after her arrival.

Helena May wrote to Nathan of how her husband 'had
a letter from Lady Piggy and I am wondering how she and
Lady Lugard will get on'.[24] From K.P Stollard, Matron of the
Victoria Hospital, came a note of thanks for some beautiful
feathers, to which she added, 'What Lady Piggott will say
when she sees them, I do not know.'[25] Emily Hatton, in a
letter which must reflect previous conversations, wrote,

I wish I had some real spicey gossip to amuse you with but the
only news I have heard is that the (RE) Hope of the Piggies has
gone and engaged himself to quite an ordinary young lady of
Gibraltar (this is not a limerick) rejoicing in the still more ordinary
name of *Smith*!! I should love to hear Lady Piggy's tongue wag
on the subject . . . I must say I rather admire the young man's
pluck, don't you? I should have thought him too "mother pecked"
to have dared . . . [26]

Isabel Slade tells how she met Mabel in Cambridge
'looking rather a wreck I thought.' And goes on to say,

You have probably heard that Lady Lugard is busy improving our
frivolous minds, first by a course at Mothers' meetings at which
we all sat round and sewed waistcoats for our husbands (Signor
Volpicelli and Mr Dunn being only half women were allowed to
sit still and listen) while her ladyship read out loud 'Somebody's

Rise of Civilisation in Europe', quite above my head but I got a good deal of amusement out of it and then in the pauses we had scraps of useful information thrown to us such as that Euclid's system of mathematics is still taught in English schools and we had no idea how wonderfully they assist the reasoning powers, etc. etc. . . . [27]

In a later letter, Isabel writes of Sir Frederick Lugard, 'No one seems to think him worthy of description . . . he certainly doesn't look much and in defiance of proverbial wisdom *looks* do matter.' She continues, 'I think the reading society is in abeyance — at least I have heard nothing of it — and come across now no serious-minded women reading large tomes, which they slap to when the hands of the clock point 20 minutes. You see I am as bad as ever.'[28]

And so to Eleanor Hastings who writes to Nathan of the Lugards, 'He is really too retiring I think. She holds a sort of salon at all their parties with a circle of admirers listening to her theories on all kinds of subjects. She talks well of course, as you know, but one cannot call it conversation, as she appears to ignore other people's views.'[29]

The gossip, and the need to amuse Nathan with it, permeated downwards, so that soon Eleanor's young daughter Aileen was writing to him, 'Lady Lugard asked the whole class to tea at Government House, we were dreadfully afraid she would want us to read to her . . .'[30] And that in the same letter that tells how Aileen had just been bridesmaid to Flora Lugard's niece and the Lugards had taken her and the May girls on the new train.

The gossip at Nathan's court is superficially quite amusing, in a sad sort of a way; but there is more to it than that. One of the clichés of Hong Kong's history has been the exclusivity of women at the top. They were undoubtedly exclusive, in the way that other groups of women I have described were — because like finds it easier and more convenient to consort with like. The social importance of such groups, as I have suggested before, lay not so much in the divisions between them, but in the cohesiveness and, therefore, supportiveness, within each of them, in a particularly male-oriented society. The saddest part of the sagas that have been related is the destruction of that cohesiveness.

There is more to it than the loss of moral support between women. If one sees any merit in the deeds of Ladies Bountiful or Big Ladies — exclusive women at the top working together for the common good — that value during Nathan's governorship was eroded.

The Colonial Office would not have seen the issue in either of the above terms, but there is some evidence that they were aware that in one important respect Matthew Nathan fell down as Governor. When they chose his successor they could not fail to be aware of the stature of his wife, the former Flora Shaw; indeed, there is a revealing remark in the preliminary notes that Marjory Perham wrote for her biography of Frederick Lugard: 'It seems that a good woman was wanted in H. Kong and the appt was as much of *her* as of him.'[31]

How Flora was further to show her paces in Hong Kong will end the next chapter. As for her relationship with Mabel Piggott, I, too, would like to know how they got on. Flora had an imperial rather than an imperious air and I suspect there would have been mutual respect once Mabel had settled down. Unfortunately, Francis Piggott caused Frederick Lugard endless trouble until they both left in 1912.

Mabel lived until 1949, when she was 92, in her later years staying as full of character as ever but turning her enthusiasm for active sports into a passion for cricket. Her granddaughter, Diana, remembers visiting her in the Isle of Wight and how Mabel used to

sit on the verandah watching us play cricket on the lawn, guarded jealously by her small fierce Pekingese, Ting-a-ling. She was by then very crippled with arthritis and walked with crutches, but she still carried her head high and wore her hair in the Edwardian fashion of her youth. She used to read me *Lays of the Scottish Cavaliers* with great feeling in her sunny drawing room, surrounded by mementoes of her time in the Far East.[32]

CHAPTER EIGHTEEN

MISS MARTY
AND THE MARTINETS

*E*verything the twentieth century touched that had belonged to the nineteenth seemed to change colour and
shape; it is hard to imagine those acidic letters in the last
chapter being written even a decade earlier. The way Hong
Kong's education was recorded for posterity also changed
— from being the brave reports by missionary women sent
home to satisfy their committees and supporters, it becomes
the not-so-rosy memories of the girls who were taught.

The reports for public consumption in the *Female Missionary Intelligencer* were all sweetness and light — apart from
the odd death of a loyal Bible woman or promising pupil,
the odd plague which sent pupils scurrying back to their
permanent homes in China, or a typhoon that blew the roof
off; but the unpublished administrative version was not
always so sanguine.

Baxter Vernacular Schools

Miss Oxlad, a former governess, who arrived in Hong Kong
in 1864, aged 24, and left in 1876 to continue devoted service
in Japan, was no cypher. In 1876, there was an 'unhappy
difference' between the missionaries and Bishop Burdon over
the translation of the 'Divine Name' into Chinese which
threatened the future of the Baxter schools.[1] Then there was
the problem of the Government Inspector of Schools, Dr
Frederick Stewart, a secular disciplinarian, having 'an objec-

tion to doing business with ladies'.[2] But by and large, the Baxter Schools, teaching in the vernacular, flourished, with the help of a regular infusion of young missionary women. They all settled down to making a serious study of the language, difficult though they found it, before hoping that they were beginning to be just a little useful.

But it is Miss Margaret Johnstone's name that deserves to live on. Born in Tasmania of Irish parents, she had been a girl in Hong Kong, a pupil, even, at Miss Baxter's school. At 25, in 1874, she became a missionary teacher with the FES, moving to the CMS in 1899 when the FES ceased its activities, and she devoted herself to the Chinese community until 1907, dying in England in 1909, aged only 58, after some years of illness. She opened several vernacular day schools on the Island, in Kowloon, and, after 1898 (and the treaty with China), in the New Territories, as well as running the Baxter Mission. By 1904 there were eight and the missionary teachers superintended them through weekly visits.

Fairlea

The Baxter Mission was based at Fairlea, a large house in Bonham Road. It was a centre for women's work — sending out Chinese Bible women into the community, visiting Chinese families, and visiting women in hospital and prison. Now Fairlea was also to become a school. By 1880, the original English language school that Mrs Smith had initiated — the Diocesan Native Female Training School — having already mutated, now no longer accepted girls and became the English language Diocesan Boys' School. Miss Johnstone therefore took over the education of the girls that remained there, moving them to Fairlea in 1892. In 1895 there were 35 Chinese girls there, 13 Eurasians and five Europeans. In 1904 some Chinese girls were still being taught there in a way to enable them 'faithfully to do their duty in that station of life in which God had placed them'.[3] In the intervening period, however, the whole scholastic endeavour based at Fairlea, excluding the vernacular schools, had begun to separate into three strands: the Diocesan Girls' School, St Stephen's Girls College and Heep Yunn.

Diocesan Girls' School

The Diocesan Girls School (DGS) came into being in 1899, moving 20 European and Eurasian girls from Fairlea to rambler rose-covered Rose Villas in Bonham Road, with Miss Elizabeth Skipton BA as headmistress, and Miss Maud Hawker as her assistant. Maria Fincher, a very young orphan girl at the school from 1904, remembers a story of a robber trying to choke Miss Skipton and Miss Hawker saving her. Miss Skipton is described by Maria as 'a lovely person, but a martinet ... nice looking, with deep set piercing blue eyes'.[4] Jean Gittins (née Ho Tung) remembers her as 'a dedicated woman who tempered a stern discipline with the warmness of a kind and gentle heart'.[5] She was also cat-mad and reigned for 22 years, until 1921.

The school expanded slowly, growing from 36 girls to 83 in 1905 and 150 in 1925. Its girls were expected to become — if they did not marry — nannies or teachers of small children. By 1912, it had to move over to Kowloon — where it still is today — and Maria Fincher mentions morning prayers, with sleepy heads meekly lowered and the prayer: 'Dear God, please help us to pay this awful, dreadful debt of $1,300.'

In 1913, Miss Janet Fernie conducted an experiment into new Montessori teaching methods, using little girls who had been in the school for several months, and wrote up her experiment in an appendix to the education section of the 1913 Administrative Report. But what Maria Fincher remembers of her is her height and her elegance and her engagement to a drunken lawyer who gave her an engagement ring of two crossed pearls, before breaking it off and marrying a woman with a poodle which had anti-social habits in the lobby of the Hong Kong Hotel.

Miss Ferguson, who was headmistress from 1921, was not liked by Maria, whereas Jean Gittins suggests that she was well-loved. Her successor on her death in 1925, Miss Sawyer, was even less liked by both Maria and Joyce Anderson (now Symons), a third Eurasian girl, who went to the school in 1926 and was later to become headmistress herself. Jean Gittins notes that it took Miss Sawyer a while to settle down when she arrived from Poona in 1922. She was at first 'high-handed', but after a particularly unpleasant incident, Miss Sawyer apologized and was forgiven, at least by Jean. Neither Miss Ferguson nor Miss Sawyer was qualified, and perhaps for that reason they behaved more unreasonably. The 12 European members of staff under Miss Sawyer were also untrained, although some of them were good teachers. Joyce Anderson Symons remembers Miss Sawyer in 1929: 'standing very rigid, with her blond, straight hair, she frightened us all'.[6]

Frightened those young girls may have been but those who succeeded in life, like Maria, Jean, and Joyce, proudly stood their ground. Miss Gibbins, who was the headmistress when the Japanese invaded in December 1941, and who was interned in Stanley Camp where she successfully ran a school, was universally loved and admired, and it was under her that Joyce Symons started her teaching career in the school, though she learned about racial prejudice in the staff room, as well.

St Stephen's Girls' College

Another school had grown up in Fairlea's shade, one started by Winifred Carden in a room at Breezy point, with eight pupils under ten. St Stephen's Girls College, with 31-year-old Miss Carden as its headmistress, formally opened in 1906. In 1923, Fairlea and St Stephen's were to move into shared premises — an 'uneasy' partnership imposed on them by government allocation of land and lack of CMS funds for separate buildings — which endured until 1937. While Fairlea, which was to move to Kowloon and become part of Heep Yunn, was for Chinese girls, taught in Chinese, St Stephen's benefactors, men such as Sir Kai Ho Kai, educated in Britain (and in memory of whose English wife Alice he had earlier founded a hospital) saw the need for the creation of a pool of wives for Chinese boys who had been educated in Britain or at the boys' school, St Stephen's College. Over the years, it was very much a school in which governors' wives would interest themselves: Lady May allowing the school to use the tennis courts at Mountain Lodge on certain days of the week, and Lady Stubbs helping with a new site.

Miss Middleton-Smith, the first headmistress to be vividly remembered, arrived to teach in about 1914, accompanying her brother who had come to join the University staff. She became headmistress in 1920. Ellen Tsao (now Ellen Li CBE, LLD, JP, wife of Dr Li Shu-pui) arrived from Vietnam, via school in Amoy, in 1924, with attitudes that were not those of Hong Kong. She found Miss Middleton-Smith 'very British'. She was tall, austere-looking, 'always well-dressed and elegant, in silk, white and brown, not flashy, and nicely cut'. Miss Middleton-Smith, while being something of a martinet, liked beautiful things. She liked to take four or five of her loveliest boarders in their last year to dances at the University, dressed in long skirts, silk, of course.[7]

Miss Middleton-Smith was followed, in 1929, by Miss E. S. Atkins, who put the girls into uniform. She was a missionary, red-faced, stooped, who had come out to the school in 1919 as a geography teacher and while not so good to look at, she was better loved. Miss Atkins was interned in Stanley during the War and returned to the school after it, retiring in 1949.

St Paul's Girls' College

Another missionary school that grew up as a twin of a boys' school was St Paul's Girls' school. Miss K. Stewart, who had helped Miss Carden in the early days of St Stephen's was responsible for this girls' school which started in a small way in Elgin Street in 1914 and later, in 1923, moved to Caine Road, and then, in 1925, to Kennedy Road. By that time it had a Chinese headmistress, Dr F.C. (Katie) Wu, who was still there, with an MBE, when it became St Paul's Girl's College in 1930. Kathleen Stewart had, meanwhile, married

E.W.L. Martin. From Stella Benson's description of her following dinner there in 1922 one picks up her attitude towards missionaries which is elsewhere in her diary expressed even more strongly:[8] 'Mrs Martin is a very obvious bright chaste type of ex lady teacher in missionary schools . . . it was a rather sticky missionary kind of dinner.'[9] A similar antipathy existed elsewhere in the community and contributed to the conflicts in the education system which have already been discerned.

Belilios School

Meanwhile, side by side with what were essentially missionary and private schools,[10] there was a government school for girls. In 1888, when Ernst Eitel, then Inspector of Schools, first suggested the idea, the missionary schools for girls were mainly teaching in Chinese, after the unhappy experience of teaching them English in earlier days. He proposed a school, similar to the Central School for boys, where girls would be taught in English.

The first headmistress, Miranda Mann, arrived in 1890 and opened the school with 20 pupils, which quickly rose to 45 and necessitated new premises. A Jewish merchant and philanthropist, E.R. Belilios, who felt strongly about the education of women, stepped in and Belilios School was opened in 1893. By 1898 it had 539 pupils, of whom 233 were British. The growth in the number of women teachers working for the government is also indicative of change; in 1904 there were three, in 1940, 33.[11]

Of the Belilios headmistresses, Nora W. Bascombe, who arrived at the school in 1922 (after 8 years at the DGS) and became principal in 1939, is best captured by her successor's 'in memoriam' of 1949. Miss Thom started, 'Miss Bascombe had a sincere love of humanity though at times she had a contrary way of showing it.'[12] For Miss Bascombe, in order to hide her 'real softness of heart,' had to cultivate 'an abrupt manner'. The rest of the obituary is panegyrics. Miss Bascombe, too, was interned in Stanley camp.

Miss Marty started teaching at Belilios School, aged 33,

in 1929. She was a member of a French mercantile family established in Hong Kong and Indo-China in the previous century. Stella Benson writes rather enigmatically of her in her diary on 20 June 1930, '[Met] a Madame Marti — a truculent looking thin young woman perhaps rather rarely studioesque (rarely so for Hong Kong).' What she means by 'studioesque' in describing a woman who taught art and was a painter herself, you can guess as well as I.

It is from an article that Michelle Marty contributed to the Belilios *School Journal* twenty years later that one gets a real feeling of the school and, indeed, Hong Kong at that time. She describes the environs of Gough Street where the school then was, with all the vibrant traditional Chinese urban life around, and goes on to discuss the static nature of Chinese traditional 'art', as opposed to the life and grace of the products of Chinese street artisans.

To the east was the European prostitutes' area but she does not, understandably, mention these establishments which were rather obvious, if only for their fine red curtains; they were, after all, on their way out. But in 1894, when the school was new, two women visiting Hong Kong to collect information about the trafficking in Chinese women prostitutes, Mrs Elizabeth Andrew and Dr Katharine Bushnell, noted of the 'fine new building of the Girls High School' that it was 'within five minutes walk' of brothels, 'glaringly numbered', the 'huge figures eight or ten inches high, of red on a white background'. As they said, the school children could not fail to see the numbers nor the prostitutes 'sitting conspicuously on their balconies'.[13]

Of her pupils, and one of her colleagues, Michelle Marty wrote,

At first all the faces in the school seemed strangely alike; they were copies of a single image. Eyes cast to the ground, the girls muffled in silence on the soft pads of their slippers, one had the exasperating impression of treading the same corridor; the only relief was a needlework mistress with crushed 'lily' [bound] feet stumbling about and swaying in a sort of awkward grace. There were no cars in that part of town, girls were carried in palanquins with drawn curtains like deities on a floating fairyland, their eyebrows shaved off and replaced by a finely pencilled black arch, and their glossy hair neatly plaited.[14]

Michelle Marty's memories of those earlier days confirm what Stella Benson suggests, that she was sensitive, literary and intelligent. The memories of some girls suggest that not all teachers were so gifted, and Stella's own experiences as a teacher for one term at the Diocesan Boys' School are not likely to change anyone's opinion. One should bear in mind Stella's finely-honed pen and the fact that the better women teachers probably went to the girls' schools where their jobs had some sort of status.

Stella explained her own teaching on 16 February 1920: 'I am to teach a class of 40–50 Chinese boys, on a variety of subjects ranging from the life of Christ to elementary scientific experiments.' The school was badly run and everyone suffered from that. As for her colleagues, Stella wrote:

The other teachers are flat stale trivial women: a grey worn voluble person who quotes Hubby and kiddies all the time, my Miss Fiddes [an acquaintance from Helena May], at this institute entirely unimaginative and unambitious but more refined than the others, a Mrs Thompson who says she is a bundle of nerves and so sensitive and clasps her heart elaborately when a pin drops, and quotes her doctor, Mrs Connor, pretty and spoilt and second rate but, smiley at least . . .[15]

The University of Hong Kong

In 1912, the principal of St Stephen's College, Miss Carden, asked the University of Hong Kong if it would admit girls. The answer was no. The University had just opened and its creation reintroduces Flora Lugard to the story.

While Stella Benson, as an intellectual, was unhappy and frustrated in Hong Kong, Flora Lugard found a way of sailing through or above the fact that the colony was not a centre of intellectual stimulation. She found something constructive to do with her intellect, while at the same time enjoying a married and domestic life that had not been hers until she was fifty (1902). Being an imperialist, as well, she managed to combine the happiness of her new marriage with her gubernatorial duties and create out of them a Government House of some style.

In many ways, Flora Shaw Lugard ignored her past, to a degree that is quite disconcerting when one reviews what that had been. The story I tell in the Preface epitomizes it. A woman who had not only been a journalist on *The Times* (of London) in the days before women journalists, but who had also headed their Foreign and Colonial desk which she expanded and developed, and who was an expert on Africa to whom experts deferred, was satisfied now, between 1907 and 1912, with holding large and successful social gatherings at a Government House she had redecorated and refurnished.

As previous chapters have shown, she did more than that. She was a Big Lady *par excellence*. Whatever Isabel Slade and Eleanor Hastings may have spitefully written of her, Helena May's reaction and assessment is more likely to be the prevailing one:

Lady Lugard is very charming I think and has such a sweet face. I like her very much indeed and am quite sure we are all very lucky in having such a nice governor's wife ... [she] is the most wonderfully energetic person I ever met — she is always doing something. Twice a week regularly she and the ADC visit either schools, or soldiers' wives and families — and she is going to have all the schools, and soldiers' and policemen's children to tea in turn.[16]

Helena May did not know with what foresight she spoke when she added, 'She must be much stronger than she looks, to do so much without being tired.' Flora was not stronger than she looked, and her health was to collapse several times during Lugard's governorship of Hong Kong, necessitating long stays in England and major operations. The ADC whom Helena mentions was Captain Taylor, whom Flora's niece, Hilda Brackenbury, was about to marry. Unfortunately, Hilda died of blood poisoning a few weeks after her wedding and left a hole in Flora's life that could never be filled. But she had one demanding and imperial task yet to tackle: a university for Hong Kong.

The University of Hong Kong is always called Sir Frederick Lugard's creation. At the time it was known in Colonial Office circles as 'Lugard's pet lamb'. It was no more popular a proposition among most of the taipans of the colony; Lugard had to fight for it. But it was by no means only his fight and without Flora at his side with her broadsword, it would not have been won. Lugard proved that when he wrote to Flora in December 1909: 'All my other public schemes have been my own ... this is yours. I took it up at your strong instigation ... If it goes through to success the credit will be yours.'[17]

That Flora was interested in education, in its broadest sense, has already been illustrated. She had not had a university education herself — even by 1909 few women had — but she was highly self-educated, in the way that many notable nineteenth- and early twentieth-century women were. In her early youth she had access to the Royal Artillery Library at Woolwich, where her father served, and by 13 she already had responsibility for the education of her siblings — she was one of fourteen. Later she was to tutor the children of family friends, while her own reading was given more direction by friendship with John Ruskin. Her first writing, a children's novel, was published in 1877. But her development, encouraged by George Meredith, who was interested in the intellectual equality of women and men, soon led her to a course of reading in history, economics, and politics, and thus to international affairs and journalism.

Flora was not 'charitable' in the traditional sense, in the way that the Big Ladies were although, or because, she had had experience of social conditions and charity work in London slums. She was more interested in change. As a journalist, she had been in a position to effect it through influence; now the plan for the university would be part of a similar ethos. No doubt, too, she saw it as a suitable monument to her husband's time in Hong Kong — a time which he neither welcomed nor enjoyed after the freedom and challenge of Nigeria. It is possible only to reconstruct

Flora's motives (rather than present them) because her husband, while helping her first biographer, following her death in 1929, did not allow her access to Flora's papers and on his death in 1945, gave instructions that they be destroyed. Among his own massive papers, only a few pages of her diary, hardly more than engagements, remain of her time in Hong Kong.

Flora was used to the mechanisms of power in Whitehall, and her enforced visits to London allowed her to lobby the Colonial Office. It was undoubtedly her intervention that prompted the crucial cable from Lord Crewe allowing the university to go ahead. In Hong Kong itself, her charm and intelligence and the social life she had created gave her unique opportunities. The impetus for the project existed, in the sense that increasingly the Chinese saw the English language as access to economic power; a university was the obvious consummation of the development of education. But it was not Chinese philanthropists who responded initially to the Lugard proposition; it was H.N. Mody, a sickly and elderly Parsee who took warmly to Flora; their relationship was the key. Mody offered to finance the university, but only partly, and he fixed a time limit for the rest of the money to be found. In London, Flora went round the offices of the men who ran the major Hong Kong companies and put the facts and arguments to them across their desks. Even so, the money was not enough and more effort was needed, particularly from Flora. As well as her lobbying, she pulled strings to get Mody an encouraging knighthood.

When the foundation stone was laid, in March 1910, Flora was in London having an operation. In his speech Mody paid warm tribute to her and after the event Lugard wrote, 'You will like dear old Mody's reference to you — he almost worships you, dear old man — when he read that part in a voice of feeling and an almost reverential tone, there was great applause.'[18]

The University was opened two years later, but it was only for male students. That would not have impinged upon Flora. She was no feminist, but was in the tradition of women who succeed themselves and see no incongruities. In 1916 she was made a Dame for her war work on behalf of refugees, an award very much in her own right, but she was against the campaign for female suffrage — a symbol of women's release generally into the public arena. Ironically, the law giving the vote to women over 30 was overshadowed in 1918 by World War I, a tragedy which released women in Britain more practically from life lived only in private.

After the first request for admission to the University in 1912 by St Stephens College for Girls, further requests followed but it was not until 1921 that a breach was forced. Not surprisingly, when Rachel Irving, daughter of the Director of Education, wanted to go to the University, wheels were put in motion. An application went to the Attorney General and a resolution was formulated. After a great deal of debate, the University Council passed it and women were admitted, Rachel being the first. It was Bella Southorn who in 1928, aroused interest in the building of a women's hostel; Michelle Marty later became its warden, as well as teaching French at the University.

The first Hong Kong-born woman graduate was Irene Hotung (now Dr Irene Cheng) and the first woman in the medical school was her sister Eva Ho. Eleanor Thom, later headmistress of Belilios School, graduated in 1926, and later gained a doctorate in education. By now women teachers were increasingly not only university graduates but also educationalists.

Those Chinese women graduates of the 'twenties and 'thirties were not only an example of a radically different life for Chinese women, they were also to play their part strongly in effecting continuing change. Earlier in the century, however, as Part IV shows, it had been a new kind of expatriate woman who provided the momentum for change. They were different from the missionaries in that it was reform they were after, not relief. They were different from the Big Ladies because they were activists rather than patrons and often their struggle was also partly against the

Establishment. It did not make any difference to women, European or Chinese, that there was no democracy in the colony — their protest, by virtue of the less obvious restraints on their sex, was essentially part of their private life.

IV
DEAR COMRADES

CHAPTER NINETEEN

MRS LITTLE
AND BIG FEET

'Instead of a hop, skip, and a jump, with rosy cheeks like the little girls of England,' wrote Alice Little of many six-year-old girls in China, 'the poor things are leaning heavily on a stick somewhat taller than themselves, or carried on a man's back, or sitting sadly crying'.[1] She was describing the process whereby little girls' feet were tied up tightly in long bandages so that over a period of years they became bent inwards to form a shape only three inches long known, by those who found them beautiful, as 'golden lilies'.

Alicia arrived in China in 1887 and she was to campaign successfully against bound feet both there and in Hong Kong. It would be a mistake, however, to think that no one, foreign or Chinese, had previously shown concern. Missionaries had worked against the custom in their own areas from the time they arrived in China. Mrs Smith, wife of the Bishop of Hong Kong, wrote in 1862 of her pity for some of the suffering girls at the Diocesan Native Female Training School and even told of how one girl who wanted to have her feet unbound had 'obtained her father's permission but the mother is decidedly opposed to her wishes'.[2] Mothers were concerned that their daughters, rendered ugly, would not find husbands.

Henrietta Shuck, twenty years earlier, described how the mother of one of her girls bound her daughter's feet when she was already in her teens, in order to satisfy the demands of a prospective bridegroom's family.[3] But Lydia Smith found that boys who had received a Christian education preferred girls with natural feet.

As early as the Taiping Rebellion, feet were unbound in those areas of Southern China where it had most success but binding still remained widely prevalent elsewhere in all classes of Han Chinese, as opposed to the foreign Manchu ruling class; indeed, attempts by Manchu emperors over the centuries to outlaw it were ignored.

In Hong Kong before 1841 bound feet among mainly fishing people was not customary, but as soon as the influx from China started, it became so and, in spite of the number of missionaries in such a small area, it continued. Not only did Michelle Marty's colleague in the late 1920s still 'stumble and sway' on her 'crushed lily feet', but even today it is not impossible to see an elderly woman whose feet were bound well over half a century ago.

Opposition to the custom was not only on the grounds of aesthetics or knowledge of the dreadful pain some little girls experienced during the long process, and the pain a fifty-year-old woman could still feel, as her feet bled from too much standing. From a medical point of view, too, bound feet could lead from suppuration to gangrene and amputation, and all sorts of pelvic disorders and diseases.

As a writer interested in women's issues and fascinated by China, Alicia Little made it her business to find out all about bound feet. Not being a woman doctor who could treat the victims, nor a missionary who could persuade individual women to unbind their own feet and not bind those of their daughters through Christian conviction, she decided to campaign publicly to eliminate the custom throughout China.

Alicia and her campaign were well suited. Born in Madeira in 1845, the youngest daughter of Calverley Bewicke of Leicestershire and Mary Hollingsworth, she was educated by her father. Finding herself with little taste for the triviality of the social life she was expected to enter in England, she became a novelist with a sharp and critical eye, as well as serving on several philanthropic committees. In 1885, she published *Mother Darling* in which she advocated reform of the law concerning the custody of children — to establish the rights of mothers and their children. Archibald Little, whom she married in 1886, when she was 41 and he was 48, was an Old China Hand. He had arrived in Hong Kong in 1859 as a tea taster for Siemssen and Company but left them in 1862, after a spell in Canton and Shanghai, to set up as an independent merchant, first in Kiukiang and later in Shanghai. He was also a pioneer in opening up steam communication on the upper Yangtze. His work enabled Alicia to travel widely, to write and to publish. He gave her campaign his full support.

Alicia's description in *Intimate China* (1899) of how the Natural Foot Society felt its way forward is as touching as her exposé of the details and history of bound feet is saddening, even sickening. She leavens further details of the campaign, including her visit to Hong Kong in 1900, with humour in *Land of the Blue Gown* (1912). With her husband's contacts she could make a start but buttonholing 'Tsai, the good-natured Governor of Shanghai' across the Chief Justice's dining table was not enough.

In 1895, therefore, Alicia called together ten immediately responsive foreign women in Shanghai to form a committee. They knew their ambitious objective; how to proceed was not quite so simple. None of them spoke or read Chinese though they had access to those who did. Their first move was to circulate a poem written by a woman of Hankow and translated by a missionary into English. They also came upon a tract written by another missionary and they tailored it to their purpose, but how should they direct propaganda into the Chinese community? How, for example, should that tract be translated — into Shanghainese dialect to make it more accessible, perhaps? But women could not read. Were they aiming at women or men? Even discussing the subject in public was risqué; it was, after all, to do with sensuality. In the end they decided, fortunately as it turned out, to translate into the 'dignified Wenli of the Chinese classics.'[4] One mandarin responded to the extent of releasing his own pent up feelings on the subject into an even more elegant tract more accessible to his fellows, and copies of that were delivered by the Natural Foot Society to 10,000 students going up to Chungking for the Mandarin examination.

At the same time, elegant, bound-footed women attended a drawing-room meeting. All agreed that foot binding was 'no use.' But, they added, it could only be given up 'by degrees'.[5] The committee drew up a petition intended for the Emperor, whose mother ruled in all but name, which was signed by nearly every foreign woman in the Far East. They never knew if it was received but, in 1902, along with other delayed reforms, a decree was to be passed outlawing footbinding. Some suggest that it was a sop to the foreign women in Peking whom the Dowager was trying to cultivate following the Boxer rebellion, but such a law in itself, as past imperial decrees had proved, would have been ineffectual without the campaign that began to build up steam in the late 1890s among Chinese women and men, including viceroys of provinces. Some upper-class Chinese women came forward and started a non-Christian school which required its pupils to unbind their feet; at the same time, 1,000 women were addressed in a silk factory by foreign and Chinese women.

In 1900, the year that she was vice-president of the Women's Conference in Shanghai, Alicia set off on a campaign tour of Southern China, Hong Kong and Macau. She spoke, through an interpreter, at public meetings in several major towns and thousands of leaflets were taken home from them. In Canton she managed to gain an interview — in spite of the British Consul — with the influential Viceroy Li Hung-chang (and later wrote his biography). As she left his presence, having persuaded him to write a suitable message on her fan to display at other meetings, he grumbled, 'You know if you unbind the women's feet you'll make them so strong, and the men so strong too, that they will overturn the dynasty.'[6]

And so Alicia arrived in Hong Kong. There had been some attempt by Europeans to persuade her that there were no bound feet in the colony. They were certainly not obvious but that was because small-footed women left their homes only rarely, and then in a covered chair. But Alicia knew better. In Canton she had been taken to meet two daughters of the biggest Chinese property owner in Hong Kong. Laden with jewels, sitting almost in the dark, their feet bound, they had shrunk from their first foreign woman. On the steamer from Canton, the captain had told Alicia how women 'were carried on board pick-a-back by their men servants, just as sacks might be carried'.[7] Thus, while Alicia held a well-attended public meeting for Chinese men, and addressed the boys school, Queen's College, she knew that she must somehow talk to the women as well.

Mention of foreign women's activities in Hong are rare in accounts of its history, but one writer who does mention Alicia Little's visit mocks the naivety of her address to the 500 Queen's College boys. He writes of how 'the tall English lady (tightly bound at the waist be it said) lectured them on this indelicate subject'.[8] It is unlikely that Alicia, who expressed herself forcefully on the unsuitability of restricting European fashions being maintained in the East, would have been 'tightly bound' on this occasion. Moreover, it is certainly a red herring to equate, as was often done, the wasp waist with bound feet.[9] The former is qualitively different and has choice, age and impermanence as ingredients.

Alicia was hot and bothered when she arrived at the meeting, her chair-carriers having lost their way to the College and made her late. She had to overcome that and any embarrassment she may have felt, for she was convinced that the attitudes of the boys must be challenged, that they had to stop wanting wives with bound feet, before mothers could stop crippling their daughters. And if only ten of those youths — who came from China as well — were mature enough to understand what she was saying, it had been worth her standing exposed, perhaps to ridicule, on that platform.

Her meeting with the Chinese women of Hong Kong was to be rather different. For a start, Edith Blake, the governor's wife, offered to hold it at Government House where no Chinese woman had ever before been invited. An embryonic branch of the Natural Foot Society had been set up with Lady Blake's daughter Olive as its secretary.

How the two Blake women had become involved is not clear. It is possible to recreate just a faint impression of the governor's wife. From the biography of her husband's successor, Frederick Lugard, it seems that Government House during Edith Blake's time was a bit dowdy, but Edith was not without an appreciation of beauty, at least in its natural surroundings. She not only sent plants from wherever her husband was posted to the Botanic Gardens at Kew, in London, but she also painted Hong Kong and Chinese plants. One of them, an oak with a particularly long acorn, was named after her *Quercus edithae* at Kew.[10] Is it too far-fetched to suggest that her love of nature attracted her to the campaign to promote natural feet for women?

Whatever the reason, she spared no effort that day at Government House, including arranging for the route the guests would take to the ballroom to be lined with shrubs and plants, the way the Chinese like things. The organizers had sent out 70 invitations and invited husbands to a function in a separate room to encourage the women to attend but the ballroom looked very big. The Admiral's wife said bravely that it would not matter if no one came. Edith Blake responded, 'Oh, some are sure to come, and we'll have them in the drawing room and shut up the ballroom, if they're very few.'[11]

By some mistake, the guests' sedan chairs were left outside the gate and so, in their highly embroidered silk, they hobbled and tottered on the arms of their *amahs* to the ballroom until it was full and there were no more seats. The *amahs*, then, were asked to stand, while small daughters, some of them already with bound feet, sat on the floor. Forty seven women joined the Natural Foot Society at the meeting and one showed how she had already begun to unbind her feet, an excruciating but often successful process. Afterwards there was tea and cake in the drawing room with the Bishop's wife, Mrs Hoare — brought up in China — chatting in Mandarin, and Miss Johnstone and Miss Eyre in Cantonese.[12]

If Edith Blake and Alicia Little had not known each other before that meeting, they were friends thereafter. Later in

1900, Edith accompanied her husband on an unofficial trip through China to Peking, the first Hong Kong Governor to make such a journey, let alone a governor's wife. In Shanghai Edith visited Alicia. In an unpublished account of her trip Edith Blake writes of how the Yamen, or provincial administrator, Jao-tui had said to Alicia, 'Till now China has had but one Kun Jam [Kun Yam, Goddess of Mercy] but now you are the second Kun Jam.'[13]

No doubt Alicia was gratified — she was not beyond a little self-promotion in her writing; but she cared greatly for the well-being of women and children. After her return to England, where she was soon widowed, she continued with similar work, campaigning with Mrs Pankhurst and, as we shall see, with Clara Haslewood on behalf of *mui tsai*. She survived her husband by 18 years, and died at 81 in 1926, still travelling almost until her death.

Alicia would have liked the story, and perhaps read it in the *Female Missionary Intelligencer*, that came from Kiukiang in 1893 following the unbinding of her feet by a Mrs Huang. That summer her husband said to her, 'If you will insist on having big feet, why don't you go out and work in the fields.' 'I am willing to do so,' she replied, 'if you will bind your feet and stay in the house.'[14]

It was not only women's feet that were unbound by the campaign that Alicia Little set rolling. In 1908, the Natural Foot Society in Shanghai was taken over by Chinese women; the Revolution of 1911, in which they continued to find a voice, was only three years away. It is likely that the May Fourth Movement, begun in China in 1919, with its feminist component, influenced the decision in 1921 for the University of Hong Kong to admit women. With unbound feet and increasing education, Chinese women in Hong Kong, too, were to throw off the shackles of the past. Initially, as the next chapter continues to show, it was with the help of foreign women, but increasingly they made their own way.

CHAPTER TWENTY

MRS HASLEWOOD
AND THE *MUI TSAI*

'Lady Smale has already given money for the support of a child who had been a slave,' reported Miss Johnstone in 1881, and continued, 'She was most cruelly treated by her mistress, burned and bruised and her ankle bone broken by a blow.'[1]

The *mui tsai* system was another Chinese custom that upset foreign women, one that missionaries chipped quietly away at, as they did with foot-binding, expressing distress among themselves and providing relief. It was not unknown for a little girl to be given into the care of missionaries and then be taken back by her family to be sold.[2]

Girls tended to be sold — usually using a professional intermediary or 'pocket mother' — because of some tragedy or hardship in the family or even to pay wedding or funeral expenses. There was nothing traditionally reprehensible about letting your daughter go into a family who could afford to keep her; in return, she would give them her services. The daughter of a rich man might, for example, on her sixteenth birthday, be given a nine-year-old girl who would wait on her and bring her luck. Tragedy and hardship were rife in China; everyone benefitted from the transaction.

Often, no doubt, the girl was treated well enough, though today one would look at the psychological effects of being thus rejected by her own family and taken into another where she had an ambiguous status — part servant, part family; *mui tsai* meant, literally, 'little younger sister' — a euphemism used in southern China for the Mandarin *pei nu*, slave girl. The tradition was that, on reaching maturity, a suitable husband of her own class would be found for the girl, as one would marry off one's own daughter.

Often, however, *mui tsai* were badly treated, sometimes brutally, particularly in families that were not much better off than the one which had sold its child. Some were sold into prostitution by their new family — and it was a constant threat to ensure good behaviour; though the institution was sometimes excused as needed to save girls from having to become prostitutes. Some went the same way direct from their 'pocket mother', and that will be elaborated upon in the next chapter. Sometimes *mui tsai* became concubines, with the status of a subsidiary wife. As Maria Jaschok shows in her exploration of the rump of the *mui tsai* system, *Concubines and Bondservants* (1989), a concubine could even oust a number one wife from her position of power and privilege within the family and inherit a man's wealth after his death, but usually only through manipulation or a power struggle which scarred the women concerned for ever, as well as the children from the different unions.

The status of *mui tsai* reflected the low status of women in general, which is why some Europeans could not see why there should not be *mui tsai*. As far as others were concerned, however, what singled *mui tsai* out particularly was the money given in exchange for a young girl and the freedom that, in Western terms, thus became lost; she belonged to her new family as a chattel. Both those who campaigned to abolish the *mui tsai* system and those who were simply aware of it called the young women and little girls 'slaves'.

The first time the issue was aired in public was in 1879 when Sir John Smale, whose wife's help is mentioned by Miss Johnstone, was Chief Justice of Hong Kong. Clara Smale, who obviously shared her husband's concerns, was 'a lady of fortune' whom the elderly judge, then a widower, had married in 1873. Several cases had come before Smale of trafficking in children and in the judgement he delivered, and thereafter, he spoke out strongly against the custom, castigating the existence of 10,000 slaves in the colony and emphasizing that the system was against the law, slavery having been abolished in 1835 and its abolition confirmed in Hong Kong law in 1845.[3] The Governor, Sir John Pope Hennessy, was, not surprisingly, sympathetic, but he was on his way out and most sectors of the community criticized the Chief Justice (who had been in Hong Kong since 1861) for his outburst against a perfectly sensible, long-established Chinese custom. One rocked the boat of Chinese custom and, therefore, the governability of Hong Kong's Chinese citizens, at one's peril.

Although the Po Leung Kuk had been founded by a group of leading Chinese men in 1878 as a reaction to the then prevalent kidnapping in China of women and children for prostitution in Hong Kong, the petition to the Government which instigated its establishment carefully did not interfere, as the Colonial Office noted, with the buying and selling of children for adoption or domestic service.

Sir John Smale was not regarded as a dignified Chief Justice by those who measured such things, but he is seen as something of an early hero by those Western women who later campaigned for the abolition of the *mui tsai* system, whether the girls concerned were domestic or brothel slaves. The first women to speak out in public — through their book *Heathen Slaves and Christian Rulers*, published in the United States and perhaps never seen in Hong Kong — were Mrs Elizabeth Andrew and Dr Katharine Bushnell. They came to Hong Kong (and to Singapore) in 1894 to look into the problem of increasing prostitution, through the trafficking of Chinese women and children, on the Western coast of the United States. Much earlier than the publication of their detailed book in 1907, they corresponded with the British Colonial Office and appear to have had some influence on attempts to strengthen protective legislation;[4] but though the various laws over the years meant stronger control of prostitution, they preserved 'domestic servitude' and had little effect on the women and girls bought or kidnapped for prostitution.

The anti-*mui tsai* campaign that followed World War I concentrated its fire on the *mui tsai* system in general, with an emphasis on domestic slavery and mistreatment, rather than on prostitution. Perhaps Miss Ada Pitts, as a CMS missionary teaching at Fairlea School, felt unable to raise that issue in public, though she was to become involved in 1921 in Sybil Neville-Rolfe's work on venereal disease and, as early as 1904, she and Lucy Eyre had opened their refuge for prostitutes. Certainly Miss Pitts was the first woman to raise the subject of *mui tsai* in a public forum; the first woman, indeed, to address the Church of England's Men's Society in Hong Kong. It was the first time, too, that women were in the audience. How she raised it, and what followed, is an interesting illustration of the difference between how a missionary felt able to work within limits, and how a lay-person felt compelled to campaign without constraint. As so often with campaigning, it was pressure from all quarters that brought results, but someone or something was necessary to provide the spark.

Miss Pitts bravely raised the issue in 1918 but it was one among several social evils that she discussed in her address at St Paul's College of 17 December. In a measured way, as a result of her 17 years experience in Hong Kong, she raised the subjects of child labour, in the form of carrying loads up Victoria's steep slopes, in factories, in the home, and then the insufficiency of schools and the will of parents to send their children. She found reasons for all those shortcomings. She suggested, for example, that 'in many instances the children in this state of domestic servitude were better cared for than in their own homes'.[5] But still, 'their position was by no means an ideal one'. Reasonably she put forward remedies.

Her address was well received and fully reported. The points in her paper were raised again at the next meeting of the society, and thereafter. Francis Bowley, a lawyer who had already raised some of the same issues and was well-informed about legislation in Britain, was prompted by Miss Pitt's suggestions to propose reforms to the Sanitary Committee — a committee rather more powerful than it might sound, and one on which Dr Alice Hickling also sat, as Acting Medical Officer of Health. In 1921 Miss Pitts was still addressing the Helena May on the suffering she had seen among 'these girls' though in some families *mui tsai* were 'very, very happy'.[6]

Mrs Haslewood now enters the story; she did not see the need for such delicacy. She came to Hong Kong, heard of the *mui tsai* system and its iniquities and wrote a strongly worded letter which was published in the local press. The flame was lit and Clara Haslewood and her husband were caught up in a campaign that was to last for 20 years, to govern, if not ruin, their lives and to be, in the end, successful.

The discussion and subsequent action which Mrs Haslewood's letter unleashed, dealt with the issues that Miss Pitts had so reasonably raised. The Child Labour Ordinance, for example, was enacted in 1922 separate from *mui tsai* legislation, after work by a subcommittee of which Alice Hickling was a member. Alice made a tour of inspection of factories, gathering information about the exploitation of child labour. The commission which followed the work of the sub-committee had Ada Pitts as a member. The Child Labour Bill which placed restraints mainly on poor families who depended on the work of their children was, however, less controversial than suggesting the abolition of the *mui tsai* system which mostly affected the influential and rich Chinese. Miss Pitts, not surprisingly, was to be an essential part of the anti-*mui tsai* campaign because of her accumulation of evidence.

Clara and Hugh Haslewood arrived in Hong Kong on 15 August 1919. He was a 33-year-old retired Lieutenant-Commander who had worked before the War in the Hydrographic Department of the Admiralty and was now appointed Superintendent of the Naval Chart Depot at Hong Kong. Clara (née Taylor) was 44 and had gone to France in 1914 as a VAD (nurse of the Voluntary Aid Detachment). They were hardly immature and inexperienced in the ways of inhumanity.

A couple of months after their arrival, a sermon was

preached at St John's Cathedral the text of which they read in the newspaper the following day. It talked of the *mui tsai* system and its cruelties. It was a revelation to Clara Haslewood, one to which she immediately reacted by inviting the chaplain to dinner and learning more. She then started to do her own research, so far as a newcomer to Hong Kong could. She talked to a Chinese Christian man who was well-informed, and she talked to Dr Alice Hickling who told her, too, of the child labour in factories. But when she tried to raise the question elsewhere, she was told, 'Oh, but you see the whole question of the mui tsai system is based on an old Chinese custom with which it would not be wise to interfere.'[7] She learnt, however, that it had been forbidden in China by law since the Revolution of 1911, even if this had not been successfully enforced.

Clara wrote her letter and visited several local newspapers with it. H.A. Cartwright, editor of the *Hong Kong Daily Press*, told her that he would print anything she wrote on the subject. Another editor was more ambivalent until she mentioned his own daughter, and he saw the point. On 4 November 1919, her letter was printed in four morning and evening papers.

The letter was quite temperate, considering the furore it caused and the accusations that were to be made against it. It did talk of 'child slavery' and a 'hideous stain' — but it was the British colony (not the Chinese community) and, by implication, its administration that she considered at fault for allowing such a thing to continue. She intended, she said, to raise the matter with the British government and she asked for the support of 'those who still retain the instincts of British men and women'.[8]

The following day, during a long talk with Alice Hickling, who had now practised in Hong Kong for over fifteen years, Clara was warned to 'Expect no sympathy from Hong Kong officials in your campaign.'[9] And Cartwright told her how Miss Pitts — who was on leave at the time — had worked for years to improve the position of the *mui tsai*. He also confirmed Alice Hickling's opinion: 'Home was the only place to obtain a hearing.'[10] That day, Clara sent two cables.

One went to Lord Lee of Fareham who had introduced and piloted through Parliament the White Slave Traffic Act of 1912, when he was Member of Parliament for Fareham where Clara lived. The other was to the National Vigilance Society with whom, in the past, she had worked for the abolition of the white slave traffic. She suggested that they get in touch with John Ward MP who had passed through Hong Kong in 1917 and knew all about the *mui tsai* system. Ward, anxious not to cause trouble during the War, had done no more than get in touch with the Colonial Office and asked the Trades Union Congress to do the same, assuming that this would be sufficient to rectify matters.

In her account of the campaign, published in book form in 1930, Clara says quite unemotionally that at the end of December she and her husband sailed for England 'with the fixed resolve to publish the state of affairs on our arrival'.[11] Readers will ask themselves how a naval officer could arrive to take up a job 7,000 miles away from home in mid-August and leave at the end of December because his wife had got a bee in her bonnet about cruelty to Chinese girls. It was not quite as simple as that.

Sir Reginald Stubbs, who had been Governor only since September, was incensed by Clara's letter or, as it was to be told to the Colonial Office, letters, to the press; the chaplain's published sermon is never mentioned. He assumed, perhaps naturally because his control over his own wife has already been illustrated, that the letter was really Lieutenant-Commander Haslewood's work, and he was not going to stand for it — a man drawing a government salary, what was more! Stubbs wrote to Commodore Gurner calling attention to Mrs Haslewood's letters and her husband's encouragement of her and asked 'if such conduct was in accordance with Admiralty regulations'.[12] Gurner showed the letter to Admiral Sir Alexander Duff who in his turn informed Hugh Haslewood that 'if his wife continued her campaign he would have to go home'.[13] Haslewood refused to restrain his wife. The formula now was that he should apply 'to proceed on urgent private affairs'. He complied with the formula, thus resigning and leaving for home.

Later Haslewood and a friend, Harold Begbie, were to take up the case of his forced resignation and Stubbs was to justify himself by lies and distortion. He talked of Clara's letters and of the 'annoyance' they caused to the local Chinese community. He said that the Chinese, knowing of and respecting Haslewood's official position, would pay more attention to what she wrote and, because Haslewood encouraged his wife, they would assume that the 'exaggerated and offensive attacks' were supported by the Government. In fact, many Chinese supported what she said and told her so. He pointed out, too, that Mrs Haslewood was 'well-known to be a person of unbalanced mind'.[14] The proof of that, he maintained, was her behaviour in November 1919 when she informed the police that a child was being cruelly ill-treated in a nearby Chinese house. The child, Stubbs explained, had been adopted by a 'very respectable' family from the German Foundling Home and was having a tantrum because she had been left behind at home.

As Clara tells the story, not knowing of Stubbs' explanation to the Colonial Office, it is naturally rather different. The incident occurred between the time that she read the chaplain's sermon and when she wrote her letter. Below the Haslewood's hotel was a house owned by a Chinese who had a 'number of these unpaid slave girls'. Among them was a girl of about eight. One Saturday evening they heard 'terrible screams, in which pain and terror were dominant'. Clara had previously heard her 'crying or moaning' but this was different. The hotel owner agreed with her.

The Haslewoods immediately went to a police station where the British sergeant on duty remarked, 'It is probably a slave girl.'[15] On the Monday, the Haslewoods reported the matter to the Chief of Police, the Secretary of Chinese Affairs, and the chaplain. In was that incident that spurred Clara to her researches.

Stubbs ended his explanation to the Colonial Office by saying that a few days after his letter to Commodore Gurner he was informed that 'Mrs Haslewood's health had entirely given way and that her husband was taking her back to England at once.'[16] Begbie, two years later, assured the

Colonial Office that Clara's health had had nothing to do with Haslewood's resignation, which was forced on him by the naval authorities.[17]

Back in England, the Haslewoods started their campaign. Colonel John Ward MP had been alerted and on 26 April 1920 he aired the subject he had previously been discreet about in the House of Commons, asking if the Colonial Office proposed to 'take immediate action to remove this stain upon the British name in the Far East'.[18] The same day, a letter from Clara appeared in the *Spectator*; on 4 August there was a letter from her in *The Times* and in the autumn she started a 'systematic round of all the societies we thought would be likely to take an interest in this cause of humanity and justice'.[19] Meanwhile, Hugh Haslewood was writing to the Colonial Office.

Not surprisingly, the letters to the Colonial Office were getting nowhere; the Haslewoods had been discredited by Stubbs and the colonial government. A letter of 5 March, for example, talks of 'Mrs Haslewood's feelings I am afraid rather overcoming her and she took up the matter in a somewhat baldheaded way.'[20] So well, indeed, did Stubbs do his work that when ten years later the matter was resurrected, Helena May wrote to Matthew Nathan about a leaflet a friend had been handed in Camberley, 'I seem to remember that Mrs Haslewood was rather hysterical over it all.'[21] Madness and hysteria, the well-known ways to muzzle dissidents and denigrate women.

A reader of *The Times*, Eleanor Walker, without knowing of that campaign of vilification, and prompted by Clara's August letter to the paper, wrote to Colonel Amery at the Colonial Office reminding him that he had served with her brother, enclosing *The Times* letter, asking for information and action, and adding, 'Having known Mrs Haslewood for a great number of years, I can vouch for her sincerity and level headedness.'[22] That was the first of many letters from Eleanor Walker and the first of many from other quarters even more influential.

At the same time, Haslewood himself struggled un-availingly to get his forced resignation recognized and to clear his name and Clara's of what he knew from Colonial Office statements were distortions concerning their activities and evidence. He was constantly fobbed off, accused of providing no evidence, merely generalizations, and told that they did not know what they were talking about.

But Clara had scored a major coup by interesting the Anti-Slavery Society in the *mui tsai* case. As she recorded her victory, 'Having satisfied themselves that our statements were borne out by the facts, they asked for a number of questions to be asked in Parliament.'[23] The campaign was much helped by the fact that the Colonial Office, receiving conflicting material from several quarters and unable to rationalize their policy, began to issue contradictory statements which Clara turned into useful pamphlets.

The Archbishops of York and Canterbury weighed in on the side of the campaign at the end of 1920, writing letters to the Colonial Office which could not be faulted as a means to destabilize bureaucrats under pressure. Now the heavy women were brought in. Margery Corbett Ashby, in her capacity as recording secretary of the International Woman Suffrage Alliance (Overseas Committee) wrote to the Attorney General of Hong Kong; Viscountess Gladstone rang her friend 'Edie' at the Colonial Office and followed it up with a letter on League of Nations Union paper. She was off to a League conference and did wish 'that Winston could do something soon'.[24] By now the campaign's evidence and arguments were both sophisticated and irrefutable. They mentioned the cruelties, naturally, but their arguments centred more on the fact that slavery existed in a British Colony when it had been abolished internationally and that as the *mui tsai* system had been made illegal under Chinese law — however difficult to implement — it could not be called an inviolate Chinese custom in Hong Kong.

Winston Churchill had been made Colonial Secretary in February 1921 and, with a new minister, pressure was increased. Dorothy Gladstone's letter was followed by one from Lilian Dawson, Secretary of the Fabian Society's Women's Group (25 June 1921), one from John Harris of the Anti-Slavery and Aborigine Protection Society (10 August

1921), and Kate Trounsen of the International Woman Suffrage Alliance (14 December 1921).

The campaign was given added weight that summer of 1921 by the formation in Hong Kong in August of the Anti-*Mui Tsai* Society, a Chinese group with a woman, Mrs Ma Ying piu, on the committee. One of its aims was to counterbalance the effects on the Hong Kong government of the Chinese Society for the Protection of *Mui Tsai*, which did not want abolition since many of its members had several *mui tsai* and concubines. By 1922 the Anti-*Mui Tsai* Society had nearly 1,000 members. In their manifesto they called attention to Clara Haslewood's lead, but two other letters must have been equally sweet to her. One came in April 1921 from Alicia Little. Alicia told Clara how she could not forget attending a dying man who had asked for her and how he said to her, 'Why ... did you not fight the slavery.' The thought still troubled her that she had chosen 'the lesser evil to combat'.[25] Alicia became involved in the *mui tsai* campaign. In November came a letter from Dr Katharine Bushnell in the United States, rejoicing in Clara's efforts to put down child slavery.[26]

Sustained by the support and the momentum the campaign had generated, Clara redoubled her efforts. She spoke at meetings held by many societies throughout the country. In Gosport she had an audience of 300 working women who rose to their feet as she finished and unanimously passed a resolution calling for reform. All such resolutions were filtered upwards.

In February 1922, an appeal to Parliament for an enquiry was issued by the Anti-Slavery Society and the Archbishops of Canterbury and York took that to their Convocation. On the 15th, the Anti-Slavery Society held a meeting at Caxton Hall in London, presided over by Viscountess Gladstone, at which 20 societies were represented.

No one knew how near Churchill was to breaking. The letter from Josiah Wedgwood MP of 19 February may have been the deciding factor. He scrawled just a few lines, 'This mui-tsai business is a small thing that you might put right with credit. It must go soon, and you should do it.'[27] On

21 February, Churchill wrote to his staff, 'I am not prepared to go on defending this thing . . . I do not care a rap what the local consequences are.'[28] He allowed a month of interchange between the Colonial Office and Government House in Hong Kong before he made a statement to the House of Commons that the *mui tsai* system was to be abolished.

It was not going to be an easy time for Sir Reginald Stubbs. He had to get a Bill through the Legislative Council that would be opposed. He wrote, 'We hold our position in Hong Kong because the Chinese are satisfied to be ruled by us so long as we do not make our yoke heavy.'[29] Not only was the Chinese bourgeoisie opposed to abolition, for obvious reasons, but the Bolsheviks in Canton, who had organized a general strike in Hong Kong the year before, were supporting abolition. As a sop to the opponents of abolition, when the Bill was read a second time, Stubbs dissociated himself from 'venomous attacks' by 'ignorant people at Home' and apologized for the 'unsubtle Western mind' which failed to understand the system.[30] But he got the Bill — to Regulate Certain Forms of Female Domestic Servitude — through; Hong Kong was, after all, no democracy. And Churchill got his kudos.

Harold Begbie, in his letter to the Colonial Office of 30 May about how the Haslewoods had been treated, summed up their personal victory when he wrote:

The facts are as simple as they are incontrovertible: 1. Mrs Haslewood opposed herself to a form of child slavery which leads in numerous cases to enforced harlotry. 2. The Governor did not sympathise with her action. 3. The Naval Authorities, moved by the Governor, told Lt-Commander Haslewood that he must restrain his wife or resign. 4. Under this pressure, Lt-Com. Haslewood resigned. 5. The Governor is ordered by Mr Churchill to put an end to this slavery under the British flag.[31]

They had won. But then everything went very quiet, until 1928.

It had been assumed that when the Bill was passed in 1923 the *mui tsai* system would start along the road to abolition. What no one knew was that Churchill's successor

had agreed with the Hong Kong government that Part III
— the registration and payment of *mui tsai* and control and
inspection of their conditions — was impossible to implement; they had his permission to leave it in abeyance.

In 1928, the Anti-*Mui Tsai* Society in Hong Kong, which
had itself almost gone into abeyance, woke up to the fact
that the situation was even worse than it had been previously. They sent evidence to the Haslewoods who passed
it to the Anti-Slavery Society. A letter from the Society's
Secretary, John Harris, appeared in the *Manchester Guardian*
on 16 January 1929 and was widely circulated. The campaign was on again, with a vigour reinforced by cynicism
about government promises.

On 4 February 1929, Question Time in the House of
Commons proved awkward for the Colonial Office when
several MPs asked a string of questions on the subject. They
included Miss Ellen Wilkinson (MP for Middlesborough, a
former organizer of the National Union of Women's Suffrage
Societies and currently National Organizer for the National
Union of Distribution and Allied Workers) Miss Susan
Lawrence (MP for East Ham North, who chaired the Labour
Party, and was Organizer of the National Federation of
Women Workers between 1912 and 1921) and Viscountess
Astor, the first woman MP (Sutton, Plymouth).

The Colonial Office was in an embarrassing position and
on top of their failure to implement Churchill's promise to
Parliament was the fact that Cecil Clementi, Governor of
Hong Kong, now wrote them a dispatch which they could
not publish since it resurrected arguments that were history,
disputing, for example, that a *mui tsai* was a slave. What
was almost worse, a General Election was coming up;
women now had the vote. A Colonial Office memorandum
talked of the 'prospect of the Mui-tsai question being made
a "test question" by the Feminist societies which exploited
it to the full last time'.[32]

Clara Haslewood's most effective supporter in the resurrected campaign was Kathleen Simon, Joint President of the
Anti-Slavery Society. Her book *Slavery*, on the subject in
general, with a preface by her husband, Sir John Simon,

known as much for his principles as his brilliance, was published on 19 November 1929, with a chapter in it on slavery in Hong Kong. In that chapter, Lady Simon talked of Clara Haslewood's courage, and the letters between them written at this time provide a touching sidelight to relations between campaigning women: 'Dear Comrade', they start, and end, 'with love to you, your dear Comrade'.[33] Lady Simon contributed, too, by setting up a trust fund for freed *mui tsai* in China; and she was to be made a Dame in 1933.

After the election in 1929 of a Labour government, Lord Passfield, formerly Sidney Webb, was the new Colonial Secretary. He needed little prompting and in November he published a White Paper on the *mui tsai*. For the first time, the interchanges between the British and Hong Kong governments, though not the inter-departmental memoranda, entered the public domain. In August, Passfield had sent instructions to Hong Kong to bring in the neglected Part III of the Domestic Servitude Ordinance. He also approved the setting up of a Society for the Protection of Children. A new Ordinance, more carefully worded, was thus passed at the end of 1929.

Meanwhile, Kathleen Simon was addressing meetings up and down the country on the general theme of slavery, always mentioning the need to monitor the situation in Hong Kong. Clara Haslewood addressed the annual meeting of the Women's Advisory Council of the League of Nations, which included 75 nationally organized women's societies, giving the same warning, and the Council for the Representation of Women in the League of Nations. On 18 March 1930, an anti-slavery demonstration was convened by the League of Nations Union at which the Archbishop of Canterbury and Lady Simon gave the same message to an international audience. She also called upon women to 'liberate their sisters in all parts of the world'.[34]

In 1930, the Haslewoods published their book, *Child Slavery in Hong Kong: The Mui Tsai System*, to detail the system and the campaign against it over the previous 50 years, and to encourage the implementation of the new Ordinance. Kathleen Simon described Clara and Hugh

Haslewood, in a letter of 1932, as 'a pair of noble minded people who have sacrificed material gain to help abolish this crying shame on England'.[35] They should now have been able to rest, but it was not the last of the exploitation of Chinese women and children in Hong Kong. Expatriate women still had a job to do. This time, most of the action was to take place more firmly in Hong Kong itself.

CHAPTER TWENTY-ONE

STELLA, GLADYS, PHYLLIS, AND BROTHELS

ஒ৺৻৩৻৸৵

*S*tella Benson wrote disparagingly of Bella Woolf Southorn that her activities were designed to promote her husband's career. Stella was being less than generous; Bella's community involvement came from her own warm and outgoing temperament, as well as from her own sense of the responsibility that went with her position. Nevertheless, it is unlikely that Bella would ever knowingly have jeopardized her husband's career as Hong Kong's Colonial Secretary.

That is one of the ways in which Stella and Bella differed; Bella had built-in limits which were less obvious in women such as Alicia Little, Clara Haslewood, Stella Benson, Gladys Forster, and Hilda Selwyn-Clarke. For them, the campaign against an iniquity transcended the penalties. None of the husbands of the five married women campaigners seem to have resented the repercussions. Hugh Haslewood, the most affected, supported his wife's campaign without reserve. Campaigning wives who were prepared to put their husband's career at risk may be accused of not caring for them but the evidence is to the contrary. Stella Benson's marriage certainly had its ups and downs, and in its early days her husband had signs of a recurrence of syphillis contracted in China when he was very young, but Stella blamed his mother for not bringing him up properly, and, in her frank diary, her reasons for campaigning against licensed prostitution have nothing at all to do with her marriage or a wish to hurt her husband.

Several women are credited with, or blamed for, the abolition of licensed prostitution in Hong Kong. They include Lady Clementi, the Governor's wife, Mrs Wolfe, wife of the Inspector General of Police, Mrs Tratman, married to the Secretary for Chinese Affairs, and, indeed, Lady Southorn. When I asked the former magistrate Eric Himsworth, who gave the information about Mrs Wolfe, Mrs Tratman and Lady Southorn to Paul Gillingham for his book *At the Peak: Hong Kong Between the Wars* (1983), for substantiation, he told me that that was the talk at the time.

Lady Clementi's involvement is suggested by Marjory Angus for the same Gillingham chapter. The reason for that inference seems to be that Penelope Clementi read all new books bought for the Helena May Library; 'Any reference to a kiss or a cuddle and the book was removed.'[1] That might well be so, though it does not really fit in with the picture of Penelope Clementi that has emerged. It is rather a large step, however, from objecting to young British girls reading 'unsuitable' literature at the Helena May, to making sure that the licensing of Chinese prostitutes was abolished in the colony, particularly since twentieth-century governors, including Clementi, as was shown in the previous chapter, were against tampering with Chinese customs, and those women who did work against licensing ran up against the then governor, Sir William Peel.

The names of the two women who were most involved, Gladys Forster and Stella Benson, are not usually mentioned, though their part is documented. It is worth turning to Stella's diary to look at her relations with Mrs Wolfe and Mrs Tratman; were they friends and allies? Stella and her husband, James, had been told by a mutual friend in England to remember him to the Tratmans but, as Stella writes on 16 June 1930, 'I tried to, but Mrs Tratman was curiously unfriendly, though glowing like a rose to look at. (To my surprise, James who came to fetch me away called her an obvious — [sic]'[2] We will never know what James said but I surmise it did not mean that she was a feminist or protector of young girls. On 13 October, Stella went further after a dinner party at which both couples were present: 'I think [Mrs Tratman] is absolutely cold-hearted and greedy — [Her] glowing face is like a rose with grey steely balls in the heart of it for eyes.'

As for Mrs Wolfe, Stella was hardly more taken; she wrote after a tennis party on 6 December 1930, 'Mrs Wolfe had confidence enough for all — a manner that had apparently never known rebuff, fortunate woman.' Big Ladies' roles in the abolition of prostitution in fact appear to be nothing but hearsay or supposition that has now entered the history books.

By coincidence, the day following the tennis party Stella was roped in by Katherine Beavis, a friend and the wife of a local solicitor, and Gladys Forster, to sit on a local League of Nations sub-committee which Gladys was chairing and whose brief was to prepare evidence on the local situation for a visit by a League of Nations Travelling Commission enquiring into International Traffic in Women. As Stella said of a report presented to the meeting, 'The things we heard made our blood boil.'

Stella suggests that only four women on the committee knew anything about the 'traffic' and its effect on Hong Kong. Of those, three were unnamed Chinese and one was an English woman from the Salvation Army, probably Adjutant Rosa Raines, newly arrived in the colony from North China to set up an industrial refuge for Chinese prostitutes, or 'unfortunate girls'. It was these who were at issue as far as trafficking was concerned because, as Stella rather ambiguously put it on 9 December 1930, 'There are no licensed foreign prostitutes here.'

The licensing of European prostitutes was the first to be abolished, but not until the end of 1931, and there is good evidence that there were European prostitutes at the time Stella was writing, presumably licensed. The brothel madame Ethel Morrison is something of a legend of that time. A long-time resident in the colony recalled how, around 1930, Ethel had, as was her custom, breezed into the office of the Canadian Pacific Steamships Limited, where European women were discussing their passages home, in order to track down, in a carrying voice, young men who had failed to honour their chits for her establishment in Lyndhurst Terrace.[3] In May 1930, the governor informed the Colonial Office that there were six brothels with 17 European prostitutes; (there were also 222 known Chinese and Japanese brothels, with 2,657 prostitutes).[4] Surely Stella's statement is not part of European women's protective denial of the existence of European prostitutes raised in Chapter 17? Though it is certainly true that on one level even Ethel Morrison connived at that impression. When a Canadian milliner attempted to introduce Ethel to another, respectable, woman looking at hats, she was chided, by Ethel, for her lack of sensitivity.

By 5 January 1931, the League of Nations Travelling Commission on Trafficking had arrived in Hong Kong and Stella mentions that her sub-committee was talked to for an hour and a half by a Swedish member, Dr Alma Sunquist. Stella, being rather deaf, did not hear much because of Alma's Scandinavian intonation but, as she put it again, 'My blood [was] politely boiling at the very idea of traffic in women.'

What is not clear is whether or not Stella and Gladys realized how much pressure there already was on the Hong Kong government to abolish the registration of prostitutes. Did they see themselves as part of a major campaign already in progress or were they fighting dragons alone? The Colonial Office in London and the Governor had been in communication for some time before the arrival of the League of Nations Commission; they expected an adverse report on Hong Kong. While the Hong Kong government lagged, as it always had done, far behind advanced thinking on prostitution, that was not the case with all sectors of the Colonial Office and the machinery was well in motion for effecting the changes for which Stella and Gladys were to campaign.

Registration or licensing was in existence in Hong Kong illegally, as it had been since the end of the previous century when the Hong Kong government was instructed to abolish it. A Colonial Office memorandum of October 1930 criticized a recent dispatch by Sir William Peel who had suggested that local opinion was widely in favour of maintaining the status quo. Quoting from Peel's dispatch, the Colonial Office remarked that the 'system may be "more orderly than the state of affairs in London" but that orderliness is purchased at the price of recognising and maintaining large vested interests in vice in the person of brothel owners'.[5] The Colonial Office wanted at least European brothels to look as if they were about to close.

Renewed activity on the part of the Colonial Office was prompted not only by the League of Nations Commission but also by questions in Parliament by MPs such as Lady Astor, by Sybil Neville-Rolfe's report on venereal disease in the colony, which was still shaping policy, and by resolutions passed by the Association for Moral Hygiene (the new name of Sybil's organization, founded by Josephine Butler) and the National Council of Women.

By February, the local sub-committee on trafficking was ready to be dissolved; it had served its purpose. But the women had learnt that the Governor felt it had done more than that; he felt, according to Stella, that 'any enquiry into tolerated brothels here [was] unwarrantable interference'.[6] The Governor required that all such enquiry be dropped. 'Why should we drop it?' Stella asked her diary. 'We are citizens, and the enslaved girls are our sex and slaves. There may be no solution of the prostitution difficulty in a place like this ... and yet it is not interference to enquire.' And so, as Stella put it, 'Mrs Forster — a burning fanatic — wishes to make a new committee and defy the Govt.'

Stella was the only one willing to 'defy' too; though she did feel that any work they produced should represent a 'sizable body of opinion'. A few days later, Gladys was onto Stella about their new committee, warning her, however, that 'few women would support any insistence, since nearly all were wives of Govt. servants, and the Governor had had men sent home on account of their wives' tactlessness in the Colony'.[7] Gladys, Stella noted, was referring to Clara Haslewood and it is interesting that it should have been common knowledge — particularly since the Haslewoods did not mention it in their recently published book. It was perhaps that knowledge, fresh in the early 1920s, that had confined the campaign against the *mui tsai* system to British women in Britain, rather than those in the colony, even though the wives of government servants had not hesitated to support Sybil Neville-Rolfe against Sir Reginald Stubbs's wishes in 1921.

Stella considered the matter and decided that 'I am in a safer position than most, since the Governor could only indirectly and by the most determined [means] harm James' career.'[7] How Gladys felt, apart from that warning to Stella, is not recorded. However, her daughter Helen Clemetson records how during the War a colleague of her father, Professor Middleton-Smith, told her, 'You know your mother nearly lost your father his job.'[8] Helen believes that her father felt that the work should be done but would rather it had not been done by his wife. His position as Professor of Education in Hong Kong was hard fought for from a background of poverty. He certainly contributed his own writing against the *mui tsai* system. It seems, however, that it was only when he was retired, in England, after 1945, that he actively objected to Gladys's activities on behalf of women and then only because they took her away from home and her domestic duties, factors which would not have applied in Hong Kong.

Stella mused that when she and Gladys had completed their enquiries, they would, by taking advantage of Gladys's contacts, give the information to the Bishop; he in his turn might bring it 'privately to the Governor's ear in a friendly way between the soup and the fish as it were'.[9] By no other means was Peel approachable on the subject.

The following afternoon, 4 March 1931, Gladys Forster took Stella Benson in hand and over to Kowloon, to the brothel quarter of Yaumatei. By that time, Gladys had been in Hong Kong for 13 years. Lancelot Forster had come out in 1914 and taught at the boy's school, Queen's College, before moving to the University in 1920. Meanwhile, he had met Gladys in Newcastle and she came out to marry him in 1918. She was 24, and a well-educated woman herself. Although her maternal grandfather had been a miner, he had sent his daughter Elizabeth, rather than any of his sons, to Durham University. Three of her children, all girls, and including Gladys, were to follow her there; and three of Gladys's own four daughters were to go to Oxford. So, as well as the 'fanaticism' with which Stella endows Gladys, she came to her research from an academic background.

There is another quality which is illustrated by a family anecdote. As a young girl, Gladys was very 'determined'. Her mother wished to reprimand her but her father, Alfred Jennings, would say, 'No, leave her alone. It may be that in her life she is going to need that determination.'

During her early years in Hong Kong, between 1919 and 1925 Gladys had four children, all of whom, except one, she then sent home to school in England, between 1928 and 1932. It was a process which caused some anguish in the family and difficulties of readjustment on Gladys's return to England — a situation which must have been replicated in many families over the years. At some stage, Gladys also taught English at the University.

Stella's sharp pen was to linger affectionately on Gladys in 1931, when she contrasted, too, their approach to prostitution. On 11 April she wrote:

Mrs Forster lunched with us and we had a good tempered but very incompatible argument about morals. She attacks prostitution as a Christian and a moralist, I as a feminist bone-seeker (there is no bone of nature about the system of prostitution) — and James as a hard-headed practical man. The argument of James and me upholding the idea of less chastity among 'virtuous' women as a counter stimulant to prostitution, dumbfounders Mrs Forster, but she is a brave and just arguer, in spite of her Christian standpoint. We both rather like her. She is a fanatic on morals though, and introduces too much reforming emotion into this enquiry into the lot of prostitutes. I don't want to reform anybody myself — I just want everybody to be allowed to have his or her own self respect.

On 8 May, Stella continued her analysis, after Gladys, to her surprise, had expressed approval of her, having read her latest novel, *Tobit Transplanted* (1930):

254 THE PRIVATE LIFE OF OLD HONG KONG

There is something buoyant and big-dog-like about Mrs Forster. She is fat, she sweats, she is an ardent moralist, and an excellent talker — and she is charmingly honest. Today is the first time I ever heard her express a *feeling* — mostly she puts *opinions* most eloquently into words. At least, of course, her morals are founded upon *feeling*, her feeling against prostitution and in favor of total chastity for all sexes (males, females, and half-&-halfs) amounts to fanaticism. But to hear her express a personal feeling for a person (especially a disputatious non-moralist like me) was like hearing a dog mew. Both James and I felt rather warmly to her.

Some of that characterization of Gladys needs qualifying and her daughters have done so for me. Helen Clemetson admits that Stella may well have known her mother better than she: after all, she was at school in England, 'But,' Helen writes, 'I never connected her "horror of unchastity" with Christianity. I always thought of it as something in her more "social" than "Christian". She was not a fundamentalist or evangelical Christian. Just a church-going Christian.'

Both Helen and her younger sister Anne Badenoch mention Gladys's love of and talent for singing and feel that she would have liked to be an opera singer; Helen goes so far as to suggest a hankering for the music hall stage. Gladys's 'fanaticism', therefore, can more usefully be seen as a sense of the dramatic, the over-emphasis of the performer. Her overtly emotional personality was the opposite of Stella's own.

Helen accepts that Stella was probably a feminist — 'Gladys certainly was. She worked most of her life for women's causes.' She also instilled in her daughters, Anne suggests, a feeling for the situation of women.[10] Her feminism, Helen feels, was an important part of her reaction to prostitution, as well as compassion for the young girls who suffered, horror at their conditions, and a repudiation of slavery. Gladys's granddaughter, Lindsay Badenoch,[11] also feels that she had a special feeling for children, which is what many of the prostitutes were, and that empathy is born out by an incident described by Alwin Ovenell, Penelope Clementi's daughter and friend of Gladys's daughter Anne. She remembers her warm personality and a picnic where Gladys found the psychological key to teach her how to swim.[12]

The first afternoon of research was spent by Gladys and Stella at a school for prostitutes run by a Chinese woman, Mrs Ruby Mow Fung, and attended that afternoon by nine young prostitutes. At least three of the girls had been licensed at 15, though the permitted age was 21. Girls were primed to say that they were 22, which occasioned no surprise to the authorities since clerks of the Secretariat for Chinese Affairs and inspectors of police were easily bribed, usually by the brothel mistress. The latter could well afford the bribe: out of each dollar that a prostitute earned, she paid 50 cents to the brothel mistress (and 25 cents to the *amah* who was often her procuress).[13]

It is not clear at what stage Gladys Forster began a close association with Mrs Fung's school. Stella's diary that first afternoon does not suggest a direct connection, though Gladys obviously knew of it to take her there. When in 1937, back in England, Gladys had occasion to write to the Colonial Office, she says that 'for several years a Chinese friend, Mrs Mow Fung, and I had a school for prostitutes — the To Kwong Girls School'.[14] That might mean from 1931 to 1936. It is a fair assumption that Ruby Mow Fung was one of the three Chinese women on the League of Nations sub-committee referred to above.

Beatrice Pope, a teacher at St Stephen's and an unsung junior member of the local League of Nations Committee (Stella does not mention her) wrote in 1974 that Gladys

made real friends of a number of these prostitutes . . . She held a school for them on their own premises, meeting in the afternoon as the girls slept in the morning. She also used to invite them to her house on the Peak for tea . . . She was criticized by some people for letting them meet her young daughters but I daresay they did not understand who their mother's pupils were.[15]

Anne Forster Badenoch who was nine in 1931, confirms that: she knew of them simply as 'slave girls'. Elspeth was only six and Margaret and Helen were in England. To look at

the photograph of Gladys and Mrs Ruby Mow Fung with
their 'prostitutes' in Gladys's garden is to understand more
than any words or memories can convey.

The Governor and his wife were to visit the school which
he regarded highly, according to him towards the end of his
governership (1935); according to Stella it was in November
1931, at the height of their campaign. Peel does not mention
Gladys Forster's connection, though she was present at the
time. While the 'Chinese lady' was 'philanthropic', people
such as Gladys he calls, politely, 'enthusiasts'.[16] The other
more usual description of them is 'do gooders', which is
intended as more than faintly disparaging for, after all, they
were attempting to change the status quo which suited most
people, even some of the victims. Questioning whether expatriate women had the right to decide what was acceptable
treatment for Chinese women under the circumstances
described in these chapters is like asking if there is one form
of human rights for British people and another for Chinese.

Stella records how on one occasion at that time the
Governor and Lady Peel 'seemed to look icily through me,
perhaps because of the prostitute question'. But the
following day she was recognized 'from a distance'.[17] The
more she learnt of what was going on, the more dis-
illusioned she became, for it was not simply the life of the
girls, unfolded through statement after statement, that hurt;
she was made increasingly aware, too, of the corruption of
the colonial government. 'I have always innocently supposed', she wrote to a friend in March 1931, 'that English
officials were straight because they were English.'[18] She was
not naive, she had been a suffragette but somehow the
obtuseness towards child prostitution was hard to take. The
attitude of even top officials is illustrated by an entry in
Stella's diary concerning A.E. Wood, the Secretary for
Chinese Affairs, who had overall responsibility for the
refuge Po Leung Kuk; she writes of how he was *personally*
offended because Miss Raines, of the Salvation Army, reported that two rescued girls had lice in their hair'.[19] The
hypocrisy of that attitude was compounded by the discovery
that, while Chinese prostitutes for Chinese clients lived in

clean cubicles, the Big Number girls considered 'safe' for British soldiers and sailors were slatterns in their physical appearance and in the state of their quarters.

On 21 May, Stella finished writing up their research and sent it off to Gladys. A week later they submitted the contents of the report orally to the original sub-committee on trafficking and, when a couple of days after that, Stella had Gladys's final copy, she composed a careful letter to Bella Southorn and sent a copy to her for transmission upwards — 'God send it may be effective,' she wrote as she did so.[20] The same day, she started preparing further copies. In the middle of that onerous task, in the days when only carbon paper made copies, James came in and was a 'very peevish and injured martyr' because she was working after he got home.

On 5 June, Gladys and Stella came before the League of Nations Society itself and introduced their report. It was accepted and the Society decided to take it further themselves. 'Thus we shall attain our end we hope' Stella wrote, 'without getting either our husbands our ourselves into trouble.' But now another sub-committee was formed to 'revise and verify' and when it met again the two women found their report much changed, with many omissions. Stella gave way on points that would only provoke the government but stood her ground on others; and she felt that the 'balance and shape of the report is spoilt'.[21] She felt, too, that the sub-committee had spent 'about five minutes skipping through a thing we had spent months over'.

The new, emasculated report was passed by the League of Nations Society who, in their turn, said that they would send it to the government, but on 9 September Gladys showed Stella a letter from the Colonial Secretary, Tom Southorn, saying that no reform would be carried out until the report of the League of Nations Commission of Enquiry in two years time, and noting that their report was only that of a sub-committee and did not represent the opinion of the Society. At the next meeting the Society discussed, too, the Governor's request to drop the subject of Chinese brothels. By that time European brothels were scheduled to close at the end of the year. Stella lost all patience with the line taken and let it show at the meeting; Gladys was too over-come to be her usually eloquent self.

At that meeting on 6 October, though, Stella learnt that Dame Rachel Crowdy, Head of the Social Questions and Opium Traffic Section of the League of Nations — renowned not only as being the first woman head of section but also for having breathed life into an inert clause of the Charter — was expected in Hong Kong the following Thursday. Dame Rachel's views would obviously carry weight with the governments, home and colonial, and in other forums. Stella laid her plans to speak to the visitor before the Governor, with whom she would be staying. Her diary gives a lively description of the two-hour wait on the dock while she positioned herself ahead of those who had come to meet Rachel Crowdy. As so often, Stella was unwell and, al-though it was already early October, it was still very hot and there was nowhere to sit.

She had already written to Rachel Crowdy who was not, therefore, surprised when it was Stella who reached her first. They talked for 20 minutes and Stella wrote later,

She was a very honest looking woman, much younger than I expected [she was 57] and it was like a good dream, the way she welcomed me, said she liked all my books ... and announced at once that she intended to come to lunch with me that minute ... She said she could lunch with Governors any day but might never get a chance again to lunch with S Benson.[22]

Gladys joined them for lunch and they found complete agreement amongst themselves. No one who had thoroughly studied the subject, Rachel Crowdy maintained, could logically advocate state regulation and 'delay could only be accounted for by commercial expediency'. The *South China Morning Post* was to suggest on 4 December 1931 that at least 10,000 people were directly or indirectly interested financially in organized prostitution.

In spite of the success of her mission, Stella's hijacking of the Government House visitor was to bring odium which it took her weeks to live down and, during that time, she feared for her husband's career at a delicate moment. They were, however, invited to Government House again, and Stella wrote unregenerately:

After dinner Lady Peel was quite friendly and came and burbled to Mrs Stephenson and me on house-wifely subjects — a rather arrested-development type, I think, Lady Peel. She loves dancing and young men, and she has the naivete of a child rather — perhaps a rather spoilt child.[23]

A few days later, the Governor got his own back, as it were, for Stella bumped into an acquaintance, Mollie Hancock, sister-in-law of Edith Stewart Lockhart, who had been talking to Sir William about state regulation. 'Really, those poor dear ladies' he was reported as saying, 'very charming and all that, no doubt, but without any knowledge of what they're talking about.'[24] Mollie prattled on so imperviously that Stella was able to control herself; her diary received the full force of her anger, particularly the fact that Peel should talk to Mollie on the subject, rather than to responsible citizens who wished to discuss it.

In case there should be any doubt about what drove Stella and Gladys, and the strength of the evidence that fuelled their arguments, here is part of Stella's diary entry for 28 November 1931:

Mrs Forster came down to see me all morning and we drafted a letter to the Governor. She was in a weepy mood, being a very tenderhearted person; the little girl we found in the Tung Wah Hospital last summer who had been used as a slave so very drastically and was infected so seriously with syphilis that her eyes & nose were almost eaten away (I paid for treatment for her) — now seemed so much better (though permanently blind, of course) that arrangements had been made to send her to a mission home for girls in Canton. The child was very happy about this, and is, according to Mrs Forster, now a merry laughing little thing. She was to be taken to Canton on Monday — but yesterday was taken to a VD specialist for final opinion. He says she is not only incurably diseased — literally rotten with disease, so that the skin breaks at a touch — but she is also extremely infectious and will remain so — cannot possibly go to a home or be anything for the rest of her life (she is 17 now). She has all known forms of VD.

At a Government House dinner on 1 December, Peel told Stella in advance that he was about to announce the abolition, in stages, of 'tolerated brothels'. He had, he added, been disposed to do so for six months.

Stella's two-year stay in Hong Kong was drawing to a close — she left, in mid-January 1932. During her leave in England, before returning to the East, where James was to be posted to Indo-China, she wrote a sarcastic article for the *Radio Times* about the colony, not about prostitution, but about European society's obsession with playing games and lack of interesting talk, in particular about China, which might as well not exist; the article then continued with a description of a Chinese wedding she had been to. It caused great upset in Hong Kong.

Passing through the colony in September 1932, she felt some trepidation and, indeed, Gladys who met her at the docks, confirmed that she was not popular. James's career, however, seemed unharmed and Stella suggested that her article had placed them 'unwittingly in the position of People Whom it is Unwise to Offend'. Certainly Bella Southorn, acting first lady, while 'archly reproachful', was magnanimous.[25]

Gladys had other news for her, too: Stella writes of their long talk, 'She says that Dame Rachel Crowdy's explanation of the string pulling behind abolition which she claimed that she (and through her, we) inspired was untrue. It doesn't matter much, for abolition is really underway, it seems.'[26] Chinese brothels for Europeans were closed in June 1932; the last 43 houses of Chinese prostitutes for Chinese clients closed in June 1934.

Gladys was to take the last of her daughters, Elspeth, back to England in 1935 and not to return, though her husband stayed and was interned in Stanley Camp. Gladys continued to campaign on women's issues from Oxford, through, for example, the Open Door Council and the Association for Moral and Social Hygiene. The latter organization was opposing proposed laws against prostitutes. She was never as happy in England, though, as she had been in Hong Kong. As for her reputation in the colony, it seems rather to have benefitted than otherwise from her campaigning work; although she did not return after the War, she was appointed to the 1946 Cox Commission to look into the future of the University. She died in 1982, aged 88.

As for Stella, she died of yet one more attack of the weakness of the lungs that had plagued her all her life, a year after her last visit to Hong Kong, in December 1933. She was only 41. Her novels, so highly regarded in her day, seem to have fallen out of fashion. Her diaries, kept from girlhood, were handed over by her husband to Cambridge University, as she had requested, to remain unopened for 50 years. In 1984 they became available to scholars and Dr Joy Grant published a new biography in 1987. News of the time embargo reached Hong Kong on 19 April 1934. *The Hong Kong Telegraph's* headline, over a London byline, read 'Escape for Local Society? Outspoken Stella Benson Diaries.' The following day there was a spoof entry which ended, 'I loathe Hong Kong. I think it's a rotten place.'

No claim can be made that Gladys Forster and Stella Benson brought about the abolition of licensed prostitution in Hong Kong. It was a reform whose time had come because many people at all levels in many places had been working towards it for many years; Hong Kong was one of the last bastions of reaction. Detractors later argued that abolition was the direct cause of a rise in venereal disease in Hong Kong. In similar places, however, there was no such rise after abolition.[27] The point which cannot be disputed is that the State connived, by its support (through registration) of the so-called 'entertainment industry' and its vested interests, at the enslavement of women, many of them under age.

What Gladys and Stella did, as well as adding their twopenny worth to the spreading pool of twentieth-century social reform, was firstly to be true to themselves and, secondly, to lend some dignity, in both contemporary and historical terms, to a society where women were so confined to the domestic sphere that they thought they were being noble when they played bridge all day for charity.

The concept of registration of females in Hong Kong holds an ambiguity that needs, perhaps, to be pointed out and explained. The registration of prostitutes, which reformers campaigned against, was to protect the users and abusers of girls and women. The registration of *mui tsai*, which reformers campaigned for, was part of the process of abolition of the *mui tsai* or 'slave' system, and was for the protection, meanwhile, of the girls and women concerned.

In spite of the reforms between 1929 and 1934 to combat the evils of domestic and brothel slavery, the situation continued to arouse concern. What started to trouble Lady Simon was the fact that the *mui tsai* system was being perpetuated by the simple device of calling girls 'adopted daughters'.[28] They did not need to be registered under the *mui tsai* legislation and were, therefore, unprotected. In 1931, her husband, Sir John Simon, who was just about to become Secretary of State for Foreign Affairs in a new coalition government, spoke on the danger in the House of Commons.

Those who were monitoring the new legislation in Hong Kong also suggested that several thousand *mui tsai* were still unregistered and that the Secretariat for Chinese Affairs depended on the vigilance of the Anti-*Mui Tsai* Society and the Society for the Protection of Children instead of appointing proper inspectors. Calls now started for the registration of adopted daughters. Predictably, Sir William Peel resisted them.

The League of Nations, in January 1934, asked Sir George Maxwell to write a memorandum on the *mui tsai* system which the Colonial Office then sent to the Hong Kong government for comment. A sub-committee was set up under a lawyer, F.H. Loseby, consisting of, among others, Adjutant Dorothy Brazier who had recently arrived in the colony to expand the Salvation Army's work among persecuted and offending girls.

The Loseby Report was published in September 1935 and rejected most of Maxwell's suggestions; it muddied issues that had previously been clear internationally and caused disagreement within the Chinese community of Hong Kong. In London, pressure was put on the Colonial Office to institute a full-scale enquiry. The Woods Commission was, therefore, set up in 1936, and one of its three members was Edith Picton-Turbervill, a former Labour Member of Parliament. She and her companions arrived in Hong Kong for a month in May 1936.

Edith was a formidable woman of 64 who had done social work among the navvies on the railway lines in Wales when she was still a teenager and worked for the YWCA in India for six years. In spite of the disadvantages which she felt the Commission laboured under — staying at Government House and talking through an interpreter — she saw the issues quite clearly. 'Very often,' she wrote in her autobiography, *Life is Good* (1939) 'the "adopted daughters" were nothing more or less than "mui tsais" under another name. Drudges of a household at six or seven years of age, and if unfortunate, at the mercy of a cruel mistress or lustful master.'[29]

Edith soon found, 'Indeed had feared it for some time,' she wrote, 'that I would be compelled to write a Minority Report.'[30] Her colleagues felt that the current legislation could be tinkered with; she knew that new legislation was essential, even if it would offend the Chinese, for 'transferred' girls who were not called 'mui tsai' had no protection.

The Majority and Minority Reports were published in March 1937. Once again the reformers' lobby in Britain marshalled its forces, including the Haslewoods, behind Edith Picton-Turbervill's Minority Report. Gladys Forster was among those who wrote, on 2 June 1937, to the Secretary of State for Colonial Affairs. She was quite clear that 'adoption' was a frequent recourse for supplying brothels through the adoption of country girls by a 'tortoise' or 'pocket mother' who would then sell them to a brothel-keeper. She explained, too, that Chinese prostitutes habitually saved up and 'adopted' a small girl against 'their own weariness and old age'. They were not *mui tsai* but would be included in a wider registration.[31]

Neither Gladys nor Edith was to be gainsaid; it was the Minority Report that was adopted and consequent legislation introduced into the Legislative Council in April 1938. It was passed without opposition, partly because of the careful preparation by the new Governor, Sir Geoffry Northcote, and the irrefutable evidence of Gladys's letter. As Norman Miners points out, however, in 'The Abolition of the Mui Tsai System, 1925–1941', Hong Kong, as usual, managed to evade some of its instructions.[32] And he adds that in many respects the legislation was a failure. Nevertheless, in order to supervise the forthcoming changes, a European woman had been appointed Assistant Secretary for Chinese Affairs at the beginning of that year. She was Phyllis Harrop.

When Phyllis answered the advertisement at the end of 1937, she thought that she was being hired as a secretary. She was not the only applicant for the job. Ellen Li (née Tsao), a young Chinese woman originally from Vietnam educated in Amoy and at St Stephen's, Hong Kong, with a degree in sociology and banking from the University of Shanghai, also did so, but Phyllis was a statuesque, lively blonde woman from Manchester and it would be charitable to assume that it was felt that she could pursue the work required more safely than a petite Chinese woman.

Apart from her physical attributes, which can best be appreciated from the photograph of her with two Chinese women friends, Phyllis did not exactly have the qualifications that might be looked for today. She had gone to Shanghai from England in 1929 to see the world; there she worked as a secretary until an ill-fated marriage to a German baron in 1934. Having left him, she worked in Japanese-dominated Manchuria and had some contact with the world of the Secret Service. Back in Shanghai, she had left, like many others, when the Japanese bombed the city in August 1937.

But Phyllis soon found out what her new job entailed: she

was to protect the young girls of Hong Kong. Indeed, a letter from Edith Picton-Turbervill of January 1939 to solicit money from friends and organizations in Britain towards enlarging and building schools and orphanages for girls who were no longer to be *mui tsai* or prostitutes, calls Phyllis 'The Lady Protector'.[33] As Edith told it, one raid that Phyllis had conducted in person had discovered 17 transferred girls who were about to be shipped abroad.

Phyllis set about preparing herself for her real job, becoming as soon as possible proficient in Cantonese and the relevant laws of Hong Kong. She built up a staff of Chinese women not afraid to work hard, and two police inspectors and a sergeant were seconded to her. As well as that team there were about one hundred Chinese detectives.

It was not easy. The Police Department, instructed to refer to her all cases concerning women and children or family affairs, objected to having to deal with a woman. She found that notice of a forthcoming raid on a sly (illegal) brothel was leaking out so that any evidence of law-breaking had disappeared by the time the police arrived. She set out herself, secretly, with a police escort, and that is when she found the women Edith referred to. Subsequently she made a practice of going on raids and was seen as quite a character, as well as a friend, among the Chinese. Phyllis took her work seriously but she did not take herself seriously, laughingly describing her job as 'protecting way-ward girls'; people such as Emily Hahn laughed too for, as Emily told me in a recent letter, 'she looked so wayward herself'.

Edith Picton-Turbervill may have called her The Lady Protector but Phyllis gives her own formal title in *Hong Kong Incident* (1942) as *Nui Wa Man Dai Yan*.[34] It meant, literally, and inaccurately, the Lady Secretary for Chinese Affairs. But it meant colloquially 'Big Lady'. Phyllis Harrop, however much she joked, was a Big Lady in her own right.

CHAPTER TWENTY-TWO

RED HILDA AND OTHER WAR HEROINES

When Hilda Selwyn-Clarke set out for Hong Kong with her husband in the early summer of 1938, the Munich Agreement was still a couple of months away. The tension in the Far East was more palpable: Nanking had been brutally taken by the Japanese in December 1937, following the fall of Shanghai that autumn, and, as the Japanese advanced further, the colony was increasingly becoming a centre for Chinese activities. It was grossly overcrowded, making Selwyn's job as Director of Medical Services even more challenging than he had expected. There was now a population of nearly a million, of which all but 15,000 (10,000 of them British) were Chinese. From the start, Hilda herself had two concerns, population control through contraception, and support of China's efforts to repel the Japanese incursion.

When foreign women and children were evacuated from Hong Kong in July 1940, Hilda was to be the highest-ranking British woman left behind; but she was not in the tradition of Big Ladies, wives of government officials. If she had not married Selwyn in 1935 and gone to Hong Kong, she would probably have been in the British Labour government of 1945. It was not only for her red hair that Hong Kong society called her Red Hilda.

Hilda Browning was born in 1900, the daughter of a baker. She won a scholarship to her local grammar school in Horsham, Sussex, and then one to Goldsmith's College, London, where she trained to be a teacher. By the 1920s, she was a member of the Independent Labour Party (ILP) and in 1931 she fought the London Parliamentary seat of Clapham South, then firmly Conservative, for the Labour Party. There was a local council by-election in Clapham three years later and she fought for the ILP against Captain Bertram Mills of the circus family with the slogan 'Bread not Circuses'. By the time she met Selwyn, she had worked for Fenner Brockway, General Secretary of the ILP, and was now working for the Society for Cultural Relations with the Soviet Union; indeed, she arranged a medical visit for Selwyn to the USSR.[1]

Marriage, the birth of a daughter, Mary, in 1936, and being transplanted from her political and literary home ground, firstly to the Gold Coast and then to Hong Kong, had done nothing to sap Hilda's enormous enthusiasm, energy, and her commitment to causes. She was soon chairing the Eugenics League and Honorary Secretary of Madame Sun Yat-sen's China Defence League.

Family planning in Hong Kong today is a growth industry run by Chinese professionals; in the 1930s the subject was taboo, as it was in Europe and the United States almost until then. The inspiration for Hong Kong's Eugenics League came from Margaret Sanger, who had earlier been jailed in the United States for her birth-control activities. During a fleeting visit to the colony in 1936, she addressed a meeting of fifty or so people, including Chinese doctors, which Ellen Li, who was to work with Hilda in the League, remembers.[2]

During an earlier visit, in 1921, the Police Department had given Margaret their special attention because of her friendship and work with Agnes Smedley who was *persona non grata* with the British for her Indian Nationalist activities.[3] Agnes Smedley and Hilda Selwyn-Clarke were about to become friends, and later to be part of a circle of like-minded women in Hong Kong rather different from what the colony was used to in its foreign women.

Hilda visited the small office of the Eugenics League once or twice a week, helping Ellen to prepare material to be translated into Chinese. Ellen's impression was of a strong-minded woman dedicated to her work. She noted, too, that

Hilda was 'unracist', still something to marvel at in pre-War Hong Kong, though they did not mix socially.

Phyllis Harrop, who seems eventually to have been accepted by the Chinese community at many levels, tells how European and Chinese men may have lunched together but, on one occasion, when she was asked to be hostess for a British official wanting to entertain a Chinese guest in the evening, she was asked if she 'would be embarrassed to be seen in a public place with a Chinese'.[4] Phyllis, as has been mentioned, lunched with Ellen Li at the International Women's Club, which Bella Southorn had set up for just such a purpose, and Elsa Rogers, wife of the Bank of England representative in China was, as Margaret Watson Sloss describes it, 'most skilful in bringing British and Chinese residents together socially'.[5]

An interesting sidelight on how Chinese women viewed European women is Ellen's perception of Hilda in 1938. Hilda was then 38 with, as her daughter describes her, 'reddish brown hair and bright brown eyes. She was very good looking, warm in colouring and personality and athletic ... with masses of energy'. Mary remembers, too, an aura of chiffon and jade when Hilda went out dancing in the evening. To Ellen, when Hilda came in casually dressed, in flat shoes and without make-up, she was rather unfeminine, unsmart and 45 to 50. Hilda's friend, Margaret Watson Sloss, describes her as 'a handsome woman, most sexually attractive, not at all dowdy'. And Agnes Smedley called her a 'handsome woman with flaming chestnut hair and liquid brown eyes'.[6]

Selwyn, who could have been embarrassed by his wife's eugenics work, on the contrary gave the League the full backing of the Medical Department, and could do so even more confidently knowing that the Chief Medical Officer of the British Ministry of Health also approved.[7]

Madame Sun Yat-sen set up the China Defence League in 1938 and by 1939 its work included an international peace hospital, a Red Cross training school, war orphans, Chinese industrial cooperatives, an anti-Japanese University, the coordination of relief, and publicity.[8] Its main purpose was to provide money and support for Chinese endeavours inside China among the Chinese partisans who were still resisting the Japanese. Most international aid, including that of the International Red Cross, was controlled by foreigners, many of them missionaries, who spent it worthily on refugees and medical services, but inside Japanese controlled areas.[9] One of the China Defence League's fund-raising methods they called 'Bowl of Rice'; several restaurants co-operated to take their diners' money for a full meal and served them with rice only.[10]

The Chinese Nationalist government in 1938 was in Hankow which, since the loss of Shanghai the previous year, was also the main port for trade with China. The refugees there included a nest of concerned foreigners and journalists, such as Agnes Smedley who had been there since the beginning of the year, and with whom Hilda had already been in touch by correspondence. In July, Hilda flew to Hankow to inspect military hospitals and see the work of the Chinese Red Cross Medical Commission or Corps. On the same plane was an English academic turned journalist, Freda Utley. Agnes Smedley, whose life at the time was devoted to the Chinese Red Cross and, through that, to the Chinese cause, met Hilda's plane and Freda tagged along, for accommodation in Hankow was at a premium and Agnes had managed to get Hilda a room in her own modest hotel in the French concession. Most journalists stayed at the Lutheran Hostel but, as Freda wrote of Agnes in *China at War* (1939), the elderly women 'whose writ ran at the Lutheran Mission considered her to be either too dangerous a Red or too Scarlet a woman, we never quite knew which'.[11]

Agnes, after years as a writer and activist in the United States, her home, and Germany, had been in China on and off since 1929. In 1933, she had tried and failed to establish a birth control clinic in Shanghai. In 1930, she, too, had worked with Madame Sun Yat-sen but their relationship had foundered; as Agnes's biographers put it, 'Although Smedley and Mme Sun were both women of action who agreed politically and communicated perfectly in English, Mme Sun was genteel, emotionally restrained, and taciturn, whereas Smedley was coarse, tempestuous, and outspoken.'[12] At that time Agnes, aged 48, was a special correspondent, writing two articles a week for The *Manchester Guardian*, which allowed her to work without payment for the Chinese cause.

During that stay in Hankow, Hilda and Freda's nights were disturbed by heat, mosquitoes and air-raid sirens. By day Agnes introduced them to everyone who was anyone and took them to visit military hospitals; in the evening they were entertained by newspaper correspondents and military observers. Hankow was to fall in October, as was Canton. The Chinese Nationalist government withdrew to Chungking and a new wave of refugees from Canton, the poor, as opposed to the rich who had left earlier, exacerbated the situation in Hong Kong.

Hilda flew back to the colony and founded the Foreign Auxiliary of the Chinese Red Cross, for whom she built up a network of international aid. She also turned Chinese refugee centres in Hong Kong into hives of Red Cross activity; there, women and girls prepared supplies to be sent into China. The supply of drugs, dressings, instruments, antiseptics and disinfectants which Hilda stored in warehouses in Wanchai had previously gone up the Pearl River; after the fall of Canton, they had to be re-routed via Hainan Island. When the Japanese took that in 1939, they went via Haiphong in Indo-China. Later still, they went through Burma.

Hilda's work, not surprisingly, was not always smooth-running. Helen Foster Snow, one of the American writers and journalists in China during that period, suggests, from her lofty experience of talking to Mao and other Communist leaders at Yunnan, that 'Hilda had not learnt the art of dealing with the Chinese and was being blocked at every turn, for mysterious reasons. "How do you do it?" she asked me anxiously. "Never break the surface. By not trying, all things are done," I said. "In China you can never mend a piece of broken porcelain."'[13]

However that may be, a colleague of Selwyn's described Hilda as 'an electrifying woman, full of energy, vastly intelligent and widely informed, with great warmth, firmly held opinions and completely devoted to the welfare of the Chinese citizens of the Colony'.[14] And Helen Foster Snow's remarks belie the fact that Hilda managed to remain friendly with and work with both Agnes Smedley and Mme Sun Yat-sen whose personal and political relations continued to deteriorate.

Unalike as Hilda and her husband were in many ways, Dr Selwyn Selwyn-Clarke also caused a stir. He shook up the medical services of Hong Kong, made enemies and devoted admirers. Early on, he recognized the need for medical social work in the colony, won his case and approached the Institute of Almoners for help. Margaret Watson, Hong Kong's first almoner, or medical social worker, was appointed. It was into that highly charged atmosphere — though many Europeans went on living as if nothing were happening — that Margaret arrived in July 1939, just before the war in Europe broke out.

Margaret, born in 1910, and a graduate of the London School of Economics (LSE), had recently joined the Colonial Service in the hope of being posted to Hong Kong. She had decided that she wanted to sample another culture after seven years in an ophthalmic hospital in the East End of London, a searing experience which built on the radicalism she had imbibed at the LSE. She was to train four Chinese social workers by the end of the year and lay the ground for what was to become a flourishing and essential part of the health services, invaluable as regards nutrition, housing and hygiene as refugees continued to pour in.[15]

She was also drawn warmly into Hilda and Selwyn's circle of uncolonial friends and political activity, and she and Hilda were to stay firm friends for nearly 30 years, until the latter's death in 1967. Mary Selwyn-Clarke, now Dr Seed, describes Margaret as her second mother, for the three of them were to share a room in Stanley internment camp.

Another member of that circle, described by Margaret as an 'attractive, amusing, intelligent, friendly acquaintance', was Emily Hahn. Hilda and Margaret, though radical, were quite conventionally British, though Margaret describes

Hilda as 'an emotional and passionate person'. Eric Himsworth says of Margaret (to both Margaret and Mary Seed's amusement), 'She was a jolly good looking girl, tall with golden hair and a quiet disposition.'[16] Emily, a 34-year-old American, was overtly Bohemian. Agnes Smedley's biographers describe Emily, or Micky as she was better known to her intimates, as 'a short, heavy-set, handsome young woman with jet black hair. She sashayed down Chinese streets in minks, smoking a black cigar. Her trade mark was a pet gibbon riding on her shoulder — intended, she said, to ward off unwanted men.'[17]

Emily, also a university graduate, had spent time with the Red Cross in the Belgian Congo and taught English in Shanghai. Now she was a writer, working on a biography of the famous Soong sisters — she, too, therefore, had her relationship with Mme Sun. In Shanghai she was involved with a Chinese poet who, when it came to the shake-up of nationalities to avoid internment, she described as her husband, but by early 1941, she was pregnant by Charles Boxer, Japanese scholar and British army officer, and after the War her husband, but then married to someone else.

Into this somewhat unorthodox circle of women, in the Summer of 1940, rampaged Agnes Smedley. Since the fall of Hankow, two years earlier, she had travelled with the Chinese guerrilla army; earlier she had joined the end of the Long March and caused chaos there among women barely out of bound feet and rejoicing in being the only wife of their husband (instead of one of several) by her radical feminism and anti-marriage views. Now Agnes was too ill to remain alongside the partisans.

One wonders how she would have coped in Hong Kong if it had not been for Hilda and her circle. What is impressive about Hilda is that she cared not only on the rarified heights of great causes but also on the lower, equally important slopes of personal relationships. The British authorities had been monitoring Agnes's activities ever since the beginning of her involvement with the Indian Nationalists in 1918, when she was arrested in New York. As she left the plane in Hong Kong on 26 August 1940, she was taken into custody and appeared in court the following morning. She was accused not only of supporting Indian independence but also of being a woman of questionable moral character. Her reply to the judge has as many mythical versions as much of the rest of her life, but the most appropriate is, 'Yes, she had slept with many men. But if one of them had been English, she simply couldn't remember because "he made so little impact on me".'[18] The case was dismissed. Agnes was allowed to remain in Hong Kong for medical treatment, as long as she made no speeches and indulged in no political activities.

In her book *Battle Hymn of China* (1944) Agnes tells none of that story, nothing of her arrest. She merely says that an immigration officer paid her taxi fare to the Peninsula Hotel, where Hilda came for her the following morning. Hilda took her straight to Queen Mary Hospital, where Margaret Watson worked, to have her gall bladder examined. She lay there, her boiler suit removed, in a rather inappropriate pink silk nightdress bought for her by Hilda, and before she left the hospital after her operation had written a scathing indictment of Hong Kong's social conditions in two instalments for the *South China Morning Post*, with data supplied by Hilda and signed 'American Observer'.[19] As part of her convalescence, she spent a month or so in Margaret's flat, attached to the hospital. There, as Margaret explains, she came to know Agnes and acquire 'considerable respect and admiration' for her. The political stimuli, in spite of the strictures placed upon her, looked up after Agnes's arrival.

Just before that, in July 1940, came the order for the evacuation of women and children from Hong Kong. Only women essential for the colony's war effort were allowed to stay. Strictly speaking, Hilda's work with the Eugenics League and for the Chinese war effort did not count. A day had been appointed for registration; on that day, Hilda and her daughter travelled up-river to visit the British Consul from Canton on the small island where the Japanese allowed him to be nominally active. Later, therefore, the ships were to sail without them or Emily Hahn, or, more obviously, for she was part of essential medical services, Margaret Watson.

All that added to Hilda's unpopularity in some circles. But as Selwyn later wrote rather proudly of his wife, the Governor, Sir Geoffry Northcote, 'showed a kindly disregard for the reputation that Hilda's independent outlook — much more than mine — was gaining in Hong Kong. In that environment one did not have to be very far left of centre to be talked about.'[20] Agnes Smedley wrote of her guardian angel in Hong Kong:

As the wife of a high official, she might easily have been content to give her patronage to organisations. But she came from the British labour movement, and thus did not scorn to do her own typing, telephoning, and similar work. In her office I met every kind of relief worker from Hong Kong and China ... Officials called Hilda utterly unscrupulous — words which, in the mouths of such individuals, always amused me. Some men held that she twisted the Governor ... round her finger. When it came to her aims, Hilda was certainly tough as nails.[21]

After July 1940, Hilda and other expatriate women who had managed to stay — there were 1,000 of them when the Japanese invaded, though that figure included some who had drifted back after evacuation — started medical training, in anticipation of what was then inevitable. The Auxiliary Nursing Service had been formed in March 1939 and attached to the Hong Kong Volunteers under the charge of Nina Valentine, wife of Selwyn's deputy.

Agnes was holding private political meetings and giving lectures, but fretting. She was able to help China, and particularly the new Chinese woman whom she much admired, only tangentially. She was interested in Emily Hahn's book on the Soong sisters but did not regard them as the 'only capable women of China'.[22] Agnes supplied funds to and organized medical treatment for the novelist Hsio Hung, for example, but her tuberculosis did not clear up and she died, aged 28, three days after the invasion. Agnes, realizing that her own health would not allow her to return to China, even if she were wanted there, and that when the Japanese invaded her fate would be unenviable, returned to the United States in May 1941.[23]

The Japanese crossed over the border into the New Territories at 8 a.m. on 8 December 1941, at the same moment that they bombed Pearl Harbour and invaded Malaya. The British and Punjabi troops, who were more than half expecting them, though not their efficiency, fell back.

In the New Territories, 34-year-old Mildred Dibden, who had been a missionary with the Bible Churchman's Missionary Society in Hong Kong since 1931, now ran the Fanling Babies Home. She had received a telephone call in those early hours and had managed to get 34 older children packed into a lorry that came for them. But it had not yet returned for the remaining 54 infants, Mildred and her English assistant Ruth Little and the staff of 17 Chinese nurses and *amahs* when they saw the first Japanese soldiers moving towards the house. The commanding officer merely issued orders that no one should go outside but later more soldiers forced their way in. Mildred, a baby in her arms, was struck across the face with a rifle butt when she tried to prevent the rape of a young *amah*. Cots were overturned, and one baby was trampled to death. Following that night of terror, they were left alone and somehow Mildred kept her orphanage open throughout the War.[24]

Dorothy Brazier's Salvation Army Home for women and children was in Kowloon. The fall of the peninsula was imminent and Europeans were being evacuated; but Chinese were not allowed to cross the harbour. Dorothy wrote later, 'We looked at our "family" — our girls saved from lives of shame, our children no relatives to go to, our precious babies, and could not find it in our hearts to leave them.'[25] By the third afternoon, Kowloon was 'without law of any kind' and the electricity had been cut off when the British forces left. The following morning, Mrs Bander, a 70-year-old English woman stood outside their door ready to collapse. Her Chinese neighbour had called at noon the previous day saying that he would come to take her house at 5 o'clock. She waited for her husband's return; he did not come but her Chinese neighbour did, shooting her dog and handing her its lead as he saw her off. Dorothy took her in and hid her. By the time the Japanese reached the Home, the British were shelling Kowloon from the Island. The Japanese were peremptory but no one was harmed. Dorothy and her assistant Doris Lemmon also continued, somehow, to run their Home during the war, receiving help, for example, from Mr and Mrs Kastman, a German couple.

On the Island, Phyllis Harrop was working at Police Headquarters and by 9 December discovered that she was also working for the Chinese Secret Police, part of the Chungking government. Those women who were senior secretaries, a relatively recent innovation in government departments, and Constance Murray in the Chief Justice's Chambers, now came into their own, providing calm and efficiency in the midst of disintegration, and solidarity among themselves as the Island waited to be overrun.

Looting and air-raids started to take their toll; Brenda Morgan, a Canadian military sister, was killed when her hosptial was shelled on 14 December. Mrs Gwen Priestwood had been in China since 1919, now she was a lorry driver, borrowed from the Auxilliary Nurses by the Defence Services, driving through the air raids, at first in a bright yellow milk float which was later painted a dull grey. On 17 December the Japanese tried to force the Island's surrender. Two launches with a white flag, a British woman hostage, Mrs C. R. Lee, wife of the Secretary to the Colonial Secretary, and a pregnant Russian woman whom Mrs Lee had insisted should be brought over to hospital, arrived to bring the proposal which the new governor, Sir Mark Young, rejected. The incident was witnessed and photographed by an American journalist, Gwen Dew, who happened to be on the dock when the boat pulled in.[26]

The Japanese landed on the Island on the night of 18–19 December and immediately established a strong foothold. By now there was no water and no light. Emily Hahn's daughter, Carola, had recently been born. The registration of her birth had caused upset in an administration unused to unmarried mothers, until Margaret Watson intervened. Michelle Marty who had also, in her day, had a daughter outside marriage, befriended Emily and they maintained their friendship after the War. But now the friendship between Hilda and Margaret on the one hand, and Emily on the other, was to be tested and found wanting.

Emily, in *China to Me* (1944), criticizes Hilda for her inflated view of her own political importance and concern over her own fate when the Japanese finally arrived; and she criticizes Margaret and, indeed, any other women involved in the medical profession whom she encountered in those days, for her superiority and authoritarianism, as hospitals filled with the wounded. She found them ultra-critical of her when she put Charles, who was also wounded, ahead of Carola in her concerns and left her new baby in the charge of others while she set up camp in the hospital where Charles was being treated. The women all lived together at Queen Mary Hospital for a short time and they said harsh things to each other, things which are perpetuated in Emily's book. As Emily says in the foreword to the 1986 reprint, she never thought the people about whom she was so candid would read it.

Margaret Watson says generously, 'I must confess to having been very rude to Emily Hahn which in retrospect I much regret. The circumstances were, to say the least, unusually stressful.' But she also says, unrepentantly,

During the hostilities, I was alarmed by her rather unscrupulous use of people to achieve her ends. The dislike which she engendered arose out of this and not ... out of disapproval of her unmarried state with a child. We had too many urgent, painful and tragic concerns of our own to occupy us.

Gwen Priestwood wrote later, 'I know that, all through the siege, people squabbled over trifles. Lifetime friendships exploded with the bombs. Bosom companions quarrelled — over nothing.'[27]

As the Japanese swept towards Victoria, their behaviour was sickening towards women — Chinese, Eurasian and European, including nurses in hospitals. By being behind the wheel of her van, instead of in her grey cotton Auxiliary Nurse's uniform with its white headdress, Gwen Priestwood avoided being at the Jockey Club, then a hospital, when its nurses were repeatedly raped. Gwen Dew, in her attempt to make a proper record of that period in *Prisoner of the Japs* (1943) describes how Marie Paterson, a volunteer nurse, physically violated but with her spirit intact, escaped from that nightmare. 'I just crawled until I reached help,' Marie explained.[28] The British army post she struggled up a hill to through Japanese scouting parties managed to rescue and treat the other nurses.

On Christmas Day at St Stephen's College, also then a hospital, nurses were unable to stop 52 of their military patients from being bayonetted to death. Then those women were raped throughout the day and night and three of them were murdered, including Mrs Begg, wife of a wounded Volunteer who was a patient there. The Governor had no choice but to surrender that day. 'Apparently we were all to be shot, the newly widowed Volunteer later recalled, 'and it was only the news of the surrender that saved us.'[29]

The following day, Phyllis Harrop, watching the troops in a victory parade, realized the implications and approached the Japanese consulate. Later, Selwyn-Clarke's deputy took her to meet the Japanese Director of Medical Services and they discussed the question of prostitutes and the brothel system. Phyllis explained that there were no licensed houses but that she knew where many of the prostitutes lived. She writes about it dispassionately in *Hong Kong Incident* but, however unsavoury it sounds, her action must have saved lives and untold distress. Unfortunately, she was unable to prevent her own *amah* from being raped in her flat while she was away from it.

By 16 January 1942, most British people — army and civilian — were interned. Phyllis was not because, with the approval of her own government, she made use of her old German passport. She escaped from Hong Kong, the first British person to do so, on 27 January 1942, and made her way through Southern China to Chungking. Her relations with the Chinese over the previous three years bore on that escape and she took with her information helpful to both the British and Chinese governments. Gwen Priestwood escaped, too, as she describes in *Through Japanese Barbed Wire* (1943), in a party from Stanley camp on 20 March, and the same moonless night, unknowing, another party escaped which included Elsie Fairfax Cholmondeley, a British woman who had worked on a radical Chinese journal advocating agrarian reform, and who was a friend of Agnes Smedley. The escape of the two parties caused a worsening of conditions in the camp.

Emily Hahn was not interned because she claimed her Chinese poet as a husband, and when the second lot of Americans were evacuated on 1 September 1944, she went with them, writing her book on her return to the United States — the fate of Charles Boxer then unknown. Michelle Marty gave the Japanese problems: if she was born in Hong Kong, she must be Chinese. She was not, therefore, interned. Her health was not helped by the conditions endured by those outside though her daughter tried to get medicines into the occupied territory for her.[30]

Gwen Dew was involved in the siege of the Repulse Bay Hotel and later well enough treated, in the same hotel as Mrs Lee who had acted as hostage, by the Japanese who hoped to use her help for propaganda purposes. When she failed to co-operate she went into Stanley with four duffle bags containing 'six hundred yards of khaki, two hundred pairs of khaki three quarter stockings, a hundred pairs of shorts, several dozen shirts, a hundred scarves, needles, thread, buttons, elastic'.[31] She was later repatriated with other American internees.

Those women were independent before the War. Ellen Field was very much the 'little woman'; in *Twilight in Hong Kong* (1962) she places great emphasis initially on that mentality. Her later exploits seem, therefore, all the more outstanding. She had reached Manila with the evacuated wives and her three small daughters in the summer of 1940, but turned back to Hong Kong. With the same unfocused obstinacy, she refused to leave her home in Kowloon until it was almost too late in December 1941, and then did so in high heels and overladen with luggage. She just made it across the harbour with the help of two passing Canadian soldiers. Then, her husband and father interned, her flat wrecked, penniless, Hong Kong and the easy life she had known in ruins about her, she took charge of her own life and became a war heroine.

She claimed an Irish grandmother, thus avoiding internment, and moved into the flat of an interned friend. She began preparing sensible, self-sacrificing parcels for her husband and father interned in the Shamshuipo camp in Kowloon and for the owner of her flat and one of the Canadian soldiers who had helped her to cross the harbour. Then, seeing through the barbed wire the desolation of the Canadian soldiers who had arrived in Hong Kong without families just before the Japanese invaded, she was inspired to extend her activities. With the help of Dr Selwyn-Clarke and a Japanese Lutheran pastor acting as an interpreter in Shamshuipo, she organized regular deliveries, which she accompanied herself into the camp, of essential supplies, starting with medicines and foods for invalids. Later, her relationship with the Japanese military hierarchy precarious because of her quick temper and highly developed sense of patriotism, she persuaded them, none the less, to allow in sports equipment. At the same time, apparently unknown to anyone but the Chinese agent who had approached her, she acted as a decoy for a network organizing the escape of British soldiers. Whenever she was in trouble, she flashed her identity card in the name of Ellen O'Rourke with the attached photographs of her three daughters. They grew up quickly and bravely during the years that were to follow, providing her with cover and sustenance as well as much cause for guilt. The Japanese pastor, John Watanabe, called her 'the Colonel'; but she writes in the middle of it all, 'Oh, if only I were a man.'[32] She herself escaped to Macau by boat in 1944.

Hilda Selwyn-Clarke was not interned at the beginning because the Japanese needed Selwyn's services; indeed, though kept under house arrest in St Paul's (French) Hospital, they were not formally arrested for 18 months and then he was brutally tortured for, during those months, as well as working tirelessly to maintain the colony's public health system, he also ran a network of support for those interned. Ellen's account mentions only his involvement with her own enterprise. But his work was much more wide-spread, including Stanley camp where the civilians were interned. There he used among others, Margaret Watson, who chaired the International Welfare Committee, to keep him informed of needs.[33] She received an MBE after the war. Ellen mentions Hilda only in passing, and Hilda made no record but in his autobiography Selwyn writes, 'In the account which follows I shall have to correct a passage in the Official History of the Second World War, since it attributed to me a piece of service for which most of the credit should have gone to Hilda — and some of it, even, to our five-year-old Mary.'[34]

Hong Kong under Japanese occupation and life in the internment camps over three and a half years is another story. All that should be added here to the account of Hong Kong and the private life of its women that came to an abrupt end in December 1941 is that when Red Hilda came out of Stanley in 1945 her hair was white.[35]

NOTES

Notes to Chapter 1

1. Clara Elliot, Unpublished Letters to Lady Hislop 1832–40, 4 November 1839. All other quotations from Clara are from the same source; dates will be given here if not in the text.
2. Unpublished Letters to Julia Baynes, 1827–31, 19 November 1830.
3. Gideon Nye, *The Morning of My Life* (1873), p. 70.
4. Jardine Matheson Papers, B7/27/1268.
5. Peter Ward Fay writes in his otherwise excellent *The Opium War 1840–1842* (1975), '[Elliot] left no diary, no private papers, and never set down his reminiscences, nor did his wife though she survived him.' p. 308.
6. Charles Elliot, Unpublished Letters to Lady Hislop 1833–65, 13 November 1833. All other quotations from Charles are from the same source; dates will be given here if not in the text.
7. Fay, *The Opium War 1840–1842* (1975), p. 82.
8. Clara Elliot, Unpublished Letters, 9 November 1834.
9. Clara Elliot, Unpublished Letters, 31 August 1840.
10. Charles Elliot, Unpublished Letters, 10 May 1834.
11. Clara Elliot, Unpublished Letters, 24 August 1834.
12. Two versions of Harriet Low's Journals have been published. The one by her daughter, Katharine Hilliard, is the one consulted by this author, not the one by her granddaughter Elma Loines, which was not available. There is, however, a much longer, unpublished version annotated by Arthur Hummel in the Library of Congress. This quotation, and others that I call 'unpublished', has been taken from that version which I have seen in typescript. They may have appeared in Loines.
13. Katharine Hilliard, *My Mother's Journal* (1900), 18 October 1829.
14. Harriet Low, Unpublished Journals, 21 March 1832.
15. Low, Unpublished Journals, 21 March 1832.
16. Low, Unpublished Journals, 18 November 1829.
17. Low, Unpublished Journals.
18. Hilliard, *My Mother's Journal*, 14 May 1832.
19. Low, Unpublished Journals.
20. Low, Unpublished Journals, 8 May 1831.
21. From genealogical material supplied by descendants.
22. Lady Napier, Unpublished Letter of 19 August 1834.
23. Clara Elliot, Unpublished Letters, 15 March 1836.
24. Low, Unpublished Journals, 1 November 1831.
25. Clara Elliot, Unpublished Letters, 9 November 1834.

26. Clara Elliot, Unpublished Letters, 9 November 1834.
27. Low, Unpublished Journals, 3 September 1831.

Notes to Chapter 2

1. Clara Elliot, Unpublished Letters, 15 March 1836.
2. Clara Elliot, Unpublished Letters, 9 November 1834.
3. Charles Elliot, Unpublished Letters, 17 February 1837.
4. Clara Elliot, Unpublished Letters, 25 February 1838.
5. Charles Elliot, Unpublished Letters, 21 March 1839.
6. Clara Elliot, Unpublished Letters, 1 May 1839.
7. Harriet Low, Unpublished Journals 1829–1834, 23 August 1830.
8. Frederick W. Williams, *The Life and Letters of Samuel Wells Williams* (1889), p. 93.
9. Williams, *Life and Letters*, p. 93.

Notes to Chapter 3

1. J.B. Jeter, *A Memoir of Henrietta Shuck* (1846), p. 144.
2. Clara Elliot, Unpublished Letters, 4 November 1839.
3. Arthur Waley, *The Opium War Through Chinese Eyes* (1958), p. 62.
4. Waley, *The Opium War Through Chinese Eyes*, p. 63; John Slade, (Editor of *Canton Register*) *Narrative of the Late Proceedings and Events in China* (1840), p. 147.
5. Clara Elliot, Unpublished Letters, 4 November 1839.
6. Slade, *Narrative of Events*, p. 147.
7. CMS Papers, C CH/082/1–3, Letter from Caroline Squire, 16 November 1839.
8. Clara Elliot, Unpublished Letters, 4 November 1839.
9. Squire, 16 November 1839.
10. Clara Elliot, undated letter, lacking beginning, probably early 1840 (folio 28).
11. Charles Elliot, Unpublished Letters. This letter is wrongly placed, I believe, in folios.
12. Clara Elliot, undated letter, folio 28, probably early 1840.
13. Clara Elliot, Unpublished Letters, 25 February 1838.
14. Anne Noble, *A Letter Describing her Suffering After the Wreck of the Kite* (1841), p. 5.
15. Noble, *A Letter*, p. 8; Peter Ward Fay, *The Opium War 1840–1842* (1975), says she was pregnant, p. 256.
16. Noble, *A Letter*, p. 11.
17. Noble, *A Letter*, p. 7.
18. Michael Levien, *The Cree Journals* (1981), 26 September 1840.

19. Edward Cree, Unpublished Journals, vol. IV, 7 December 1840. Levien and Cree are from the same original unpublished source.

20. Cree, Unpublished Journals, vol. IV, 3 October 1840.

21. LMS/CWM China 1843–72, box 4, folder 2, Lockhart's diary.

22. Noble, *A Letter*, p. 14.

23. LMS/CWM box 4, folder 2, printed circular letter of 10 July 1841 with handwritten addition.

24. W. P. Bernard, *Narrative of the Voyage of the Nemesis* (1844), vol. I, p. 438.

25. Capt. Sir Edward Belcher, *Narrative of a Voyage Round the World* (1843), vol. I, p. 225.

26. Fay, *Opium War*, p. 311.

Notes to Chapter 4

1. Harriet Low, Unpublished Journals, 20 June 1831.

2. Edward Cree, Unpublished Journals, vol. IV, 1840–1, p. 56.

3. William Tarrant, *The Early History of Hong Kong* (1862), July 1841.

4. Cree, Unpublished Journals, vol. IV, 5 July 1840.

5. Osmond Tiffany, *The Canton Chinese* (1849), p. 259.

6. Tiffany, *The Canton Chinese*, p. 259.

7. Cree, Unpublished Journals, vol. VIII, ? October 1844.

8. Alexander Fraser, *The Frasers of Philorth* (1879), p. 195; Rebecca Kinsman, 'Life in Macao in the 1840s' (1950), vol. 86, p. 28.

9. Mary Sword, Social Letters to Her in Macao 1837–1845, 15 November 1844.

10. Henry T. Ellis, *Hong Kong to Manila* (1859), p. 4.

11. Cree, Unpublished Journals, vol. XI, 16 February 1848.

12. Sword, Letters to, 15 November 1844.

13. Sword, Letters to, 3 April 1845; 16 May 1845.

14. Sword, Letters to, 3 May 1845.

15. Cree, Unpublished Journals, vol. VIII, 6 February 1844 & Michael Levien *Cree Journals* (1981), 20 January 1845.

16. Levien, *Cree Journals*, 14 February 1845.

17. Cree, Unpublished Journals, vol. IX, 12 March 1845.

18. Levien, *Cree Journals*, 16 March 1845.

19. Levien, *Cree Journals*, 17 March 1845.

20. Levien, *Cree Journals*, 5 May 1845.

21. Levien, *Cree Journals*, 21 October 1845.

22. Cree, Unpublished Journals, vol. IX.

23. Cree, Unpublished Journals, vol. XI, 25 March 1848.

24. Levien, *Cree Journals*, October 1849, p. 204.

25. Cree, Unpublished Journals, vol. XII, 11 March 1849.

Notes to Chapter 5

1. W. P. Bernard, *Narrative of the Voyage of the Nemesis 1840–1843* (1844), vol. II, p. 468.
2. Edward V. Gulick, *Peter Parker and the Opening of China* (1973), p. 99.
3. George B. Stevens, *The Life, Letters and Journals of Peter Parker* (1896), p. 229.
4. Stevens, *The Life, Letters and Journals of Peter Parker*, p. 232.
5. Bernard, *Voyage of the Nemesis*, vol. II, p. 468.
6. William Tarrant, *The Early History of Hong Kong* (1862), p. 49.
7. Tarrant, *The Early History of Hong Kong*, p. 50.
8. Tarrant, *The Early History of Hong Kong*, p. 77.
9. William Low, *Canton Letters* (1848), 28 September 1839, p. 22.
10. William Griffis, *A Maker of the New Orient* (1902), 29 March 1844.
11. LMS/CWM, box 4, folder 2.
12. Edward Cree, Unpublished Journals, vol. VII, 16 October 1843.
13. Cree, Unpublished Journals, vol. VII, 18 October 1843.
14. Cree, Unpublished Journals, vol. VII, 20 October 1843.
15. Cree, Unpublished Journals, vol. VII, 22 October 1843.
16. Cree, Unpublished Journals, vol. VIII, 4 February 1844.
17. Cree, Unpublished Journals, vol. XI, 6 March 1848.
18. Cree, Unpublished Journals, vol. IX, 8 October 1845.
19. Hong Kong Museum of Art, *Gateways to China* (1987), p. 36.
20. Austin Coates, *Whampoa* (1980), p. 25.
21. Albert Smith, *To China and Back* (1974), p. 55.
22. George Preble, *The Opening of Japan* (1902), p. 308.
23. Preble, *The Opening of Japan*, p. 381.
24. Preble, *The Opening of Japan*, p. 390.
25. Nora Clarke, *The Governor's Daughter Takes the Veil* (1980), p. 24.
26. There is some discrepancy over which sisters were in Hong Kong. Emily certainly was; Edith must have been since she contributed to the Ladies Patriotic Fund Bazaar (for the Crimean War) in Macau on 31 January 1855. It is fair to assume that Mary was since 'Miss Bowring' (i.e. the eldest) is sometimes referred to, e.g. Preble, p. 308.
27. Clarke, *The Governor's Daughter Takes the Veil*, p. 86.
28. Clarke, *The Governor's Daughter Takes the Veil*, p. 87.
29. George Wingrove Cooke, *China: and Lower Bengal* (1858), p. 11.
30. Alfred Weatherhead, 'Life in Hong Kong 1856–1859', p. 6.
31. Ida Pfeiffer, *A Lady's Voyage Round the World* (1988), p. 44.

Notes to Chapter 6

1. Edward Cree, Unpublished Journals, vol. VII, 14 May 1843.
2. G. M. Theal, *History of South Africa since 1795* (1908), pp. 50–2.

3.   William Tarrant, *The Early History of Hong Kong* (1862), p. 80.

4.   Cree, Unpublished Journals, vol. III, 18 July 1843.

5.   Maggie Keswick, *The Thistle and the Jade* (1982), p. 39.

6.   Alexander Fraser, *The Frasers of Philorth* (1879), vol. III, 11 November 1842, p. 151.

7.   Fraser, *The Frasers of Philorth*, vol. III, p. 157.

8.   Fraser, *The Frasers of Philorth*, vol. III, p. 164. In quoting Cree and developing the Morgan story from Lord Saltoun's letters, note must be made of an entry from the diary of Admiral Sir Thomas Cochrane on 2 July 1842: 'Mrs Morgan and her mother were to have dined with me today but sent their excuses on the ground of being indisposed — which so far was very well — but the best of it was that she begged Mr M might be excused because when she was unwell she did not like him to be away — this is *uxoriousness* with a vengeance.'

9.   Fraser, *The Frasers of Philorth*, vol. III, 10 November 1842, p. 151.

10.   Carl T. Smith, 'Notes'.

11.   Cree, Unpublished Journals, vol. IX, 17 October 1845.

12.   Major W. H. Poyntse, *Per Mare Per Terram* (1892), p. 153.

13.   Fraser, *The Frasers of Philorth*, vol. III, 28 May 1843, p. 192.

14.   James Norton-Kyshe, *The History of the Laws and Courts of Hong Kong* (1971), vol. I, pp. 99–100.

15.   Carl T. Smith 'Notes'.

16.   Norton-Kyshe, *The History of the Laws and Courts of Hong Kong*, vol. I, p. 333.

17.   Carl T. Smith, 'Notes'.

Notes to Chapter 7

1.   G. B. Endacott, *A Biographical Sketch-book of Early Hong Kong* (1962), p. 94.

2.   CO129/158, 15 July 1872, p. 254; CO129/161, 15 May 1872, p. 156.

3.   Letter from descendant to Hong Kong PRO.

4.   Michael Levien, *Cree Journals* (1981); Edward Cree, Unpublished Journals, vol. VIII.

5.   Carl T. Smith 'Notes'.

6.   Carl T. Smith 'Notes'.

7.   Carl T. Smith 'Ng Akew, One of Hong Kong's Protected Women.' (1970); see also James Endicott's will in the PRO Hong Kong.

8.   Probate Records, PRO Hong Kong.

9.   Albert Smith, *To China and Back* (1974), p. 63.

10.   Carl T. Smith 'Notes'.

11.   Carl T. Smith, *Chinese Christians* (1985), p. 200.

12. *Female Missionary Intelligencer*, vol. 4–9, 1 December 1864, p. 240.

13. Endacott, *A Biographical Sketch-book of Early Hong Kong*, p. 125.

14. Alfred Weatherhead, Unpublished 'Life in Hong Kong 1856 –1859', p. 3.

Notes to Chapter 8

1. Michael Levien, *The Cree Journals* (1981), 17 May 1843, p. 120.

2. Levien, *The Cree Journals*, 2 August 1843, pp. 123–4.

3. Keith Sinclair, *A Soldier's View of Empire 1831–1892* (1982), p. 40.

4. Sinclair, *A Soldier's View of Empire*, pp. 41–2.

5. John Ouchterloney, *The Chinese War* (1844), p. 486.

6. Edward Cree, Unpublished Journals, vol. VII, September 1843.

7. George D'Aguilar, Unpublished 'Pencillings on the Rock' (1853), p. 132.

8. J. B. Jeter, *A Memoir of Henrietta Shuck* (1846), pp. 198–9, 19 December 1843.

9. Sinclair, *A Soldier's View of Empire*, pp. 70–1.

10. H.J. Lethbridge, *Hong Kong: Stability and Change* (1978), p. 203.

11. Colin Crisswell, *The Royal Hong Kong Police 1841–1945* (1982), p. 77.

12. A water-colour of that date by the journalist Charles Wirgman entitled 'Chinese nursemaids on parade ground Hong Kong' illustrates the point.

13. Harriet Low, Unpublished Journals.

14. Charles Elliot, Unpublished Letters to Lady Hislop 1833–65, 19 January 1834.

15. Mary Sword, Unpublished Social Letters to Her, 8 April 1845.

16. See also James Norton-Kyshe, *The History of the Laws and Courts of Hong Kong* (1971), vol. II, p. 350.

17. Carl T. Smith 'Notes'.

18. Carl T. Smith 'Notes'; gives source as CSO1094, 23 April 1869.

Notes to Chapter 9

1. The story first surfaced in the 1890s; then in 1928 it was told in *The South China Morning Post* by someone who remembered it from forty years earlier. It was picked up by John Luff in *Hong Kong Cavalcade* (1968); by the biographer of Emily Bowring in *The Governor's Daughter Takes the Veil* (1980); and finally repeated in "Historical Byways' in *The South China Morning Post* on 18 December 1988.

2. John Luff, *Hong Kong Cavalcade* (1968), p. 14.

3. W.C. Hunter, 'Journal of Occurences at Canton' (1964), p. 40.
4. Jardine Matheson Papers, 15 July 1834, B7/27/1268.
5. Carl T. Smith 'Notes'.
6. Edward Cree, Unpublished Journals, vol. VIII, 1 December 1844. Since W. (William) Bowra had a wife, and brought her out on the same ship as Rosa, it is more likely that Rosa looked after bachelor Charles.
7. Michael Levien, *The Cree Journals* (1981), 14 February 1845.
8. Charles Drage, *Servants of the Dragon* (1966), p. 64.
9. George Preble, *The Opening of Japan* (1902), p. 71.
10. H.J. Lethbridge, 'Caste, Class, and Race' in *Hong Kong Stability and Change* (1978), p. 163–88, [p. 164–5].
11. Preble, *The Opening of Japan*, p. 312.
12. Albert Smith, *To China and Back* (1974), p. 65.
13. E.J. Eitel, *Europe in China* (1983), p. 405.
14. *Hong Kong Daily Press*, 2 January 1868.
15. Colin Crisswell, *The Royal Hong Kong Police 1841–1945* (1982), p. 76.
16. Alfred Weatherhead, Unpublished 'Life in Hong Kong 1856–1859', p. 2. The engravings of Murdoch Bruce, architect-engineer confirm this.
17. Ray Strachey, *The Cause* (1978), p. 49.
18. Martha Vicinus, *A Widening Sphere* (1977), p. xvi. The number of single women between the ages of 15 and 45 rose from 2,756,000 in 1851 to 3,228,700 in 1871.
19. Carl T. Smith, in conversation with the author.

Notes to Chapter 10

1. LMS/CMW box 5, folder 1, 22 May 1850.
2. J. B. Jeter, *A Memoir of Henrietta Shuck* (1846), p. 188.
3. Jeter, *A Memoir of Henrietta Shuck*, pp. 208–9.
4. Jeter, *A Memoir of Henrietta Shuck*, p. 205.
5. Jeter, *A Memoir of Henrietta Shuck*, p. 216.
6. Waltraud Haas, *Texts and Documents*, (1989), p. 48.
7. *Female Missionary Intelligencer*, vol. I, 1854, p. 136.
8. LMS/CWM, box 5, folder 3, 26 October 1852.
9. He is known in other sources as the Reverend Ho Fuk-tong.
10. LMS/CWM, box 4, folder 4.
11. CMS/C CH/03b/11B, 19 August 1851.
12. CMS/C CH/03b/11B.
13. CMS/C CH/03b/11B.
14. CMS/C CH/03b/11B.
15. George Smith, *A Narrative of an Exploratory Visit* (1847), p. 512.
16. Nora Clarke, *The Governor's Daughter Takes the Veil* (1980), p. 91.

17. William Lobscheid, *A Few Notes on the Extent of Chinese Education* (1859), p. 4.
18. Clarke, *The Governor's Daughter Takes the Veil*, p. 118.
19. Joyce Smith, *Matilda* (1988), p. 64.
20. Clarke, *The Governor's Daughter Takes the Veil*, p. 139.

Notes to Chapter 11

1. William Lobscheid, *A Few Notes on the Extent of Chinese Education* (1859), p. 5.
2. *Female Missionary Intelligencer*, vol. 1, 1854, p. 141. Hereafter *FMI*.
3. FES/AM1, Minute 727, 14 June 1839.
4. Of the blind girls sent to England, one at least, Agnes Gutzlaff, fulfilled all Mary's hopes: she arrived back in China in 1857 to become a teacher of blind girls herself; *FMI* vol. IV.
5. *FMI* vol. 1–3, new series, 28 November 1859, p. 70.
6. W. Featherstone, *The Diocesan Boys School* (1930), p. 14.
7. *FMI* vol. 1–3, 1 February 1860, p. 22.
8. *FMI* vol. 1–3, 1 August 1860, p. 132.
9. *FMI* vol. 4–6, 1 January 1861, p. 5.
10. *FMI* vol. 4–6, 1 January 1861, p. 6.
11. G.B. Endacott, *A Biographical Sketch-book of Early Hong Kong History* (1962), pp. 154–5.
12. Edward Suter, *History of the Society for Promoting Female Education in the East* (1847), p. 279.
13. Details from CMS Register contained in letter to the author of 1 February 1990 from Rosemary Keen of CMS.
14. *FMI* vol. 7–9, 1 November 1865, p. 194.
15. *FMI* vol. 7–9, 1 November 1865, p. 196.
16. E.J. Eitel, 'The Protestant Missions of Hong Kong' (1875), p. 26.
17. Eitel 'The Protestant Missions of Hong Kong', pp. 26–7.
18. *FMI* vol. 7–9, 1 November 1865, p. 199.
19. *FMI* vol. 7–9, 2 May 1864, p. 90; Miss Eaton is generally said to have taken over the school earlier but the *FMI* records are clear.
20. *FMI* vol. 4–6, 1 January 1861, p. 6; and 1 July 1862, p. 122.
21. Diocesan Girls' School, *A Brief History 1860–1977*, p. 1.
22. *FMI* vol. 4–6, 1 November 1861, p. 202.
23. *FMI* vol. 7–9, 2 May 1864, p. 90.
24. *FMI* vol. 7–9, 1 August 1864, pp. 159–60.
25. FES/AM3, Minute 3969, 16 July 1863.
26. *FMI* vol. 7–9, 1 December 1864, pp. 240–1.
27. *FMI* vol. 9, 1 April 1865, p. 72.
28. FES/AM3, Minute 4250, 9 February 1865.
29. FES/AM3, Minute 4250, 9 February 1865.
30. Featherstone, *The Diocesan Boys School* (1930), pp. 94–5.

31. Featherstone, *The Diocesan Boys School*, p. 92.

32. Featherstone, *The Diocesan Boys School*, p. 93.

33. *FMI* vol. 7–9, 1 November 1865, p. 197.

34. *FMI* vol. 7–9, 1 December 1865, p. 202.

35. *FMI* vol. 7–9, 1 December 1865, p. 203.

36. FES/AM3, Minute 4371, 19 October 1865.

37. Endacott in *A Biographical Sketch-book*, p. 154, says that this story refers to Miss Baxter; Featherstone in his history of the schools, p. 48, says, 'The Lady Superintendent having been robbed carried a pistol and nearly shot a friend …'

38. FES AM3, Minute 4463, 18 January 1866.

39. See, for example, FES AM1, Minute 890, 25 June 1840, the treatment of a Miss Woodman.

40. In dedicating his history of Hong Kong to his wife, Eitel called Mary Ann 'Winefred nee Eaton'. E.J. Eitel, *Europe in China*.

41. She is called variously: Miss Randle, Blue Book 1866; Miss Randall, Blue Book 1867; Rendle, Featherstone p. 132; Randel, Eitel 'Materials for a History of Education in Hong Kong', p. 352.

42. Featherstone, *The Diocesan Boys School*, p. 95.

43. *FMI* vol. 10–11, 1 June 1869, p. 91.

44. E.J. Eitel, 'Materials for a History of Education in Hong Kong' (1890–91), p. 350.

45. Anon. *Dates and Events Connected with the History of Education* (1877), p. 14.

46. LMS/CWM China 1843–1872, box 6, folder 5, October 1868.

Notes to Chapter 12

1. Millicent McClatchie, unpublished, 'In Varying Scenes and Climes 1895–1899', 27 August 1895, pp. 19–20.

2. Lady Brassey, *A Voyage in the Sunbeam* (1984), p. 395.

3. Isabella Bird, *The Golden Chersonese* (1879), pp. 37–8.

4. Isabella Bird, Unpublished Letters to her Sister, 9 January 1879.

5. Joyce Smith, *Matilda* (1988), p. 79.

6. Smith, *Matilda*, p. 53.

7. Matilda Sharp, Unpublished Letters, 31 March 1867. Unless otherwise stated, quotations are from the same source; a reference will only be given if the date is unclear from the text.

8. Sharp, Unpublished Letters, 26 April 1867. *Pidgin* was not a baby talk devised by expatriate women to talk to their servants, as is sometimes suggested, but evolved, before Hong Kong, as an international trading language at a time when Chinese were forbidden from teaching 'barbarians' their language. It offers some explanation for the misunderstandings and tensions that arose.

9. Sharp, 10 October 1875.

10. Sharp, 10 August 1866; 10 July 1866.

11. Sharp, 29 May 1867.

12. Sharp, 26 September 1866.

13. Sharp, 12 February 1859.

14. Sharp, March 1865.

15. *Female Missionary Intelligencer*, vol. 22, 1880, p. 18.

16. Sharp, 2 June 1862.

17. Helen Legge, *James Legge* (1951).

18. Sharp, 19 September 1877.

19. Sharp, 19, 21 December 1875. Matilda notes one of the problems of such marriages on the couple's return to China: the husband would marry a Chinese wife as well. The consequences of such unions were given a thorough public airing in 1898, as Norton-Kyshe discusses, vol. II, pp. 519–21. The case of Annie Lee in the twentieth century is discussed by Emily Hahn, p. 203–6, and Joyce Smith, pp. 127–128.

20. Constance Gordon Cumming, *Wanderings in China* (1888), p. 80.

21. There is more than one version of this story but I choose to follow that of Carl T. Smith in 'The Hong Kong Amateur Dramatic Club and its predecessors' (1982) pp. 228–9.

22. CO129/207, p. 251.

23. Mrs Archibald Little, *In the Land of the Blue Gown* (1912), p. 11.

24. Wei Tao-ming, *My Revolutionary Years* (1943), p. 12.

25. Shiona Airlie, *Thistle and Bamboo* (1989), p. 39.

26. Mabel Cantlie, Unpublished Diaries, 17 September 1889. All quotations are from the same source; references will only be given if dates are unclear from the text.

27. Cantlie, 29 January 1890.

28. Cantlie, 6 January 1890.

29. Carl T. Smith 'Notes'.

Notes to Chapter 13

1. *Hong Kong Daily Press*, 18 January and 19 January 1880.

2. *Daily Press*, 22 April 1870.

3. *Daily Press*, 13 January 1869.

4. Probate Calendar, 20 November 1883.

5. Edward J. Bristow, *Prostitution and Prejudice* (1982).

6. *Daily Press*, 25 October 1883.

7. G. B. Endacott, *A History of Hong Kong* (1964), p. 65.

8. Norman Miners, *Hong Kong Under Imperial Rule* (1987), p. 191.

9. Miners, *Hong Kong Under Imperial Rule*, p. 191.

10. CO129/522 p. 46 'Notes on Reprinted Papers from 1880 to 1900'.

11. Parliamentary Papers, vol. 3, 1882–99, p. 267.

12. Miners, *Hong Kong Under Imperial Rule* (1987), p. 192.

13. Benjamin Scott, *A State of Iniquity* (1894), p. 23.

14. Edward J. Bristow, *Vice and Vigilance* (1977), p. 83.

15. Bristow, *Vice and Vigilance*, p. 81.

16. Parliamentary Papers, Sir W. Des Voeux to Lord Knutsford, 1889 LV p. 163 No. 22.

17. H.J. Lethbridge, *Hong Kong: Stability and Change* (1978), p. 199.

18. CO129/352 p. 418, United States Ambassador to FO 1 September 1908.

19. CO129/522 p. 76, Sir W. Peel to CO, 22 May 1930; CO129/533 pp. 49–63 'Commission of Enquiry into the Traffic in Women and Children in the East'.

20. *Hong Kong Telegraph*, 31 March 1888.

21. CO129/533 pp. 49–63, 'Commission of Enquiry into the Traffic in Women and Children in the East'.

22. Mrs Archibald Mackirdy, *The White Slave Market* (1912), p. 73. Mrs Mackirdy was also known as Olive Christian Malvery.

23. *Daily Press*, 3 February 1883.

24. *Daily Press*, 13 November 1885.

25. CO129/349 p. 403, Lugard to British Consul General, Shanghai, 26 October 1908.

26. CO129/352 p. 418, United States Ambassador to FO, 1 September 1908.

27. CO129/349, p. 40, Lugard to the Earl of Crewe, 14 December 1908.

28. *Daily Press*, 1 November 1863.

29. *Daily Press*, 10 January 1891.

30. *Daily Press*, 9 December 1891.

31. Miners, *Hong Kong: Stability and Change* (1978), p. 198.

32. Wills File 80 of 1920, No. 3369.

33. Carl T. Smith 'Notes' and *Daily Press*, 22 or 26 September 1896.

34. Smith 'Notes'.

35. Anna Clark 'Whores and Gossip: Sexual Reputation in London 1770–1825' (1989), p. 238.

36. *Daily Press*, 19 September 1890.

37. Hong Kong Benevolent Society *Annual Report* 1906.

38. Mackirdy, *The White Slave Market*, p. 8.

39. *Daily Press*, 16 August 1892 and Smith 'Notes'.

40. See 'Correspondence regarding measures to be adopted for checking the spread of venereal disease (Ceylon, Hong Kong and Straits Settlements)' 18 November 1898. Acting Governor Major Gen. W. Black to Mr Chamberlain, p. 589.

41. 'Further correspondence ... in continuation of [c. 9253]', 17 January 1900. Sir Henry Blake to Mr Chamberlain, para. 3, p. 265 (HMSO 1906).

Notes to Chapter 14

1. Jean Cantlie Stewart, *The Quality of Mercy* (1983), p. 53; all other quotations are directly from Mabel's Unpublished Diaries; 1894 was missing when the author read the diaries.
2. Sir William Des Voeux, *My Colonial Service* (1903), pp. 201–2.
3. Mabel Cantlie, Unpublished Diaries, 18 May 1893.
4. Cantlie, 21 September 1893.
5. Nathan Papers, 246–437, 1 July 190?.
6. Veronica, *The Islanders of Hong Kong* (1907), 'To a Hospital Nurse' II.
7. Nathan Papers, 342, letter 6 n.d.
8. Vincent H. Jarret, 'Old Hong Kong', vol. II D–H, pp. 566–8, Hospitals.
9. *Government Gazette* 'Medical Report on the Epidemic of Bubonic Plague in 1894' by Dr Lowson, Government Civil Hospital, 13 April 1895, p. 396.
10. Jarret, 'Old Hong Kong', vol. II D–H, p. 527.
11. G.H. Choa, *The Life and Times of Sir Kai Ho Kai* (1981), p. 20. Other sources say that Alice died of typhoid, and that the child did not die but was taken back to England to be brought up by the Walkden family. Another mystery about Alice is her maiden name; while Choa calls her the daughter of John Walkden, Brian Harrison calls her Whitcome (p. 6) or Whitcombe (index).
12. Edward Hamilton Paterson, *A Hospital for Hong Kong 1887– 1987* (1987), p. 30.
13. Paterson, *A Hospital for Hong Kong*, p. 33.
14. Alice Memorial and Nethersole Hospitals *Annual Reports* 1903–6.
15. James Sibree, *A Register of Missionaries* (1923), No. 1163.
16. Margaret Watson Sloss, tape to the author, December 1989.
17. CO129/487 'Infant Welfare in Hong Kong' E.R. Hallifax, p. 163.
18. Nathan Papers, 351–2, p. 127, 13 March 1928.
19. Lady Ride, in conversation with the author.
20. Jarret, 'Old Hong Kong', The Dispensary Movement, p. 55.

Notes to Chapter 15

1. Asile de la Sainte Enfance, 'Almost as Old as Hong Kong' (1973), p. 3.
2. Argus *Hong Kong Telegraph*, 25 August 1899.
3. Vincent H. Jarret, 'Old Hong Kong' (1933–5).
4. Matilda Sharp, Unpublished Letters, 16 November 1865.
5. Samuel Couling, *Encyclopaedia Sinica* (1983), p. 51.
6. Hildesheim Missionary Society for Blind Girls, *Annual Report* 1904.

7. Victoria Home and Orphanage, *Annual Report* 1903 (1904).

8. Hong Kong Refuge for Chinese Women and Girls, *Annual Report* 1904–1905.

9. Edward J. Bristow, *Vice and Vigilance* (1977), p. 237.

10. Flora Lugard, Unpublished Diary, 14 August 1907. This visit is the only reference to Flora Lugard's work that could tie in with the Mackirdy allusion in 'Queens Women' (Chapter 13, note 38), though the latter seems to refer to European women.

11. Lugard, Unpublished Diary, 15 August 1907.

12. Asile de la Sainte Enfance 'Almost as Old as Hong Kong' (1973), p. 5.

13. See her obituary in *The Times*, 5 August 1955.

14. Mrs C. Neville-Rolfe, Confidential Report, April 1921, p. 5, CO129/472 p. 360.

15. E. Lau, 'The Role of Hong Kong Women in Society During the Interwar Period' (unpublished BA dissertation 1982).

16. The Helena May *A Short History*.

17. Nan Severn, Unpublished Letters, 21 February 1921.

18. Severn, Unpublished Letters, 25 February 1921.

19. Stella Benson, Unpublished Diaries, 25 February 1920.

20. Benson, Unpublished Diaries, 22 October 1930.

21. Benson, 18 August 1930.

22. Benson, 20 September 1930.

23. Benson, 15 November 1930.

Notes to Chapter 16

1. Nan Severn, Unpublished Letters; all quotations are from the same source; references will only be given if the date is unclear from the text.

2. Stella Benson, Unpublished Diaries; all quotations, except where specified, are from the same source; references will only be given if the date is unclear from the text.

3. Information from Nan's daughter, Claudia Severn, and from *Girton College Register*.

4. Severn, Unpublished Letters, 12 February 1921.

5. Severn, 25 February 1921.

6. Benson, Unpublished Diaries, 20 March 1920 and 25 April 1920.

7. Mrs C. Neville-Rolfe, Unpublished Confidential Report (1921) p. 2, CO129/472.

8. Neville-Rolfe, Confidential Report, p. 8.

9. CO129/483 p. 71, letter from Mrs C. Neville-Rolfe to Ormsby-Gore, 29 June 1923.

10. See her obituary in *The Times*, 5 August 1955.

11. Isabella Bird, Unpublished Letters, 3 January 1879.

NOTES TO PAGES 189–199 295

12. G.B. Endacott, 'They Lived in Government House', (1981).

13. G.B. Endacott, *A Biographical Sketch-book of Early Hong Kong* (1962), p. 50.

14. William Des Voeux, *My Colonial Service* (1903), p. 230.

15. Des Voeux, *My Colonial Service*, p. 241.

16. Alwin Clementi Ovenell prepared a detailed paper for the author based on her mother's diaries and her own recollections. All other quotations come from the same source.

17. Benson, Unpublished Diaries, 11 September 1930.

18. Obituary, *The Times*, 6 December 1960.

19. Nathan Papers, 351–2, p. 128, 7 January 1928.

20. Nathan Papers, 351–2, p. 124, 5 April 1928.

21. Ellen Li in conversation with the author.

22. Unpublished letter to Bella Woolf Southorn, Leonard Woolf papers. The Club closed about 15 years ago because it could no longer make ends meet.

23. Joy Grant, *Stella Benson* (1987), p. 303, quoting letter in Berg Collection, New York Public Library, early 1933.

24. Benson, Unpublished Diaries, 26 July 1931.

25. Story told to the author by Austin Coates, who heard it from Claude Burgess, post-war Colonial Secretary, Hong Kong.

26. Benson, Unpublished Diaries, 27 July 1931.

27. Bella Woolf, Unpublished Letters, 19 November 1913.

28. Woolf, Unpublished Letters, 13 November 1959.

Notes to Chapter 17

1. Nathan Papers, 342, letter 147. Permission to quote from Nathan's personal papers was denied by the copyright holder.

2. Geoffrey Sayer, *Hong Kong 1862–1919* (1975), p. 95.

3. Sayer, *Hong Kong 1862–1919*, p. 91.

4. Ronald Hyam 'Empire and Sexual Opportunity' (1986) p. 39.

5. A.P. Haydon, *Sir Matthew Nathan* (1976). Nathan's biographer pays some attention to his ambivalent relations with women, giving as his reason his determination 'not to sacrifice his career standing ... on the altar of convention and sexual gratification', (p. 19). Haydon also suggests that for Nathan 'A woman's place was in the home, but not his home.' Mary Kingsley's biographer, Katherine Frank, in detailing Nathan's relations with her subject, is understandably less generalized. Nathan used Mary's position as a renowned Africanist to his own advantage but when the attentions of this 'handsome man ... possessed of a muted but compelling charm' caused her to write a letter revealing her interest in him as a person, he behaved with neither wisdom nor compassion. Frank, *A Voyage Out*, pp. 289–308.

6. Haydon, *Sir Matthew Nathan*, pp. 109–10.

7. Haydon, *Sir Matthew Nathan*, p. 110.

8. H.J. Lethbridge, *Hong Kong: Stability and Change* (1978), p. 182.

9. Shiona Airlie, *Thistle and Bamboo: The Life and Times of Sir James Stewart Lockhart* (1989), pp. 81–4.

10. Airlie, *Thistle and Bamboo*, p. 84.

11. Peter Wesley-Smith 'Sir Francis Piggott' (1982), p. 268.

12. Wesley-Smith 'Sir Francis Piggott' p. 265, quoting Mabel Piggott to Mrs Chamberlain, private, 7 November 1901, CO167/741.

13. Nathan MS 118: no. 106.

14. Nathan Papers, 342, letter 136, 27 December 1906.

15. Nathan Papers, 342, letter 121, 11 October 1906.

16. Alexander Grantham, *Via Ports* (1965), pp. 16–17.

17. Sir William Des Voeux, *My Colonial Service* (1903), p. 197.

18. Nan Severn, Unpublished Letters, 24 January 1911.

19. Nan Severn, Unpublished Letters, 6 February 1921.

20. Nathan Papers, Unpublished Diaries 1881–1936, 38–42, 13 February 1907.

21. *South China Morning Post*, 9 February 1907.

22. Nathan Papers, Unpublished Letters from Mabel Piggott, 342, letter 156, 7 March 1907.

23. Nathan Papers, 342, letter 149, 2 March 1907. There is a horrible irony in Mabel raising the C.N.A. with Nathan following her 'rejection' by him. Mary Kingsley had raised exactly the same subject under similar circumstances seven years earlier. Frank, *A Voyage Out*, p. 305.

24. Nathan Papers, 346–7, n.d.

25. Nathan Papers, 346–7, 20 January 1908?

26. Nathan Papers, 346–7, 18 April 1909? Emily Hatton's view of Mabel's future daughter-in-law has, fortunately, an antidote. Mabel's granddaughter, Diana Piggott, writes of her Aunt 'Juanita' that she was 'no "ordinary young lady", but a sterling character, firm as the Rock where she was born, and with a quite exceptional sense of humour. She and my uncle were married in Gibraltar Cathedral on 11 December 1909. Much later my aunt and her brothers and sisters donated some fine doors to the Cathedral in memory of their parents, who were members of an old-established Gibraltar family ... My uncle, who became a Major-General, had a lifelong association with Japan, where he was very highly regarded right to the end of his life.' (28 March 1990) I am confident that 'Juanita's' children will see the malicious letter from Emily Hatton as more of a commentary on her and Matthew Nathan than on Miss Smith.

27. Nathan Papers, 346–7, 1 July?

28. Nathan Papers, 346–7, no. 179/81, 7 November ?

29. Nathan Papers, 346–7, 4 October 1907.

30. Nathan Papers, 346–7, no. 194.

31. Perham Papers, Rhodes House, 302/8/Folio 5b.

32. I am particularly grateful to Diana Piggott for continuing to

allow me to use this quotation from an earlier letter, even after she had read the completed chapter which, not suprisingly, saddened her.

Notes to Chapter 18

1. FES/AM4, Minute 6360, 24 February 1876.
2. CMS, C CH/050/74–75, Memoranda as Regards the Baxter Memorial Schools, April 1878.
3. Baxter Schools *Annual Report* (1905).
4. Maria Fincher in conversation with the author; all other quotations from Maria are from the same source.
5. Jean Gittins, *Eastern Windows, Western Skies* (1969), p. 27.
6. Joyce Symons, autobiography in preparation.
7. Ellen Li in conversation with the author.
8. Stella Benson, Unpublished Diaries, 5 March 1920, and Joy Grant, *Stella Benson* (1987), p. 147.
9. Stella Benson, Unpublished Diaries, 9 October 1922.
10. By 1920 there were over 2,250 female students enrolled in religious schools.
11. Civil Service Lists.
12. Belilios School *Journal* (Diamond Jubilee 1950) 'In Memoriam'.
13. Elizabeth Andrew, *Heathen Slaves and Christian Rulers* (1907), p. 124.
14. Belilios School *Journal*, pp. 42–3.
15. Benson, Unpublished Diaries, 8 March 1920.
16. Nathan Papers, 346–7, 11 August 1907 and 6 October 1907.
17. Margery Perham, *Lugard: The Years of Authority* (1960), p. 348 (2 December 1909).
18. Perham, *Lugard*, p. 351 (16 March 1910).

Notes to Chapter 19

1. Mrs Archibald Little, *Intimate China* (1899), p. 139.
2. *Female Missionary Intelligencer*, vol. 4–6, 1 July 1862, p. 121.
3. J. B. Jeter, *A Memoir of Henrietta Shuck* (1846), p. 210.
4. Little, *Intimate China*, p. 150.
5. Little, *Intimate China*, p. 152.
6. Little, *In the Land of the Blue Gown* (1912), p. 210.
7. Little, *In the Land of the Blue Gown*, p. 214.
8. Nigel Cameron, *Hong Kong: The Cultured Pearl* (1978), p. 145.
9. See quotation from Lord Macartney, not a contemporary of Mrs Little, and Cameron's comment in *Barbarians and Mandarins* (1989), p. 366; also Abby Jane Morrell *Narrative of a Voyage* (1833), p. 38.
10. D.A. Griffiths 'The Hong Kong Botanical Gardens' (1986).
11. Little, *In the Land of the Blue Gown*, p. 216.

12. *Hong Kong Weekly Press*, 10 March 1900, p. 164.
13. Edith Blake, typescript of 'A Journey in China' (1900), p. 5.
14. *Female Missionary Intelligencer*, vol. xiii, 1893, p. 21.

Notes to Chapter 20

1. *Female Missionary Intelligencer* new series, vol. 1, 1881, pp. 146–7.
2. *FMI* vol. 1–4, 1854, p. 134.
3. Elizabeth Andrew, *Heathen Slaves and Christian Rulers* (1907), p. 9.
4. *British Parliamentary Papers* (1971) 'Correspondence regarding the measures to be adopted for checking the spread of venereal disease', p. 6.
5. *Hong Kong Daily Press*, 19 December 1918.
6. *Hong Kong Telegraph*, 27 October 1921.
7. Mrs H.L. Haslewood, *Child Slavery in Hong Kong* (1930), p. 20.
8. Haslewood, *Child Slavery*, p. 22
9. Haslewood, *Child Slavery*, p. 23.
10. Haslewood, *Child Slavery*, p. 24.
11. Haslewood, *Child Slavery*, p. 24.
12. CO129/461, p. 419, 10 July 1920.
13. CO129/478, letter of 30 May 1922 from Harold Begbie.
14. CO129/461, letter of 10 July 1920 from Sir R. Stubbs.
15. Haslewood, *Child Slavery*, pp. 13–14.
16. CO129/461, 10 July 1920.
17. CO129/478, 30 May 1922.
18. Haslewood, *Child Slavery*, p. 37.
19. Haslewood, *Child Slavery*, p. 39.
20. CO129/466, p. 239.
21. Nathan Papers, 351–2, 1 November 1929.
22. CO129/466, 7 August 1920.
23. Haslewood, *Child Slavery*, p. 39.
24. CO129/473, p. 146.
25. Haslewood, *Child Slavery*, p. 50.
26. Haslewood, *Child Slavery*, p. 64.
27. CO129/478, p. 315.
28. CO129/478, p. 297.
29. CO129/478, p. 766, 16 September 1922.
30. Haslewood, *Child Slavery*, p. 75.
31. CO129/478, p. 551.
32. CO129/514, 10 April 1929.
33. Anti-Slavery Society Papers, 19 August 1931.
34. Haslewood, *Child Slavery*, p. 124.
35. Anti-Slavery Society Papers, Lady Simon to Hon. Mrs Cyril Arlington, 15 November 1932.

Notes to Chapter 21

1. Paul Gillingham, *At the Peak: Hong Kong Between the Wars* (1983), p. 110.
2. Stella Benson, Unpublished Diaries; all quotations, except where stated, are from the same source; references will only be given if the date is unclear from the text.
3. Letter from John Howard to H. J. Lethbridge, 31 July 1974.
4. CO129/522, 22 May 1930.
5. CO129/522, Summary of printed correspondence on this question covering years 1857–1900.
6. Benson, Unpublished Diaries, 11 February 1931.
7. Benson, 20 February 1931.
8. Detailed letter to the author from Helen Forster Clemetson; other quotations and information are from the same source.
9. Benson, 20 February 1930.
10. Anne Forster Badenoch, in conversation with the author, followed by letters.
11. Lindsay Badenoch, in conversation with the author.
12. Alwin Clementi Ovenell, letter to the author, mostly about her own mother.
13. Benson, 4 March 1931.
14. CO825/23/550 19/37 no. 36, letter from Gladys Forster to W.G. Ormsby Gore, 2 June 1937.
15. Letter from Beatrice Pope to H.J. Lethbridge, 21 June 1974.
16. Sir William Peel, Unpublished autobiographical manuscript, pp. 147–8.
17. Benson, 21 and 22 March 1931.
18. R. Ellis Roberts, *Portrait of Stella Benson* (1939), letter to Laura Hutton, 21 March 1931, p. 406.
19. Benson, 3 November 1931.
20. Benson, 1 June 1931.
21. Benson, 15 June 1931.
22. Benson, 22 October 1931.
23. Benson, 13 October 1931.
24. Benson, 9 November 1931; by 13 November when Mollie had tea with Gladys and Stella, she was denying the previous conversation and quoted the governor as saying that their report was intelligent and interesting and that he agreed with it almost in its entirety.
25. Benson, 28 September 1932.
26. Benson, 28 September 1932.
27. See CO129/533 p. 26, 29 September 1931, CO to Governor: 'I am advised that expert medical opinion no longer views such a system as providing any real safeguard against the spread of venereal disease and that the abolition of tolerated houses in Celyon and Malaya has not led to any increase ...'

28. Anti-Slavery Society Papers, draft letter from Sir John Simon to Sir George Maxwell, 15 January 1933.

29. Edith Picton-Turbervill, *Life is Good* (1939), p. 299.

30. Picton-Turbervill, *Life is Good*, p. 301.

31. CO825/23/550 19/37 No. 36, letter from Gladys Forster to W.G. Ormsby Gore, 2 June 1937.

32. Norman Miners, *Hong Kong Under Imperial Rule* (1987), p. 187.

33. Anti-Slavery Society Papers, January 1939.

34. Phyllis Harrop, *Hong Kong Incident* (1943), p. 46.

Notes to Chapter 22

1. Sir Selwyn Selwyn-Clarke, *Footprints* (1975) and tape from Mary Selwyn-Clarke Seed to author, November 1989. All quotations from Mary come from the same tape.

2. Conversation with Ellen Li, 23 September 1989.

3. Margaret Sanger, *Margaret Sanger: An Autobiography* (1970), p. 349.

4. Phyllis Harrop, *Hong Kong Incident* (1943), p. 60.

5. Tape from Margaret Watson Sloss to the author November 1989; all other quotations from Margaret come from the same tape.

6. Agnes Smedley, *Battle Hymn of China* (1944), (republished as *China Correspondent*, 1984), p. 159.

7. Selwyn-Clarke, *Footsteps*, p. 55.

8. *China Defence League: Report and Survey of Projects 1938–39.*

9. Smedley, *Battle Hymn of China*, p. 156.

10. G. B. Endacott, *Hong Kong Eclipse* (1978), p. 42.

11. Freda Utley, *China at War* (1939), p. 41. Freda was, at that time, and in her book, friendly-disposed towards Agnes Smedley but later she became actively anti-Communist and the relationship deteriorated. In 1938, Freda's disillusionment with Soviet Communism was already pronounced. She had been a member of the Party in Britain, travelled to the USSR and eventually married a Russian, Arkadi Berdichevsky. She lived in the USSR until 1936 when Arkadi was arrested and disappeared during Stalin's purges.

12. Janice R. and Stephen R. Mackinnon, *Agnes Smedley: Life and Times of an American Radical* (1988), p. 169.

13. Helen Foster Snow, *My China Years* (1984), p. 310.

14. Bowie, Donald C., 'Captive Surgeon in Hong Kong: The Story of the British Military Hospital 1942–1945', *Royal Asiatic Society Journal*, vol. 15, 1975, pp. 150–290.

15. 'The Silver Jubilee of Medical Social Work in Hong Kong 1930–1964'.

16. Conversation with Eric Himsworth.

17. Mackinnon, *Agnes Smedly*, pp. 229–30.

18. Mackinnon, *Agnes Smedly*, p. 225.

19. *South China Morning Post* 21, 26, 27, 28 September 1940.

20. Selwyn-Clarke, *Footprints*, p. 58.

21. Smedley, *Battle Hymn of China*, p. 355.

22. Smedley, *Battle Hymn of China*, p. 362.

23. In 1949, Agnes was accused of being a Soviet spy; in the same year the Peoples Republic of China was established. In an effort to avoid the unpleasantness caused by the charge, and loss of earnings, and to enjoy the changes in China, she set off for China via England. She lived in Hilda Selwyn-Clarke's flat in London for some time in 1949–50, writing, but growing increasingly depressed and ill. Then she moved to Oxford to stay with Margaret Watson who had married the former vice-chancellor of the University of Hong Kong, Duncan Sloss. Margaret took Agnes to hospital where she had an operation which led to her death the following day, 6 May 1950. Margaret was at her side; her last friends, therefore, were those from Hong Kong, as referred to in the Preface. The charge against Agnes is discussed in the Mackinnon biography of her. Margaret says of her political views, 'Irrefutable evidence has been produced both for and against this propositon [that she was a Soviet agent in China and elsewhere] I remain unconvinced either way.' Agnes's ashes are in Peking.

24. Jill Dogget, *The Yip Family of Amah Rock*, (1969).

25. Unpublished report, Salvation Army archives, Hong Kong, 'The Work Carried on during the Japanese Occupation', p. 1.

26. Gwen Dew, *Prisoner of the Japs* (1943), p. 149.

27. Gwen Priestwood, *Through Japanese Barbed Wire* (1943), p. 18.

28. Dew, *Prisoner of the Japs*, p. 149.

29. John Stericker, *A Tear for the Dragon* (1958), p. 151; Gwen Dew also describes the incident and names the nurses, pp. 136–8.

30. Letter from Emily Hahn to the author, 30 December 1989.

31. Dew, *Prisoner of the Japs*, p. 227.

32. Ellen Field, *Twilight in Hong Kong* (1962), pp. 130 and 137.

33. After the War Margaret worked as librarian at the Institute for Social Anthropology in Oxford, and then, on Duncan Sloss's death became a post-graduate lecturer in sociological theory and social policy, as well as Deputy Director of the Samaritans in Oxford and Chair of the Community Health Council.

34. Selwyn-Clarke, *Footprints*, p. 71.

35. After the War, Hilda returned with Mary to live in England (though Selwyn stayed on in Hong Kong and then, between 1947 and 1951 was Governor of the Seychelles; he was knighted in 1951). She worked with the China Campaign Committee and from 1950–62 as Secretary of the Fabian Colonial (later Commonwealth) Bureau. Between 1952 and 1965 she was the Labour member for Fulham on the London County Council, where she also chaired the Health Committee and was vice-chair of the Education Committee. She died in 1967.

BIBLIOGRAPHY

Unpublished Documents:
Private, Missionary, and Government

Anti-Slavery Society, Rhodes House, Oxford, Mss Brit Emp 225–K25/ 2. (including Lady Simon).

Basle Mission, (Evangelical Missionary Society of Basle) Basle, Switzerland.

Baynes, Julia (Lady), letters to her, 1827–31, in the family's possession.

Benson, Stella, Diaries etc, Cambridge University Library, Add 6762– 6802.

Bird, Isabella, Letters from, 1878–9, Archives of John Murray, London.

Blake, Edith (Lady), Typescript of 'A Journey in China, Korea and Japan', 1900, Cambridge University Library, Add 8423.

Caine, William, Letters from descendant to PRO Hong Kong, 1984, PRO Admin file PRO/REF/147.

Cantlie, Mabel (Lady), Diaries kept by, 1889–91 and 1893, in the family's possession.

Church Missionary Society (CMS), Missions of the East Asia (Group 1) Cttee, vol. 2 China Missions 1834–1934, Birmingham University Library.

Cochrane, Admiral Sir Thomas, Journals 1842–46, National Library of Scotland MSS 2599–603.

Colonial Office Records, CO129, PRO Hong Kong; otherwise PRO London.

Cree, Edward, Journals, National Maritime Museum, Greenwich.

D'Aguilar, Lt-Gen. Sir George, 'Pencillings on the Rock' (1853) and 'Scrapbook', Royal Commonwealth Society, London, MS1853.

Elliot, Admiral Sir Charles, Letters to Lady (Emma) Hislop, 1833–65, National Library of Scotland, MSS. 13135–6.

Elliot, Clara (Mrs Charles) Letters to Lady (Emma) Hislop 1832–40, National Library of Scotland MS13137 ff 4–37.

Fabian Colonial Bureau, 1950–1962, Rhodes House, MSS Brit Emp S365.

Female Eductional Society (FES), Catalogue of Papers 1834–99, Birmingham University Library.

Jardine Matheson Papers, Cambridge University Library.

Lau, E., 'The Role of the Hong Kong Woman in Society During the Interwar Period' (BA dissertation, 1982, photocopy in History Workshop, University of Hong Kong).

London Missionary Society (LMS/CWM), CWM China 1843–72, School of Oriental and African Studies (SOAS), G1 Ultra Ganges Box 3–7.

Low, Harriet, Journals, manuscript in Library of Congress.

Lugard, Flora (Lady), Lugard Papers, Rhodes House, Oxford, MSS Brit Emp S.67.

McClatchie, Millicent, Typescript, 'In varying Scenes and Climes 1895–1899', PRO Hong Kong, HKMS no. 127.

Moloney, James, Journal 1801–21, India Office, London, ref 10R Neg 11666.

Napier, Elizabeth (Lady), Letters to the Hon. & Rev. Henry Alfred Napier, in the family's possession.

Nathan, Sir Matthew, MS Nathan, Rhodes House, Oxford, 38–42 (diaries 1881–1939); 340–342 (Helena May & Emily Hatton); 346–347 (Mabel Piggott); 351–352 (Penelope Clementi).

Neville-Rolfe, Mrs C. & Hallam, Dr R., National Council for Combating Venereal Diseases, Commissioners' Confidential Report, April 1921, CO129/472, pp. 356–82.

Overseas Nursing Association, Papers, Rhodes House, Oxford, MSS Brit Emp. S.400.

Peel, Sir William, Manuscript of Autobiography, Rhodes House, Oxford, Brit Emp. S.208.

Probate Calendar, A21 SOP/PRO, PRO, Hong Kong.

Salvation Army, 'The Work Carried on During the Japanese Occupation' and 'Home for Women and Girls 1931–1941', Headquarters, Hong Kong.

Severn, Margaret Annie (Nan) (Lady) Letters Home 1921–1925, Severn Family Papers, Rhodes House, Oxford, Mss Ind. Oc. S176.

Sharp, Matilda, Letters, in the family's possession.

Simon, Lady (see Anti-Slavery Society).

Smith, Carl T., Card index system of Hong Kong ('Notes').

St John's Cathedral Register, PRO Hong Kong (Baptism HKMS36) (Marriage 1838–76 & 1928–1975 HKMS40) (Death 1853–93 & 1917–30 HKMS44).

Sword, Mary Parry (Mrs John), Social letters to her in Macao 1837–45 (including Emily Kerr) Sword Family Papers, Pennsylvania Historical Society, Ms Collection.

Weatherhead, Alfred, 'Life in Hong Kong, 1856–1859', transcript donated by family to Hong Kong Government; photocopy in Library of University of Hong Kong.

Woolf, Bella (Lady Southorn) Letters, 1913–60, Leonard Woolf Papers, Document Dept. Sussex University.

Published Works

Adams, Carol, *Ordinary Lives a Hundred Years Ago* (London, Virago, 1982).

Airlie, Shiona, *Thistle and Bamboo: The Life and Times of Sir James Stewart Lockhart* (Hong Kong, Oxford University Press, 1989).

Alice Memorial and Nethersole Hospitals (LMS) *Annual Report* (Hong Kong, 1903–6).

Andrew, Elizabeth and Bushnell, Katharine, *Heathen Slaves and Christian Rulers* (Oakland, Cal. Messiah's Advocate, 1907).

Andrew, Kenneth, *Hong Kong Detective* (London, John Lang, 1962).

Angus, Majorie, *Bamboo Connection: Recollections of the China Coast* (Hong Kong, Heinemann, 1985).

Antrobus, Eleanor, 'Memoir of Mabel Piggott', *Journal of the Royal Empire Society* (London, May–June 1949).

Argus (pseud.) 'Asile de la Sainte Enfance', *Hong Kong Telegraph* (25 August 1899).

Asile de la Sainte Enfance, *Almost As Old As Hong Kong 1848–1973* (Hong Kong, 1973).

Barr, Pat, *The Memsahibs: The Women of Victorian India* (London, Secker & Warburg, 1976).

Baxter Schools (CMS), *Annual Report* (Hong Kong, 1905).

Belcher, Capt. Sir Edward, *Narrative of a Voyage Round the World . . . in HMS Sulphur 1836–1842*, 2 vols. (London, 1843).

Belilios School, *Journal*, Diamond Jubilee (Hong Kong, 1950).

Bell, Anne Olivier (ed.), *The Diary of Virginia Woolf* (London, Hogarth Press, 1977).

Bell, Moberly E., *Flora Shaw* (London, Constable, 1947).

Benson, Stella, 'Stella Benson Goes to a Chinese Wedding', *Radio Times*, vol. 35, no. 449 (London, May 1932).

—— *The Poor Man* (London, Macmillan, 1922).

—— *Tobit Transplanted* (or *The Far Away Bride*) (London, Macmillan, 1931).

Berlin Foundling House, Bethesda, *Annual Report* (Hong Kong, 1904–1906).

Bernard, W. D., *Narrative of the Voyage of the Nemesis 1840–1843*, 2 vols. (London, 1844).

Betty, *Intercepted Letters* (Hong Kong, 1905).

Birch, Alan & Cole, Martin, *Captive Years: The Occupation of Hong Kong 1941–45* (Hong Kong, Heinemann in Asia, 1982).

Bird, Isabella, *The Golden Chersonese: Travels in Malaya in 1879* (Kuala Lumpur, Oxford University Press, 1967; first published 1883).

Blake, Clagette, *Charles Elliot RN* (London, Cleaver-Hume Press, 1859).

Boase, Frederick, *Modern English Biography* (London 1865).

Bowen, Sir .F., *Thirty Years of Colonial Government*, S. Lane-Poole (ed.), 2 vols. (London, Longman, 1889).

Bowie, Donald C., 'Captive Surgeon in Hong Kong: The Story of the British Military Hospital 1942–1945', *Journal of the Royal Asiatic Society*, vol. 15 (Hong Kong, 1975).

Bowring, Sir John, *Autobiographical Recollections* (London, H.S. King, 1871).

Brassey, Lady, *A Voyage in the Sunbeam* (London, Century, 1984; first published 1878).

Bridgman, Eliza (Gillet), *Daughters of China or Sketches of Life in the Celestial Empire* (New York, 1853).

Bridgman, Eliza (ed.), *The Pioneer of American Missions in China* (New York, A.D.F. Randolph, 1864).

Bristow, Edward J., *Prostitution and Prejudice: The Jewish Fight Against White Slavery 1870–1939* (Oxford, Clarendon Press, 1982).

—— *Vice and Vigilance: Purity Movements in Britain Since 1700* (Dublin, Gill & Macmillan, 1977).

British Parliamentary Papers China 1882–1899 (Shannon, Irish University Press, 1971).

Brittain, Vera, *Testament of Youth 1900–1925* (London, Virago, 1978; first published 1933).

Bruce, Murdoch, *Hong Kong Illustrated in a Series of Lithographs* (Hong Kong, 1846).

Burke's Colonial Gentry (Baltimore, Genealogical Publishing Co., 1970).

Burke's Genealogical Peerage, Baronage and Knightage & Heraldic History of the Landed Gentry, P. Townsend (ed.) (105th edn. 1970).

Cameron, Nigel, *Barbarians and Mandarins: Thirteen Centuries of Western Travellers in China* (Hong Kong, Oxford, University Press, 1989; first published 1970).

—— *Hong Kong: The Cultured Pearl* (Hong Kong, Oxford University Press, 1978).

Canton Register.

Cheng, Irene, 'Women Students and Graduates', in Brian Harrison (ed.) *University of Hong Kong: The First Fifty Years 1911–1961* (Hong Kong University Press, 1961).

—— *Clara Ho Tung: A Hong Kong Lady, Her Family and Her Times* (Hong Kong, Chinese University Press, 1986).

China Directory & China Directory and Chronicle.

China Mail.

Chinese Repository (1833–51).

Choa, G. H., *The Life and Times of Sir Kai Ho Kai* (Hong Kong, Chinese University Press, 1981).

Clarabut, Cecil (ed.), *Some Letters of Stella Benson 1928–1933* (Hong Kong, Libra Press, 1978).

Clark, Anna, 'Whores and Gossip: Sexual Reputation in London, 1770–1825', in Arina Angerman *et al.* (ed.), *Current Issues in Women's History* (London, Routledge, 1989).

Clarke, Nora and Riva, Sister Lina, *The Governor's Daughter Takes the Veil: Sister Aloysia Emily Bowring* (Hong Kong, Canossian Missions Historic Archives, 1980).

Clementi, Penelope, *Through British Guinea: To the Summit of Roraima* (London, 1920).

Coates, Austin, *A Macao Narrative* (Hong Kong, Oxford University Press, 1987).
—— *China Races* (Hong Kong, Oxford University Press, 1983).
—— *Macao and the British 1637–1842: Prelude to Hong Kong* (Hong Kong, Oxford University Press, 1988; first published 1966).
—— *Whampoa: Ships on the Shore* (Hong Kong, South China Morning Post, 1980).
Collis, Maurice, *Foreign Mud: Anglo-Chinese Opium War* (Singapore, Graham Brash, 1980; first published 1946).
Colonial Nursing Association, Hong Kong Branch *Annual Reports* (Hong Kong, 1904–6).
Cooke, George Wingrove, *China: And Lower Bengal* (London, 1858).
Couling, Samuel, *The Encyclopaedia Sinica* (Hong Kong, Oxford University Press, 1983; first published 1917).
Crawford, Anne *et al. The Europa Biographical Dictionary of British Women* (London, Europa, 1983).
Crisswell, Colin, *The Taipans: Hong Kong Merchant Princes* (Hong Kong, Oxford University Press, 1981).
Crisswell, Colin and Watson, George, *The Royal Hong Kong Police 1841–1945* (London, Macmillan, 1982).
Croll, Elisabeth, *Wise Daughters From Foreign Lands: European Women Writers in China* (London, Pandora, 1989).
Crowe, Duncan, *The Victorian Woman* (London, George Allen & Unwin, 1971).
Cumming, Constance Gordon, *Wanderings in China* (London, William Blackwood, 1888).
Dates and Events Connected with the History of Education (Hong Kong, 1877).
Davis, John F., *Sketches in China*, 2 vols. (London, 1841).
Dean, William, *The China Mission: Embracing a History of the Various Missions . . . with Biographical Sketches* (New York, Sheldon, 1859).
Debrett's Peerage and Baronetage, Patrick Montague-Smith (ed.) (London, 1980).
Des Voeux, Sir William, *My Colonial Service* (London, John Murray, 1903).
Dew, Gwen, *Prisoner of the Japs* (New York, Alfred Knopf, 1943).
Dictionary of American Biography.
Dictionary of National Biography.
Diocesan Girls' School, *A Brief History 1860–1977* (Hong Kong, 1977).
Diocesan Girls' School and Orphanage *Annual Report* (Hong Kong, 1902–6).
Diocesan School and Orphanage, *Annual Report* (Hong Kong, 1903–6).
Doggett, Jill, *The Yip Family of Amah Rock* (Hong Kong, 1969).
Dollar Directory (Hong Kong, 1939).
Downing, C. Toogood, *The Fan-Qui in China in 1836–7*, 3 vols. (Shannon, Irish University Press, 1972; first published 1838).

Drage, Charles, *Servants of the Dragon Being the Lives of Edward and Cecil Bowra* (London, Peter Dawney, 1966).

Eames, James Bromley, *The English in China (1600–1843)* (London, Curzon Press, 1974; first published 1909).

Eden, Emily, *Letters from India* (London, 1872).

Eitel, E. J., 'The Protestant Missions of Hong Kong' (lecture given 30 November 1875) *Chinese Recorder* vol. VII, No. 1, 1876, pp. 21–29.

—— *Europe in China* (Hong Kong, Oxford University Press, 1983; first published 1895).

—— 'Materials for a History of Education in China', *China Review* XIX(5) (1890–1), pp. 308–24, XIX(6) (1890–1) pp. 335–68.

Ellis, Henry T., *Hong Kong to Manila and the Lakes of Luzon* (London, 1859).

Endacott, G. B., and Birch, Alan, *Hongkong Eclipse* (Hong Kong, Oxford University Press, 1978).

Endacott, G. B., and She, Dorothy, *The Diocese of Victoria* (Hong Kong, Kelly and Walsh, 1949).

Endacott, G. B., *A History of Hong Kong* (Hong Kong, Oxford University Press, 1973).

—— *Government and People in Hong Kong 1841–1962: A Constitutional History* (Hong Kong, University Press, 1964).

—— *A Biographical Sketch-book of Early Hong Kong* (Singapore, Eastern Universities Press, 1962).

—— *They Lived in Government House*, Newspaper Clippings from the *China Mail* 29 March 1965–24 July 1965 (Hong Kong, 1981).

Evans, D. E. E., *Constancy of Purpose: Faculty of Medicine University of Hong Kong* (Hong Kong, University Press, 1987).

Fawcett Society Library, Biographical Newspaper File (London).

Fay, Peter Ward, *The Opium War 1840–1842* (North Carolina, University Press, 1975).

Featherstone, W., *The Diocesan Boys School & Orphanage Hong Kong: The History and Records 1869–1929 with reference to . . . The Diocesan Native Female Training School . . . 1860* (Hong Kong, DBS, 1930).

Female Missionary Intelligencer (FMI) vols. 1–XVIII, 1854–1899 (London).

Field, Ellen, *Twilight in Hong Kong* (London, Frederick Muller, 1960).

Forbes, R. B., *Personal Reminiscences* (Boston, 1878).

Forster, L., *Echoes of Hong Kong and Beyond* (Hong Kong, 1933).

—— 'The Mui Tsai or Slave Girls in China', *St John's Review*, no. 7, vol. 3, pp. 16–20 (Hong Kong, November 1930).

—— *The New Culture in China* (London, George Allen & Unwin, 1936).

Fowler, Marian, *Below the Peacock Fan: First Ladies of the Raj* (Canada, Viking, 1987).

Frank, Katherine, *A Voyage Out: The Life of Mary Kingsley* (London, Corgi, 1988).

Fraser, Alexander (17th Baron Saltoun), *The Frasers of Philorth*, 3 vols. (London, 1879).

Further Correspondence relating to measures adopted for checking the spread of venereal disease in continuation of [c.9253] Straits Settlements; Hong Kong; Gibraltar (HMSO, 1906).

Gillingham, Paul, *At the Peak: Hong Kong Between the Wars* (London, Macmillan, 1983).

Gittins, Jean, *Eastern Windows, Western Skies* (Hong Kong, SCMP 1969).

—— *Stanley: Behind Barbed Wire* (Hong Kong, University Press, 1982).

Government Blue Books, Hong Kong.

Grant, Joy, *Stella Benson: A Biography* (London, Macmillan, 1987).

Grantham, Alexander, *Via Ports: From Hong Kong to Hong Kong* (Hong Kong, Oxford University Press, 1965).

Griffis, William E. *A Maker of the New Orient, Samuel Robbins Brown: Pioneer Educator in China ...* (New York, H. Revell, 1902).

Griffiths, D. A., and Lau, S. P., 'The Hong Kong Botanical Gardens, a Historical Overview', *Journal of the Royal Asiatic Society* vol. 26, 1986 (Hong Kong, 1988).

Gulick, Edward V., *Peter Parker and the Opening of China* (Harvard University Press, 1973).

Haas, Waltraud and Ken Phin Pang, *Texts & Documents: Mission History from the Women's Point of View* (Basle, Basle Mission, 1989).

Hahn, Emily, *China to Me* (London, Virago, 1987; first published 1944).

Harrison, Brian, *University of Hong Kong 1911–1961: The First Fifty Years* (Hong Kong, University Press, 1962).

Harrop, Phyllis, *Hong Kong Incident* (London, Eyre & Spottiswoode, 1943).

Haslewood, Mrs H. L., *Child Slavery in Hong Kong: The Mui Tsai System* (London, Sheldon Press, 1930).

Haydon, A. P., *Sir Matthew Nathan: British Colonial Governor and Civil Servant* (Queensland University Press, 1976).

Helena May, The, *A Short History* (Hong Kong, The Helena May, n.d.).

Hildesheim Missionary Society for Blind Girls in China *Annual Reports* (Hong Kong, 1904–7).

Hilliard, Katharine, *My Mother's Journal; A Young Lady's Diary of Five Years Spent in Manila, Macao, and the Cape of Good Hope, from 1829–1834* (Boston, George H. Ellis, 1900).

Hoe, Susanna, 'White Women in the Colonies: Were They Responsible for Setting up Racial Barriers?', *Bikmaus: A Journal of Papua New Guinea Affairs Ideas & Arts* vol. V, no. 2 (Port Moresby, June 1984).

Hong Kong Benevolent Society, *Annual Report* (Hong Kong, 1903–6).

Hong Kong Colonial Secretariat Civil List and General Orders.

Hong Kong Daily Press.

Hong Kong Museum of Art, *Gateways to China: Trading Ports of the 18th and 19th Centuries* (Hong Kong, Urban Council, 1987).

Hong Kong Nursing Institution, *Annual Reports* (Hong Kong, 1903–5).

Hong Kong Refuge for Women and Girls, *Annual Report 1904–5* (Hong Kong, 1905).

Hong Kong Telegraph.

Hughes, Robert, *The Fatal Shore: A History of the Transportation of Convicts to to Australia 1787–1868* (London, Pan, 1988).

Hunter, Jane, *The Gospel of Gentility: American Women Missionaries in Turn of the Century China* (New Haven, Yale University Press, 1984).

Hunter, William C., *Bits of Old China* (London, 1885).

—— *The 'Fan Kwae' at Canton 1825–1844* (London, 1882).

—— 'Journal of Occurrences at Canton: During the Cessation of Trade at Canton 1839', in W. Ellsworth (ed.) *Journal of the Royal Asiatic Society* vol. 4, (Hong Kong, 1964).

Hutcheon, Robin, *Chinnery: The Man and the Legend* (Hong Kong, Form Asia, 1975).

Hyam, Ronald, 'Empire and Sexual Opportunity', *Journal of Imperial and Commonwealth History* vol. XIV, no. 2, pp. 34–89 (London, January 1986).

Jarret, Vincent H., 'Old Hong Kong' compiled from *South China Morning Post* (Hong Kong, 1933–5).

Jaschok, Maria, *Concubines & Bondservants: The Social History of a Chinese Custom* (London, Zed Books, 1988).

Jeter, J. B., *A Memoir of Henrietta Shuck: The First American Female Missionary to China* (Boston, Gould Kendall & Lincoln, 1846).

Keswick, Maggie, *The Thistle and the Jade: A Celebration of Jardine Matheson & Co* (London, Octopus, 1982).

King, C. W., and Lay, G. T., *Notes of Voyages*, 2 vols. (New York, 1839).

King, Frank and Clarke, Prescott, *A Research Guide to China Coast Newspapers 1822–1911* (Cambridge, Mass., Harvard University Press, 1965).

Kinsman, Rebecca, 'Life in Macao in the 1840s, Letters to her Family', in Mrs Frederick C. Munroe (ed.) *Essex Institute Historical Collections* (Salem, 1950–2, vol. 86–8).

Ladies Recreation Club, A History (Hong Kong, 1983).

Lane-Poole, S., *The Life of Sir Harry Parkes* (Wilmington, Del., Scholarly Resources Inc., 1973; first published 1894).

Legge, Helen, *James Legge: Missionary and Scholar* (Edinburgh, 1951).

Legge, Rev. James, 'The Colony of Hong Kong'(Hong Kong, 1872).

Lethbridge, H. J., *Hong Kong: Stability and Change* (Hong Kong, Oxford University Press, 1978).

—— 'Prostitution in Hong Kong: A Legal and Moral Dilemma', *Hong Kong Law Journal* (1978).

Levien, Michael (ed.), *The Cree Journals* (Exeter, Webb & Bower, 1981).

Little, Mrs Archibald, *Intimate China: The Chinese as I Have Seen Them* (London, Hutchinson, 1899).

—— *In the Land of the Blue Gown* (London, 1912).

Lobscheid, William, *A Few Notes on the Extent of Chinese Education* (Hong Kong, China Mail, 1859).

Loseby, F.H. 'Mui Tsai in Hong Kong' *Hong Kong Legislative Council Sessional Papers* 1935, pp. 195–282.

Loviot, Mme Fanny, *A Lady's Captivity Among the Chinese* (London, 1858).

Low, William, *The Canton Letters of, 1839–1841*, Duncan Phillips (ed.), (Salem, 1848).

Luff, John, *Hong Kong Cavalcade* (Hong Kong, South China Morning Post, 1968).

—— *The Hong Kong Story* (Hong Kong, South China Morning Post 1960).

Mackenzie, Keith, *Narrative of the Second Campaign in China* (London, 1842).

Mackinnon, Janice R., and Stephen R., *Agnes Smedley: The Life and Times of an American Radical* (London, Virago, 1988).

Mackirdy, Mrs Archibald, and Willis, W.N., *The White Slave Market* (London, 1912).

Mattock, Katherine, *This Is Hong Kong: The Story of Government House* (Hong Kong, Information Service, 1978).

McPherson, Dr D., *Two Years in China: Narrative of the Chinese Expedition* (London 1843).

Miners, Norman, *Hong Kong Under Imperial Rule 1912–1941* (Hong Kong, Oxford University Press, 1987).

Minett, Ethel M. 'The School Medical Service in Hong Kong', *Oversea Education* vol. III, No. 4, July 1932 (London).

Morrell, Abby Jane, *Narrative of a Voyage to . . . the China Sea etc.* (New York, 1833).

Morrison, Robert, *Memoirs of the Life and Labours . . .* compiled by his widow, K. Morrison (London, Longmans, 1839).

Morse, Hosea Ballou, *The Chronicles of the East India Company Trading to China, 1635–1834* 5 vols. (Oxford University Press, 1926–9).

Nicolson, Nigel, (ed.) *The Letters of Virginia Woolf* (London, Hogarth Press, 1975–80).

Noble, Anne, *A Letter Describing Her Suffering After the Wreck of the Kite* (Macau, 1841).

Norton-Kyshe, James William, *The History of the Laws and Courts of Hong Kong*, (Hong Kong, Vetch & Lee, 1971; first published 1898).

Nye, Gideon, *The Morning of My Life 1833–1839 in China* (Canton, 1873).

Ouchterloney, John, *The Chinese War* (London, Sanders & Otley, 1844).

Paterson, Edward Hamilton, *A Hospital for Hong Kong 1887–1987* (Hong Kong, Nethersole Hospital, 1987).

Pearce, T. W., 'Ernst John Eitel . . . An Appreciation', *The Chinese Recorder* (Hong Kong, 1909).

Perham, Margery, *Lugard The Years of Authority 1898–1945*, vol. 2 of 4 vols., (London, Collins, 1960).

Pfeiffer, Ida, *A Lady's Voyage Round the World* (London, Century, 1988; first published 1851).

Picton-Turbervill, Edith, *Life is Good* (London, Frederick Muller, 1939).

Piggott, F. S. G., *Broken Thread* (Aldershot, Gale & Polden, 1950).

Piggott, Mabel, 'You Would Hardly Believe it', *Nineteenth Century and After*, 68, 148 (London, 1910).

Pope-Hennessy, James, *Verandah: Some Episodes in the Crown Colonies 1867–1889* (London, George Allen & Unwin, 1964).

Poyntse, Major W. H., *Per Mare Per Terram: Reminiscences of Thirty Two Years ... Service* (London, 1892).

Preble, Rear Admiral George, *The Opening of Japan: A Diary of Discovery in the Far East* (Oklahoma, University Press, 1902).

Priestwood, Gwen, *Through Japanese Barbed Wire* (New York, D. Appleton-Century, 1943).

Prochaska, F. K., *Women and Philanthropy in Nineteenth-Century England* (Oxford, Clarendon Press, 1980).

Quincy, Joseph (ed.), *The Journals of Major Samuel Shaw: The First American Consul at Canton* (Boston, 1847).

Raven, Susan and Weir, Alison, *Women in History: Thirty-Five Centuries of Feminine Achievement* (London, Weidenfeld & Nicolson, 1981).

Ride, Sir Lindsay,'The Old Protestant Cemetery in Macao', *Journal of the Royal Asiatic Society* vol. 3 (Hong Kong, 1963).

Roberts, R. Ellis, *Portrait of Stella Benson* (London, Macmillan, 1939).

Royal Commission on Historical Manuscripts, *Private Papers of British Colonial Governors 1782–1900* (London, HMSO, 1986).

Rules and Regulations for Her Majesty's Colonial Service (London, Eyre & Spottiswoode, 1867, 1908).

Sanger, Margaret, *Margaret Sanger: An Autobiography* (Elmsford, New York, Maxwell Reprint, 1970).

Sayer, Geoffrey, *Hong Kong 1841–1862: Birth, Adolescence & Coming of Age* (Hong Kong, University Press, 1980; first published 1937).

—— *Hong Kong 1862–1919: Years of Discretion* (Hong Kong, University Press, 1975).

Scott, Benjamin, *A State of Iniquity: Its Rise Extension and Overthrow* (New York, August M. Kelley, 1968; first published 1894).

Scott, John Lee, *Narrative of a Recent Imprisonment in China After the Wreck of the Kite* (London, Dalton, 1840).

Selwyn-Clarke, Sir Selwyn, *Footprints: The Memoirs of* (Hong Kong, Sino-American publications, 1975).

Sibree, James, *A Register of Missionaries* (London, 1923).

—— *Fifty Years in Madagascar: Personal Experiences of Mission Life and Work* (London, Hodder & Stoughton, 1924).

Simon, Lady, *Slavery* (London, 1929).

Sinclair, Keith (ed.), *A Soldiers View of Empire: The Reminiscences of James Bodell 1831–92* (The Bodley Head, 1982).

Sirr, Henry, *China and the Chinese* (London, 1849).

Slade, John, *Narrative of the Late Proceedings and Events in China* (Macau, 1840).

Smedley, Agnes, *Battle Hymn of China* (London, Victor Gollancz, 1944).

Smith, Albert, *To China and Back: Being a Diary Kept Out and Home* (Hong Kong, University Press, 1974; first published 1859).

Smith, Carl T., *Chinese Christians: Elites Middlemen and the Church in Hong Kong* (Hong Kong, Oxford University Press, 1985).

—— *The Diocese of Hong Kong & Macao 1849–1974: A Brief History* (Hong Kong, Diocesan Office, 1974).

—— 'Ng Akew, One of Hong Kong's "Protected" Women', *Chung Chi Bulletin*, no. 46, (June 1966).

—— 'The Hong Kong Amateur Dramatic Club and its Predecessors', *Journal of the Royal Asiatic Society* vol. 22 (Hong Kong, 1982).

Smith, George, *A Narrative of an Exploratory Visit To Each of the Consular Cities of China etc.* (London, 1847).

Smith, Joyce Stevens, *Matilda: Her Life and Legacy* (Hong Kong, Matilda Hospital, 1988).

Snow, Helen Foster, *My China Years* (London, Harrap, 1984).

Society for the Protection of Children, *Annual Report* (Hong Kong, 1934).

South China Morning Post. (SCMP).

St John's Review (Hong Kong 1929–).

St Stephen's Girls' College, *A Short History 1906–1966* 'News Echo' (Hong Kong, 1966).

Stericker, John, *A Tear for the Dragon* (London, Arthur Barker, 1958).

Stevens, George B., *The Life, Letters and Journals of . . . Peter Parker MD* (Wilmington, Del., Scholarly Resources, 1972; first published 1896).

Stewart, Jean Cantlie, *The Quality of Mercy: The Lives of Sir James and Lady Cantlie* (London, George Allen & Unwin, 1983).

Strachey, Ray, *The Cause: A Short History of the Women's Movement in Great Britain* (London, Virago, 1978; first published 1928).

Suter, Edward, *History of the Society for Promoting Female Education in the East* (London, 1847).

Tarrant, W., *The Early History of Hong Kong to the Close of 1844 . . . A Series of Articles Reproduced from the Friend of China* (Canton, 1862).

—— *The Hongkong Almanac & Directory* (Hong Kong, 1846)

Taylor, Sir Henry, *Autobiography* (London, 1885).

Theal, G. M., *History of South Africa since 1795*, vol. III *Cape Colony 1840–60* (London, 1908).

Thomas, W. H. E., *Vanished China: Far Eastern Banking Circles* (London, 1952).

Thomson, John, *The Straits of Malacca Indo-China & China* (London, 1875).

Tiffany, Osmond jr., *The Canton Chinese: or The American Sojourn in the Celestial Empire* (Boston, 1849).

Times, The.

Trollope, Joanna, *Britannia's Daughters: Women of the British Empire* (London, Hutchinson, 1983).

Uglow, Jennifer (ed.), *The Macmillan Dictionary of Women's Biography* (London, Macmillan, 1982).

University of Hong Kong, *Directory of Women Graduates* (1961).

Utley, Freda, *China at War* (London, 1939).

Veronica, *The Islanders of Hong Kong; Being a Series of Open Letters* (Hong Kong, 1907).

Vicinus, Martha, (ed.), *A Widening Sphere: Changing Roles of Victorian Women* (London, Methuen, 1980).

Victoria Home and Orphanage, *Annual Report* (Hong Kong, 1903–6).

Waley, Arthur, *The Opium War Through Chinese Eyes* (Stanford, University Press, 1958).

Wei, Tao-ming, *My Revolutionary Years* (New York, Scribner, 1943).

Wesley-Smith, Peter, 'Sir Francis Piggott: Chief Justice in His Own Cause', *Hong Kong Law Journal* 12, 260, (Hong Kong, 1982).

Who's Who in the Far East 1906–1907 and 1907–1908.

Williams, Frederick W., *The Life and Letters of Samuel Wells Williams* (New York, 1889).

Woods, W. W. 'Mui Tsai in Hong Kong and Malaya', *Report of Commission* (London, HMSO, 1937).

Woolf, Bella, *Chips of China* (Hong Kong, Kelly and Walsh, 1930).

—— *Under the Mosquito Curtain* (Hong Kong, Kelly and Walsh, 1935).

Woolf, Leonard, *An Autobiography: Growing Up 1904–1911* vol. 1 of 2 vols. (London, Hogarth Press, 1970).

Wright, Arnold, & Cartwright, H. A. (eds.), *Twentieth Century Impressions of Hong Kong etc.* (London, Lloyds Greater Britain Publishing, 1908).

Wylie, Alexander, *Memorials of Protestant Missionaries to the Chinese* (Shanghai, 1867).

INDEX